Early Families of Somerset
and
Fayette Counties Pennsylvania

Keith A. Dull

HERITAGE BOOKS
2006

HERITAGE BOOKS
AN IMPRINT OF HERITAGE BOOKS, INC.

Books, CDs, and more—Worldwide

For our listing of thousands of titles see our website
at
www.HeritageBooks.com

Published 2006 by
HERITAGE BOOKS, INC.
Publishing Division
65 East Main Street
Westminster, Maryland 21157-5026

Copyright © 1996 Keith A. Dull

Other books by the author:
Early Families of York County, Pennsylvania, Volume 1
Early Families of York County, Pennsylvania, Volume 2
Early Families of Lancaster, Lebanon and Dauphin Counties, Pennsylvania
Early Families of Berks, Bucks and Montgomery Counties, Pennsylvania
Early German Settlers of York County, Pennsylvania

All rights reserved. No part of this book may be reproduced or transmitted in any form or by any means, electronic or mechanical, including photocopying, recording or by any information storage and retrieval system without written permission from the author, except for the inclusion of brief quotations in a review.

International Standard Book Number: 978-1-58549-324-4

This book is dedicated to my Grandfather
Leo Clifton Dull

with special thanks to
my wife Karen for her support

and the following researchers
whose work contributed to portions of this book

Roger Sims
Patricia McKinna
Carl D. Gable

TABLE OF CONTENTS

Introduction	vii
Hans Peter Doll	1
Phillip Boudemont	20
Heinrich Schlater	36
John Robinson	44
Ernst Friderich Dumbauld	48
Lohr	56
Johan Christopffel Leonhard	60
Hanss Peter Kessler	71
Jacob Shock	72
Maurer	78
Jacob Schwingell	80
Johan Nicholas Shultz	87
James Boyd	89
Jacob Jauler	95
Solomon Glatfelter	98
Clement Engle	100
Michael Engle	102
John Weimer	103
Index	111

INTRODUCTION

Compilation of these genealogies was based on research conducted at the Allen County Public Library, Fort Wayne, Indiana; Huntington County Public Library, Huntington, Indiana; Mercer County Public Library, Celina, Ohio; and the York County Historical Society, York, Pennsylvania.

Church records for the following churches were consulted:
Berlin Lutheran Church, Berlin, Pennsylvania.
Christ's Evangelical Lutheran Church, York, Pennsylvania.
Good Hope Lutheran Church.
Greenville German Reformed Church.
Middletown Lutheran Church, Maryland.
Mount Zion Lutheran Church.
Salisbury German Reformed Church, Salisbury, Pennsylvania.
Samuel's Lutheran Church.
Sanner Lutheran Church.
St. John's Lutheran Church.
St. John's Lutheran Church, Hagerstown, Maryland.
Stoyestown Lutheran Church.
Strayer's (Salem) Lutheran Church.
Strayer's (Salem) Reformed Church.
The First Reformed Church of York, York, Pennsylvania.
The Private Pastoral Records of Reverend Henry Melchoir Muhlenberg.
The Private Pastoral Records of Reverend Jacob Lischy.
Tohickon Lutheran Church.
Trinity Lutheran Church of Lancaster, Lancaster, Pennsylvania.
Wentz's Reformed Church.
Zions Lutheran Church.

The following court records were consulted:
Bedford County, Pennsylvania Deeds, Tax Records, and Wills.
Berks County, Pennsylvania Deeds, Tax Records, and Wills.
Bucks County, Pennsylvania Deeds, Tax Records, and Wills.
Fayette County, Pennsylvania Deeds, Tax Records, and Wills.
Frederick County, Maryland Deeds, Tax Records, and Wills.
Lancaster County, Pennsylvania Deeds, Tax Records, and Wills.
Lehigh County, Pennsylvania Deeds, Tax Records, and Wills.
Licking County, Ohio Deeds, Tax Records, and Wills.
Mercer County, Ohio Deeds, Tax Records, and Wills.
Northampton County, Pennsylvania Deeds, Tax Records, and Wills.
Somerset County, Pennsylvania Deeds, Tax Records, and Wills.
Stark County, Ohio Deeds, Tax Records, and Wills.

Tuscarwas County, Ohio Deeds, Tax Records, and Wills.
Washington County, Maryland Deeds, Tax Records, and Wills.
Westmoreland County, Pennsylvania, Deeds Tax Records, and Wills.
York County, Pennsylvania Deeds, Tax Records, and Wills.

The following census records were consulted:
 Fayette County, Pennsylvania 1790-1850.
 Licking County, Ohio 1820-1850.
 Mercer County, Ohio 1820-1920.
 Northampton County, Pennsylvania 1790-1800.
 Somerset County, Pennsylvania 1790-1850.
 Stark County, Ohio 1820-1860.
 Washington County, Maryland 1800-1850.
 Westmoreland County, Pennsylvania 1790-1850.
 York County, Pennsylvania 1790-1800.

Information on the European Origins of some of families has been taken from Annette K. Burgert's *Eighteenth Century Emigrants from the Northern Alsace to America.* (Camden, ME: Picton Press, 1992).

Hans Peter Doll

Hans Peter[1] had a son at Erzweiler, Ulmet Parish, Palatinate, Germany: Johannes Peter[1.1], b. in 1642.

Johannes Peter Doll

Johannes Peter[1.1] m. Gertraut, dau. of Hans Peter and Margaretha Riek, at Ulmet on May 2, 1666. She was b. at Ulmet on Feb. 13, 1641/42, and d. there in Dec., 1723. Johannes Peter d. at Ulmet on Oct. 14, 1717. They had the following children at Ulmet:
Christoffel[1.1.1], b. July 6, 1671; Anna Elisabetha[1.1.2], b. June 8, 1674; Casper[1.1.3], b. in 1676; Philip[1.1.4], b. in 1680; Johannes Christian[1.1.5], b. in 1682.

Christoffel Doll

Christoffel[1.1.1] m. Sara Catharina, dau. of Johann Peter and Anna Maria (Kappel) Schuch, at Erzweiler on March 2, 1703/04. She was b. at Rathsweiler, Palatinate, bapt. at Baumholder, Rheinland on Jan. 19, 1690, d. in Bucks Co., Tohickon Twp., Pennsylvania on April 3, 1760, and was buried at Tohickon Union Church April 4. Johann Peter and Anna Maria Schuch, had a son, Johann Christian, who was b. May 4, 1690, and later immigrated to America. Christoffel and his family set out for America on the ship *Samuel*. Christoffel d. en route, and the rest of the family arrived at Philadelphia in 1739 (except for two sons who immigrated to America in 1737). Christoffel and Sara had the following children at Ulmet:
   Anna Maria Margaretha[1.1.1.1], b. in Nov., 1705.
   Anna Catharina[1.1.1.2], b. March 14, 1707/08.
   Johann Peter[1.1.1.3], b. Sept. 22, 1709, and d. in 1714.
   Johann Christian[1.1.1.4], b. in 1712.
   Johann Peter[1.1.1.5], b. Jan. 20, 1714/15.
   Maria Engel[1.1.1.6], b. Sept. 15, 1717.
   Johann Abraham[1.1.1.7], b. April 14, 1720.
   Johann Caspar[1.1.1.8], b. Feb. 1, 1721/22.
   Johann Nickel[1.1.1.9], b. May 8, 1725.
   infant[1.1.1.10], b. July 3, 1729.

Anna Maria Margaretha Doll

Anna Maria Margaretha[1.1.1.1] m. Johan Peter, son of Jacob and Anna Catharina Mumbauer, in Erzweiler on June 12, 1727. He was bapt. in Erzweiler/Irtzweiler on March 3, 1697. Peter and Margaretha immigrated to America on the ship *Samuel* in 1739. They had the following children:
   Johan Christian[1.1.1.1], d. in 1729, aged 3/4 years.
   Johan Christian[1.1.1.2], bapt. on June 27, 1732.
   Johan Peter[1.1.1.3], bapt. on April 24, 1735.

Johan Georg Christian[1.1.1.4], bapt. on June 10, 1736.

Johann Christian Doll

Johann Christian[1.1.1.4] m. Maria Catharina Dromm at Erzweiler on Oct. 21, 1734. He immigrated to America with his brother, Johann Peter, in 1737. Johann Christian was naturalized in 1755, and resided in Philadelphia (now Montgomery) Co., Gwynedd Twp., Pennsylvania. He purchased 50 acres in Philadelphia Co. on Feb. 22, 1737, 200 acres on March 14, 1743, and 50 acres on April 25, 1750. Johann Christian and Maria Catharina had the following children:

Frederick[1.1.1.4.1], b. about 1736.
Christian[1.1.1.4.2], b. Aug. 12, 1742. He m. Elizabeth Dotterer in Montgomery Co. in 1769. He was a Captain during the Revolutionary War, and d. on Sept. 27, 1820.
Casper[1.1.1.4.3], b. June 11, 1748 (near Skippack).
Johannes[1.1.1.4.4], b. about 1750.
Valentine[1.1.1.4.5], b. about 1752. He has not been confirmed at a son of Johann Christian, but he was residing in Montgomery Co. in 1790.

Frederick Doll

Frederick[1.1.1.4.1] m. Elisabeth, and had the following children at Philadelphia (now Montgomery) Co., Germantown Pennsylvania:
Margareth[1.1.1.4.1.1], b. April 30, 1758; Anna Elisabeth[1.1.1.4.1.2], b. Dec. 14, 1759.

Casper Doll

Casper[1.1.1.4.3] m. Hannah Catherine Mathieu in Montgomery Co., New Hanover, Pennsylvania on Sept. 20, 1774. She was b. at New Hanover on Feb. 21, 1758, and d. in Mifflin Co., McVeytown, Pennsylvania on Feb. 21, 1826. Casper was a Captain during the Revolutionary War, and d. at McVeytown on July 23, 1829. Casper and Hannah had the following children:

Catherine[1.1.1.4.3.1], b. Aug. 8, 1775, and d. in June 1838. She m. Benjamin Walters.
Daniel[1.1.1.4.3.2], b. May 17, 1777, bapt. by Reverend Henry Melchior Muhlenberg, and d. before 1830. He m. Elizabeth Stanley.
Elisabeth[1.1.1.4.3.3], b. March 9 (7), 1779, bapt. by Henry Melchior Muhlenberg, and d. in 1844. She m. Casper Cosmer.
John[1.1.1.4.3.4], b. July 8, 1781.
Libby[1.1.1.4.3.5], b. about 1783, and d. in 1833.
Hannah Catherine[1.1.1.4.3.6], b. Feb. 26, 1786, and d. on Feb. 25, 1837. She m. Mehlor Ruth.
Sybel[1.1.1.4.3.7], b. Aug. 22, 1788, and d. before 1830. She m.

Abraham Copeland.
Casper$^{1.1.1.4.3.8}$, b. Dec. 25, 1791.
Mary$^{1.1.1.4.3.9}$, b. Jan. 1, 1796, and d. before 1830. She m. Isiah Van Zandt.
George$^{1.1.1.4.3.10}$, b. July 17, 1797.
Benjamin Mathieu$^{1.1.1.4.3.11}$, b. May 11, 1799, and d. before 1830. He m. Nancy Younkin.
Joseph$^{1.1.1.4.3.12}$, b. Jan. 7, 1804, and d. in 1847. He m. Jane Barkley, Jane Laird, and Martha Price.

John Dull

John$^{1.1.1.4.3.4}$ m. Margaret Betty. She was b. in Pennsylvania in 1786. They were residing in Carroll Co., Pittsburg, Indiana in Oct., 1855. They had the following children:
James C.$^{1.1.1.4.3.4.1}$, b. in 1810.
Casper$^{1.1.1.4.3.4.2}$, b. in 1815.
Benjamin$^{1.1.1.4.3.4.3}$, b. in Ohio in 1820, and m. Martha. She was b. in Ohio in 1820. They were residing in Carroll Co., Indiana in 1850.
Margaret$^{1.1.1.4.3.4.4}$, b. in Ohio in 1826.
Mary$^{1.1.1.4.3.4.5}$, b. in Ohio in 1828.
Daniel$^{1.1.1.4.3.4.6}$, b. in Ohio in 1830.

James C. Dull

James C.$^{1.1.1.4.3.4.1}$ m. Margaret. She was b. in Ohio in 1815. They resided in Carroll Co., Indiana in 1850. They had the following children:
Sarah$^{1.1.1.4.3.4.1.1}$, b. in Ohio in 1836.
Hannah$^{1.1.1.4.3.4.1.2}$, b. in Ohio in 1838.
Nancy Jane$^{1.1.1.4.3.4.1.3}$, b. in Ohio in March, 1840, and m. Bowen Wesley Speece in Carroll Co., Indiana on Oct. 27, 1859. Bowen was b. in Montgomery Co., Dayton, Ohio in March, 1830, and d. in Jasper Co., Carthage, Missouri on Jan. 18, 1915. Nancy d. in Carthage, Missouri sometime after 1910.
Rebecca$^{1.1.1.4.3.4.1.4}$, b. in Ohio in 1844.
Lydia$^{1.1.1.4.3.4.1.5}$, b. in Ohio in 1848.

Casper Dull

Casper$^{1.1.1.4.3.4.2}$ m. Mary A. She was b. in Ohio in 1818. They resided in Carroll Co., Indiana in 1850. They had the following child:
Ruthie$^{1.1.1.4.3.4.2.1}$, b. in Carroll Co., Indiana in 1849.

Casper Dull

Casper$^{1.1.1.4.3.8}$ m. Jane Junkin. He d. resided in McVeytown, Pennsylvania in Aug., 1874. They had the following children: James T.$^{1.1.1.4.3.8.1}$, b. about 1812; Hannah C.$^{1.1.1.4.3.8.2}$, b. about 1814, and m. Vance Criswell; Daniel M.$^{1.1.1.4.3.8.3}$, b. about 1816; Nancy T.$^{1.1.1.4.3.8.4}$, b. about 1818, and m. George Macklin; Margaret E.$^{1.1.1.4.3.8.5}$, b. about 1820, and m. Samuel Horning; Andrew I.$^{1.1.1.4.3.8.6}$, b. about 1822; C. Penrose$^{1.1.1.4.3.8.7}$, b. about 1824; Joseph F.$^{1.1.1.4.3.8.8}$, b. about 1826.

George Dull

George$^{1.1.1.4.3.10}$ m. Lydia Postlewait. He resided in Tippecanoe Co., Lafayette, Indiana in Oct., 1855. They had a dau.: Hannah$^{1.1.1.4.3.10.1}$.

Johannes Dull

John$^{1.1.1.4.4}$ m. Elisabeth McMeal in Montgomery Co., Germantown, Pennsylvania on Sept. 26, 1771. They had the following dau. in Montgomery Co., Worcester Twp.: Anna Maria$^{1.1.1.4.4.1}$, b. December 5, 1773, and bapt. at Wentz's Reformed Church on April 3, 1774; Hanna$^{1.1.1.4.4.2}$, b. in April, 1786, and bapt. by Reverend Henry Melchior Muhlenberg.

Johann Peter Doll

Johann Peter$^{1.1.1.5}$ m. Margaretha. He arrived at Philadelphia with his brother, Johann Christian, in the ship *Samuel* on Aug. 30, 1737. He settled in Northampton (now Lehigh) Co., Lower Macungie Twp., Pennsylvania. In 1754, Peter was a schoolmaster at Macungie, and in 1755, he was a Captain in the French and Indian War. Sometime during the winter of 1755/56, Peter and Margaretha moved to Northampton Co., Moore Twp.. On December 14, 1755, Captain Solomon Jennings and Captain (Peter) Doll, with their commands passed through Nazareth on route to the Hoeth farm with orders to search for and bury the dead, after the Indians had massacred the family of Frederick Hoeth, at his home about 12 miles east from Gnadenhutten on Pocho Pocho Creek. Doll and Jennings returned five days later to the Rose Inn just east of Nazareth. On Jan. 15, 1756, Peter's house and barn were reported burnt by the Indians. The family may have sought refuge at Macungie, which would explain the baptism of a son there in Oct., 1756. Peter's name appears on Powell relief lists from Indian attacks during this period (1755/56), while his brother, Nicholas (of Saccon and Shippach Twps.), was listed as contributing relief to the victims of these raids. by Sept., 1757, Peter had erected a blockhouse in Moore Twp., and was quartering soldiers evacuated from Fort Norris on Sept. 27. The blockhouse was situated about a mile and a half north-northwest of Klecknersville, Pennsylvania, on the banks of the Hockendauqua Creek. The blockhouse was garrisoned in Jan., 1758, served at an outpost of Fort Lehigh, had two barracks, and no stockade. Peter was appointed guardian of Johannes, son of Johan

Nickel and Maria Margaretha Heil in Moore Twp. in Sept., 1762. Peter and Margaretha had the following children:

Leonard$^{1.1.1.5.1}$, b. about 1738, and m. Margaretha Holtz/Stoltz in Bucks Co., Tohickon Twp., Pennsylvania on Oct. 15, 1760. He has not been confirmed as a son of Peter. He was a Second Lieutenant in Lewis's Pennsylvania Battalion of the Flying Camp in July-Dec., 1776.

Catherine$^{1.1.1.5.2}$, b. about 1740, and m. Frederick Hesser in Bucks Co., Tohickon Twp., Pennsylvania on Oct. 12, 1760. She has not been confirmed as a dau. of Peter.

Eva$^{1.1.1.5.3}$, b. about 1742, and m. Henry Hauser in Bucks Co., Tohickon Twp., Pennsylvania on Nov. 3, 1761. She has not been confirmed as a dau. of Peter.

John$^{1.1.1.5.4}$, b. May 20, 1753.

Anna Maria$^{1.1.1.5.5}$, b. at Macungie in Aug., 1754, bapt. at Zion's Lutheran Church on Aug. 25, 1754, and sponsored by Jacob and Anna Maria Wetzel (her mother is Magdalena on the baptism).

Johann Christophel$^{1.1.1.5.6}$, bapt. at Zion's Lutheran Church on Oct. 30, 1756, and sponsored by Peter Federolff Jr. and Maria Margaretha.

Johan Jurg$^{1.1.1.5.7}$, b. in Moore Twp. about 1758.

Elisabeth$^{1.1.1.5.8}$, b. in Moore Twp. on April 15, 1760.

Martin$^{1.1.1.5.9}$, b. about 1762. He has not been confirmed as a son.

John Dull

John$^{1.1.1.5.4}$ m. Elisabeth$^{1.1.3a}$, dau. of Andreas$^{1.1a}$ and Catharina Barbara (Bourgey) Boudemont, in Washington Co., Maryland about 1777. John was a Private in Captain Peter Rundio's Flying Camp Company, Northampton Co. Militia in 1776. John and Elisabeth resided at Washington Co., Root's Hill, near Eakles Mills, Maryland, until late 1782. In 1783, John was taxed in Somerset Co., Milford Twp., Pennsylvania. In 1785, he had 150 acres. He purchased land on Scrub Glade in 1787. He was Supervisor of the Roads and Highways for Milford Twp. in 1800. He served in the Milford Militia on Feb. 5, 1789. He resided near New Centerville, and was a trapper, trader, hunter, and farmer on Coxes Creek Glades. John d. in Milford Twp. on Nov. 20, 1835, and Elisabeth on Oct. 22, 1843. They are buried in New Centerville cemetery. They had the following children:

John$^{1.1.1.5.4.1}$, b. in Oct., 1778.

Catherine$^{1.1.1.5.4.2}$, b. in 1780.

Peter$^{1.1.1.5.4.3}$, b. June 15, 1782.

Elisabeth$^{1.1.1.5.4.4}$, b. Sept. 17 (8), 1784.

Margaretha$^{1.1.1.5.4.5}$, bapt. at Samuel's Lutheran Church on April 26, 1785.

Andreas$^{1.1.1.5.4.6}$, b. Feb. 28, 1786, and bapt. at Samuel's Church on July 31, 1787.
Frederick$^{1.1.1.5.4.7}$, b. Sept. 28, 1787.
Magdalena$^{1.1.1.5.4.8}$, b. in 1790.
Simon$^{1.1.1.5.4.9}$, b. about 1792.
George$^{1.1.1.5.4.10}$, b. March 15, 1794.
Susan$^{1.1.1.5.4.11}$, b. in 1795, and m. John Whipkey.

John Dull

John$^{1.1.1.5.4.1}$ m. Hannah$^{1.3.3.7n}$, dau. of Johan Georg and Anna Catharina Lenhart, in Somerset Co., Pennsylvania about 1799. She was b. in York Co., Newbury Twp., Pennsylvania in 1780. He was b. in Washington Co., Root's Hill, near Eakles Mills, Maryland in Oct., 1778. About 1814, John and Hannah moved to Fayette Co., Salt Lick Twp., Pennsylvania, near Champion, and in 1832, moved to Stark Co., Sugar Creek Twp., Ohio, near Wilmont. In Stark Co., John entered 320 acres of land. John d. from Asiatic Cholera on Sept. 20, 1834, and Hannah d. from the same disease on Sept. 27, 1834. They are buried in Weimer Church cemetery. A stone was erected several years after their death, by their son, Elias, but the bronze plaque, which held the inscription was melted down for the war effort. John and Hannah had the following children: Peter$^{1.1.1.5.4.1.1}$, b. June 4, 1800; Anna Maria$^{1.1.1.5.4.1.2}$, b. March 1, 1802; Joseph$^{1.1.1.5.4.1.3}$, b. Feb. 9, 1804; Philipena "Phebe"$^{1.1.1.5.4.1.4}$, b. March 7, 1806; John$^{1.1.1.5.4.1.5}$, b. Jan. 15, 1808; infant$^{1.1.1.5.4.1.6}$, b. about 1810; infant$^{1.1.1.5.4.1.7}$, b. about 1812; Elizabeth$^{1.1.1.5.4.1.8}$, b. June 4, 1813; Lenhart$^{1.1.1.5.4.1.9}$, b. Aug. 11, 1815; Jacob$^{1.1.1.5.4.1.10}$, b. May 1, 1817; Johannah$^{1.1.1.5.4.1.11}$, b. May 11, 1819; Elias$^{1.1.1.5.4.1.12}$, b. Feb. 3, 1822, bapt. June 26, 1822 at Good Hope Lutheran Church; Catherine$^{1.1.1.5.4.1.13}$, b. Dec. 27, 1824, and bapt. at Good Hope Lutheran Church.

Peter Dull

Peter$^{1.1.1.5.4.1.1}$ m. Catherine, dau. of Samuel and Elisabetha Barbara (Robinson) Schlater, in Fayette Co., Pennsylvania in 1824. Peter moved to Stark Co., Ohio with his father in 1832, and in 1840, moved to Mercer Co., Dublin Twp., Ohio, settling just North East of Shanes Crossing. He purchased 161 acres in section six in 1840, and sold it to his brothers-in-law, W. R. and P. Schlater in 1841 to purchase 183 acres in section ten. In 1842, 1853, and 1855, He purchased land in section three. From 1867 to 1882, Peter deeded all of his land in section three to Josiah, Thomas, William Dull, and Nancy Jane Hooks. In 1882, Peter sold the home farm (consisting of 100 acres) in section ten to Nancy Jane Hooks, and the remaining 83 acres to William Dull. From 1882 till his death, Peter resided with his dau., Nancy Jane

Hooks. Peter farmed northeast of Shane's Crossing until his death on April 7, 1888. Catherine was b. in Fayette Co., Salt Lick Twp., Pennsylvania on Sept. 30, 1804, d. on Oct. 8, 1882, and is buried beside Peter in Ridge cemetery in Van Wert Co., Ohio. They had the following children:

Jeremiah$^{1.1.1.5.4.1.1.1}$, b. March 1, 1826, and bapt. Jul 8, 1827 at Good Hope Lutheran Church. He m. Cynthia Ann, dau. of William and Catharine (Harp) Frysinger, in Van Wert Co., Ohio on Dec. 8, 1853, and Sarah Ann (Shaffer) Putman in Mercer Co. on April 10, 1862. Cynthia was b. in 1831, d. in Dublin Twp. in 1859, and is buried in the Old Frysinger cemetery. Jeremiah enlisted on Sept. 7, 1864, and was killed in the Civil War in Chatham Co., Savannah, Georgia on Jan. 30, 1865. He is buried in Laurel Grove cemetery in Georgia.

Mary$^{1.1.1.5.4.1.1.2}$, b. May 14, 1827, bapt. at Good Hope Lutheran Church and m. Hugh Dobson in Mercer Co. on Sept. 7, 1848. She d. in Dublin Twp. on Jan. 4, 1850, and is buried in Ridge cemetery.

Josias$^{1.1.1.5.4.1.1.3}$, b. March 5, 1830, bapt. July 31, 1830 at Good Hope Lutheran Church, sponsored by his mother. M. Mary Ann, dau. of Abraham and Martha Miller, in Mercer Co. on Nov. 10, 1854, and Mary Jane, dau. of William and Lydia (Baltzell) Dilbone, about 1889/90. Mary Ann was b. in Ohio in 1836, and d. of Typhoid in Dublin Twp. on Oct. 31, 1889. Mary Jane was the widow of Jefferson Everett. She was b. Miami Co., Ohio in Aug., 1837, and was alive in 1900. Josiah d. in Dublin Twp. on Aug. 13, 1909. They are buried in Mount Olive cemetery.

Hanna$^{1.1.1.5.4.1.1.4}$, b. Jul 10, 1832, bapt. at Good Hope on Aug. 27, 1832, sponsored by her parents. She d. before 1836.

Lucinda$^{1.1.1.5.4.1.1.5}$, b. Feb. 8, 1833, and m. Seth Temple in Van Wert Co., Ohio on Dec. 2, 1852. He was b. in 1824, and d. in Van Wert Co., Liberty Twp., Ohio on Aug. 15, 1863. Lucinda d. in Liberty Twp. on Sept. 20, 1861, and is buried beside her husband in Ridge cemetery.

Samuel$^{1.1.1.5.4.1.1.6}$, b. March 17, 1834, and brought a load of horses for his father, by way of rail to Viroqua, Wisconsin in 1851. He sold all but two teams, which he traded for land in Vernon Co., Bad Ax, Wisconsin. He m. Mary O'Leary in Vernon Co., Bad Ax, Wisconsin in Sept., 1856. Samuel sold the land in Bad Ax, and purchased land on North Clayton, where he raised his family. Later he turned the farm over to his son, John, and moved to Readstown, Wisconsin. After a short stay, they returned to North Clayton. He d. in Vernon Co., North Clayton, Wisconsin on April 21, 1918.

Hannah[1.1.1.5.4.1.1.7], b. March 10, 1836, and d. in Mercer/Van Wert Co., Ohio on Sept. 21, 1899. She m. Lafayette Frazier in Mercer Co. on April 5, 1849. He was b. in 1818, and d. in 1899.

Catherine[1.1.1.5.4.1.1.8], b. March 10, 1836, and m. Alfred Frysinger in Mercer Co. on Sept. 5, 1857. He was b. in Ohio in 1834. Catherine d. in Mercer Co., Dublin Twp. in 1907.

John[1.1.1.5.4.1.1.9], b. Feb. 8, 1837, and m. Susan, dau. of George and Katherine A. (Stophlet) Roebuck, in Mercer Co. on Jan. 1, 1860, and Louisa, dau. of William and Lydia (Baltzell) Dilbone, in Mercer Co. on Dec. 23, 1866. Susan d. in Dublin Twp. on Aug. 9, 1863, and is buried in Roebuck cemetery. Louisa d. in Dublin Twp. in 1913. John d. in Dublin Twp. on Nov. 27, 1897. John and Louisa are buried in Mt. Olive cemetery. John had a 40 acre farm on the Louis Godfrey Reserve in Dublin Twp.

William S.[1.1.1.5.4.1.1.10], b. March 15, 1840, and m. Martha Shindeldecker in Mercer Co. on Aug. 18, 1861. She was b. Oct. 22, 1838, and d. in Mercer Co., Dublin Twp., Ohio on March 24, 1925. He d. in Van Wert Co., Ohio City, Ohio on Feb. 22, 1913. He is buried in Woodlawn cemetery.

Franklin[1.1.1.5.4.1.1.11], b. in 1843, and m. Jane Miller in Mercer Co. on March 12, 1863. In the 1880's, they resided in Hamilton Co., Cincinnati, Ohio and Clermont Co., Goshen, Ohio.

Nancy Jane[1.1.1.5.4.1.1.12], b. May 12, 1848, and m. Abraham Hooks in Mercer Co. on Feb. 29, 1872. He was b. in Dublin Twp. on Dec. 28, 1851, and d. in Allen Co., Lima, Ohio on Feb. 8, 1913. She d. in Lima on Jan. 8, 1901.

Phoebe[1.1.1.5.4.1.1.13], b. March 15, 1849, and d. on Jan. 27, 1853. She is buried in Ridge cemetery.

Joseph Dull

Joseph[1.1.1.5.4.1.3] m. Elizabeth Isabell, dau. of Frederick and Christina (Wolfe) Dumbauld, in Fayette Co., Pennsylvania on March 29, 1827. She was b. in Fayette Co., Pennsylvania on Oct. 30, 1807, and d. in Licking Co., Ohio on March 21, 1881. Joseph d. in Licking Co., Liberty Twp., Ohio on Oct. 17, 1891. They had the following children:

Phebe[1.1.1.5.4.1.3.1], b. in Fayette Co., Salt Lick Twp., Pennsylvania on Jan. 7, 1829, and m. Elisha T. P. Brooks.

Christina[1.1.1.5.4.1.3.2], b. in Fayette Co., Salt Lick Twp., Pennsylvania on June 3, 1831, bapt. at Good Hope Luterhan Church on Aug. 27, 1831, and sponsored by Frederich and Susanna Dumbauld. She m. Joseph Perkins Brooks. He was b. in Licking Co., Ohio on May 29, 1831, and resided in Erie Co., Sandusky, Ohio in 1917.

Johannah[1.1.1.5.4.1.3.3], b. in Stark Co., Sugar Creek Twp., Ohio on Aug. 1, 1833, and m. Jackson Stephens in Licking Co., Ohio on July 17, 1853. Joannah d. on March 22, 1898.

Uriah$^{1.1.1.5.4.1.1.3.4}$, b. in Stark Co., Sugar Creek Twp., Ohio on Nov. 15, 1835, and m. Oelands/Lindy Ramsey. Uriah d. on Aug. 31, 1909.

Nancy$^{1.1.1.5.4.1.1.3.5}$, b. in Ohio on June 17, 1838, and m. Jared Anderson.

John$^{1.1.1.5.4.1.1.3.6}$, b. in Ohio on March 23, 1841, and m. Mary Tippett.

Elias$^{1.1.1.5.4.1.1.3.7}$, b. in Ohio on Oct. 10, 1843, and m. Caroline Wright. She was b. in 1851.

Charlotte$^{1.1.1.5.4.1.1.3.8}$, b. in Ohio on June 15, 1848, and m. Allen Stanbach/ Stanbaugh on June 23, 1875. She d. in Stark Co., Sugar Creek Twp., Ohio.

Lucenia Jane$^{1.1.1.5.4.1.1.3.9}$, b. in Ohio on June 15, 1848, and d. in Ohio on Aug. 18, 1856.

John Dull

John$^{1.1.1.5.4.1.1.5}$ m. Mary Jane Harbaugh in 1829. She was b. in Pennsylvania on Feb. 17, 1813, and d. in Van Wert Co., Wilshire Twp., Ohio on Nov. 20, 1882. John d. in Wilshire Twp. on Aug. 28, 1849. They had the following children:

Elisabeth Anna$^{1.1.1.5.4.1.1.5.1}$, b. Oct. 27, 1827, bapt. at Good Hope Lutheran Church on June 6, 1828, sponsored by her parents.

Lydia$^{1.1.1.5.4.1.1.5.2}$, b. in Fayette Co., Salt Lick Twp., Pennsylvania in 1830, and d. in 1915. She m. Samuel Krick.

Franklin Benjamin$^{1.1.1.5.4.1.1.5.3}$, b. in Stark Co., Sugar Creek Twp., Ohio in 1832, and m. Rebecca Jane Walters in Van Wert Co. on Dec. 21, 1854. She was b. Jan. 31, 1837, and d. in Wilshire Twp. on Sept. 30, 1894. Franklin d. in Wilshire Twp. in 1910.

Sarah$^{1.1.1.5.4.1.1.5.4}$, b. in Stark Co., Sugar Creek Twp., Ohio in 1834, and m. John Smith.

Joseph$^{1.1.1.5.4.1.1.5.5}$, b. in Stark Co., Sugar Creek Twp., Ohio in 1836.

George A.$^{1.1.1.5.4.1.1.5.6}$, b. in Van Wert Co., Wilshire Twp., Ohio on Sept. 27, 1841, and d. on Sept. 3, 1849.

John$^{1.1.1.5.4.1.1.5.7}$, b. in Wilshire Twp. about 1843.

Louisa Jane$^{1.1.1.5.4.1.1.5.8}$, b. in Wilshire Twp. in 1845, and d. in 1923. She m. Conrad Ault.

Mary J.$^{1.1.1.5.4.1.1.5.9}$, b. in Wilshire Twp. on Aug. 23, 1849, and d. on March 23, 1851.

Lenhart Dull

Lenhart$^{1.1.1.5.4.1.1.9}$ m. Susannah Ream in Van Wert Co., on Feb.

17, 1842. She was b. May 10, 1824, and d. in Tuscarwas Co., New Philadelphia, Ohio on Nov. 10, 1924. After Lenhart's death, Susannah m. his brother, Elias (between 1900 and 1906). Lenhart d. in Van Wert Co., Wilshire Twp., Ohio on May 8, 1892. They had the following children in Wilshire Twp.:

Celesta$^{1.1.1.5.4.1.1.9.1}$, b. Dec. 2, 1844, and m. Edward W. Robinson. Celesta d. in 1937.

James Monroe$^{1.1.1.5.4.1.1.9.2}$, b. Jan. 23, 1846, and m. Martha Ann Lintermoot in Van Wert Co. on May 17, 1868. She was b. in 1851, and d. in 1916. Monroe d. in Van Wert Co. on June 6, 1916.

Thomas Jefferson$^{1.1.1.5.4.1.1.9.3}$, b. April 7, 1848, and m. Mary Ursula Exline. She was b. in 1848, and d. in 1918.

George Washington$^{1.1.1.5.4.1.1.9.4}$, b. June 2, 1850, and d. in 1892. He m. Evaline Pickering in Mercer Co. on March 7, 1875.

Franklin Pierce$^{1.1.1.5.4.1.1.9.5}$, b. Jan. 31, 1855, and m. Hattie E. Martin in Van Wert Co. on Jan. 6, 1881. She was b. in 1862.

James Buchanan$^{1.1.1.5.4.1.1.9.6}$, b. July 11, 1857, and m. Serena Lintermoot. She was b. in Ohio in Nov., 1863. James d. in Mercer Co., Black Creek Twp., Ohio in 1945.

Lafayette Jackson$^{1.1.1.5.4.1.1.9.7}$, b. April 15, 1861, and d. in 1945. He m. Cora McKillip in Mercer Co. on Aug. 8, 1883, and Thursa Randels.

Joseph Elmore$^{1.1.1.5.4.1.1.9.8}$, b. Aug. 8, 1863, and m. Augusta Krumboltz and Frances Krumboltz.

Isabella$^{1.1.1.5.4.1.1.9.9}$, b. Aug. 20, 1865, and m. Victor Miller.

Arabella$^{1.1.1.5.4.1.1.9.10}$, b. Sept. 5, 1866, and m. Frank Cushwa/Cushman.

Mary C.$^{1.1.1.5.4.1.1.9.11}$, b. March 5, 1871, and m. Frank Estell.

Jacob Dull

Jacob$^{1.1.1.5.4.1.1.10}$ m. Harriet Ream in Van Wert Co. on Nov. 18, 1846. She was b. in Ohio on July 1, 1828, and d. in Van Wert Co., Wilshire Twp., Ohio on April 12, 1914. Jacob d. in Wilshire Twp. on Aug. 15, 1904. They had the following children in Wilshire Twp.:

Sylvester$^{1.1.1.5.4.1.1.10.1}$, bon in June, 1846, and m. Rebecca Exline.

Amos$^{1.1.1.5.4.1.1.10.2}$, b. in March, 1851, and m. Emily E. Stewart in Van Wert Co. on March 8, 1873. She was b. in 1845.

Mariah Isabell$^{1.1.1.5.4.1.1.10.3}$, b. in 1855.

Samuel$^{1.1.1.5.4.1.1.10.4}$, b. in Jan., 1858, and m. Martha J. She was b. in 1856.

Franklin Monroe$^{1.1.1.5.4.1.1.10.5}$, b. April 3, 1860, and d. on Dec. 15, 1860.

Margaret S.$^{1.1.1.5.4.1.1.10.6}$, b. in 1861.

Uriah[1.1.1.5.4.1.1.10.7], b. in 1875.
Jacob A.[1.1.1.5.4.1.1.10.8], b. in 1878.

Johannah Dull

Johannah[1.1.1.5.4.1.1.11] m. William Agler in Van Wert Co. on March 21, 1847. He was b. in Stark Co., Sugar Creek Twp., Ohio in 1824, and d. in Van Wert Co. in 1904. Johannah d. in Van Wert Co. in 1894. They had the following children in Van Wert Co.:

Mahala[1.1.1.5.4.1.1.11.1], b. in 1848, and d. 1851.

Emily Clara[1.1.1.5.4.1.1.11.2], b. Jan. 6, 1850, and m. John William Lewellen in Van Wert Co. on Jan. 2, 1870. He was b. in 1844, and d. in 1929. Emily d. in Montgomery Co., Lewiston, Michigan on Jan. 5, 1933.

Valentine[1.1.1.5.4.1.1.11.3], b. in 1852, and m. Mary Elizabeth Knight. She was b. in 1857, and d. in 1898. Valentine d. 1898.

Joseph R.[1.1.1.5.4.1.1.11.4], b. in 1854.

Naomi[1.1.1.5.4.1.1.11.5], b. in 1856, and m. Jacob Kraugh. He was b. in 1857, and d. in 1929. She d. in 1930.

Celestia[1.1.1.5.4.1.1.11.6], b. in 1859, and d. in 1876.

William[1.1.1.5.4.1.1.11.7], b. in Jan., 1862.

Willis McKey[1.1.1.5.4.1.1.11.8], b. in Jan., 1862, and m. Mary Sabina, dau. of Joshua and Elmira (Medaugh) Wagers, on July 4, 1888. She was b. in 1864, and d. in 1954. He d. in 1953.

Elias Dull

Elias[1.1.1.5.4.1.1.12] m. Jane Walters in Van Wert Co. on Sept. 3, 1850 and Susannah Ream, widow of his brother, Lenhart, between 1900 and 1907. Jane was b. Aug. 31, 1823, and d. in Wilshire Twp. on April 25, 1900. Elias d. there on Sept. 3, 1907. They had the following children in Wilshire Twp.:

Harriet Ellen[1.1.1.5.4.1.1.12.1], b. July 1, 1853, and m. John Lorenzo Hileman in Van Wert Co. on May 5, 1870. He was b. in 1848, and d. in 1918.

Hannah Lucretia[1.1.1.5.4.1.1.12.2], b. Sept. 4, 1854, and m. William Sylvania, son of Ephraim and Jane (Schlater) Medaugh, in Van Wert Co., Ohio on Aug. 7, 1873. She d. in Paulding Co., Paulding, Ohio on Sept. 11, 1882. William d. in Wilshire Twp. on June 6, 1882.

John Wesley[1.1.1.5.4.1.1.12.3], b. March 6, 1855, and m. Mary Armand Bay in Van Wert Co. on Dec. 2, 1875. She was b. in 1855. He d. in Wilshire Twp. in 1929.

William Walters[1.1.1.5.4.1.1.12.4], b. March 4, 1857, and m. Mary E. Shaffer. He d. in Wilshire Twp. on Nov. 19, 1909.

Rebecca Jane[1.1.1.5.4.1.1.12.5], b. Feb. 4, 1860, and m. Charley Blish in Van Wert Co. in 1882.

Mary Rosetta$^{1.1.1.5.4.1.1.12.6}$, b. Nov. 11, 1865, and m. Wirt A. Belden. Mary d. in Wilshire Twp. on July 9, 1890.

Catherine Dull

Catherine$^{1.1.1.5.4.1.1.13}$ m. Peter Brubaker in Van Wert Co. on Nov. 26, 1844. He was b. in Franklin Co., Pennsylvania on May 19, 1814, and d. in Van Wert Co., Liberty Twp., Ohio on July 12, 1898. Catherine d. there on July 28, 1909. They had the following children in Liberty Twp.:

- George E.$^{1.1.1.5.4.1.1.13.1}$, b. in 1846.
- Elizabeth$^{1.1.1.5.4.1.1.13.2}$, b. in 1847.
- Naaman$^{1.1.1.5.4.1.1.13.3}$, b. Dec. 12, 1849, and m. Ellen Lintermoot. She was b. in 1856.
- Elmira$^{1.1.1.5.4.1.1.13.4}$, b. Nov. 18, 1851, and d. on Sept. 2, 1853.
- Eleanor$^{1.1.1.5.4.1.1.13.5}$, b. in 1854.
- Willis$^{1.1.1.5.4.1.1.13.6}$, b. in 1857.
- Annete$^{1.1.1.5.4.1.1.13.7}$, b. in 1859, and m. --- Smith.
- Mary D.$^{1.1.1.5.4.1.1.13.8}$, b. in July, 1861, and m. Solomon, son of Isaac and Sophia (Mihm) Putman$^{1.1.8.7.2.1a}$, in Van Wert Co., Ohio in 1880.
- Hannah D.$^{1.1.1.5.4.1.1.13.9}$, b. in 1864.
- William$^{1.1.1.5.4.1.1.13.10}$, b. in 1866.

Catherine Dull

Catherine$^{1.1.1.5.4.2}$ m. John H. Pile. He was b. in Washington Co., Hagarstown, Maryland on Aug. 17, 1775, and d. in Somerset Co., Milford Twp., Pennsylvania in 1845. Catherine d. in Milford Twp. on Oct. 23, 1860. They had the following children in Milford Twp.:

- George$^{1.1.1.5.4.2.1}$, b. Feb. 10, 1797.
- John$^{1.1.1.5.4.2.2}$, b. about 1799, and m. Salome/Margaret Knable.
- Joseph$^{1.1.1.5.4.2.3}$, b. April 4, 1804, and d. in Milford Twp. on Feb. 24, 1877. He m. Mary Barkman. She was b. in 1804, and d. in 1870.
- Jonathan$^{1.1.1.5.4.2.4}$, b. Aug. 2, 1805, and d. in Somerset Co., Sculton, Pennsylvania on Sept. 7, 1889. He m. Catherine. She was b. in 1820, and d. in 1896.
- Henry$^{1.1.1.5.4.2.5}$, b. about 1807.
- Jacob$^{1.1.1.5.4.2.6}$, b. about 1809.
- Samuel$^{1.1.1.5.4.2.7}$, b. Sept. 23, 1811.
- Peter$^{1.1.1.5.4.2.8}$, b. about 1812, and d. sometime before 1845.
- David$^{1.1.1.5.4.2.9}$, b. about 1815, and d. sometime before 1845.
- Elias$^{1.1.1.5.4.2.10}$, b. June 29, 1816, and m. Mary. She was b. in 1816, and they resided in Somerset Co., Jefferson Twp., Pennsylvania.
- Elizabeth$^{1.1.1.5.4.2.11}$, b. Jan. 25, 1818.

Daniel Barnetta$^{1.1.1.5.4.2.12}$, b. Jan. 11, 1819, and d. in Milford Twp. on April 18, 1879. He m. Sarah Bearl. She was b. in 1818, and d. in 1888.

Absalom$^{1.1.1.5.4.2.13}$, b. Feb. 6, 1822, and m. Delilah. She was b. in 1833.

George Pile

George$^{1.1.1.5.4.2.1}$ m. Salome$^{1.1.8.6a}$, dau. of Andreas$^{1.1.8a}$ and Anna Elisabetha (Lenhart) Putman. She d. in Milford Twp. on Oct. 1, 1891, and George d. there on March 15, 1894. They had the following children in Milford Twp.:

Rosanna$^{1.1.1.5.4.2.1.1}$, b. in 1821, and d. in 1916. She m. William Moore and John L. Gardner. William was b. in 1811, and d. in 1852. John was b. in 1830.

Andrew$^{1.1.1.5.4.2.1.2}$, b. about 1823.

Josiah$^{1.1.1.5.4.2.1.3}$, b. in 1825, and d. in 1868. He m. Margaret Kooser. She was b. in 1828, and d. in 1911.

Mary$^{1.1.1.5.4.2.1.4}$, b. about 1827, and m. Franklin King.

Jeremiah$^{1.1.1.5.4.2.1.5}$, b. in 1829, and d. in 1926. He m. Susan Stough and Ida Lowry. Susan was b. in 1836, and d. in 1882.

Solomon$^{1.1.1.5.4.2.1.6}$, b. in 1831, and d. in 1917. He m. Sarah King. She was b. in 1837, and d. in 1908.

Samuel Pile

Samuel$^{1.1.1.5.4.2.7}$ m. Elizabeth Cable, dau. of Peter and Sarah (Cable) Dumbauld. She d. in Licking Co., Bennington Twp., Ohio on Sept. 7, 1885, and Samuel d. there on May 25, 1882. They had the following children in Fayette Co., Salt Lick Twp., Pennsylvania:

Sarah E.$^{1.1.1.5.4.2.7.1}$, b. in Oct. 28, 1833, bapt. at Good Hope Lutheran Church June 11, 1837, and sponsored by Petrus Dumbauld. She m. Henry S. Beider on Aug. 8, 1855. He was b. in Fayette Co., Pennsylvania on July 11, 1832, and d. in Licking Co., Jonestown, Ohio in 1915. Sarah d. there in 1902.

Ananias$^{1.1.1.5.4.2.7.2}$, b. and d. in 1834.

Clarissa Clara$^{1.1.1.5.4.2.7.3}$, b. Jan. 11, 1836, and m. Henry Jackson Crotinger. He was b. in Licking Co., Burlington Twp., Ohio in 1835, and d. there in 1857. Clarissa d. at Jonestown, Ohio on June 26, 1911.

Catherine Ann$^{1.1.1.5.4.2.7.4}$, b. July 25, 1838, and m. William Henry Barrick. He was b. in Licking Co., Burlington Twp., Ohio, and d. in Bennington Twp. on Jan. 30, 1920. Catherine d. in Bennington Twp. on April 13, 1874.

Austin$^{1.1.1.5.4.2.7.5}$, b. Aug. 24, 1840, and d. in Licking Co., Bennington Twp., Ohio on Nov. 11, 1906. He m. Kate Hurd in 1876. She was b. in June, 1855, and d. in Bennington Twp. in

1923.

Amanda[1.1.1.5.4.2.7.6], b. June 30, 1842, and m. Joseph Runnels in Licking Co., Ohio in 1864. He was b. in Ohio on Dec. 11, 1837, and d. in Licking Co., Liberty Twp., Ohio on Dec. 5, 1917. Amanda d. in Liberty Twp. on March 10, 1904.

Peter Dull

Peter[1.1.1.5.4.3] m. Eva K. Knable in Somerset Co., Pennsylvania in 1804. She was b. March 31, 1790, and d. in Somerset Co., Milford Twp., Pennsylvania on Sept. 19, 1861. Peter d. in Milford Twp. on Dec. 15, 1854. They had the following children in Milford Twp.:

John[1.1.1.5.4.3.1], b. Oct. 17, 1805.
George[1.1.1.5.4.3.2], b. Jan. 30, 1808.
Elizabeth[1.1.1.5.4.3.3], b. May 26, 1810.
Jacob[1.1.1.5.4.3.4], b. Dec. 3, 1812, and m. Catherine McCormick. She was b. in 1822.
Mary[1.1.1.5.4.3.5], b. about 1814, and m. --- Brant.
Peter[1.1.1.5.4.3.6], b. Sept. 23, 1816.
Anthony[1.1.1.5.4.3.7], b. Nov. 26, 1818, and d. in 1895. He m. Polly. She was b. in 1811, and d. in 1881.
Daniel[1.1.1.5.4.3.8], b. April 19, 1822, and d. on Oct. 21, 1870. He m. Margaret King. She was b. in 1827, and d. in 1870.
Sarah Salome[1.1.1.5.4.3.9], b. March 28, 1825, and d. on Sept. 18, 1883. She m. George Brant. He was b. in 1825, and d. in 1913.
Christina[1.1.1.5.4.3.10], b. Nov. 20, 1827, and m. Daniel Ressler and Jacob Brooks.
Catherine[1.1.1.5.4.3.11], b. in March, 1828.
Samuel H.[1.1.1.5.4.3.12], b. Nov. 13, 1831, and d. on July 28, 1878. He m. Cassandra Walter in Somerset Co. on Dec. 9, 1852. She was b. in 1830, and d. in 1878.

John Dull

John[1.1.1.5.4.3.1] m. Mary K. Hartzell in Somerset Co. on May 18, 1826. She was b. in 1806, and d. in 1841. They had the following children:

George Alexander[1.1.1.5.4.3.1.1], b. in 1827.
Hiram[1.1.1.5.4.3.1.2], b. in 1828.
Elizabeth Catherine[1.1.1.5.4.3.1.3], b. in 1830.
Simon Peter[1.1.1.5.4.3.1.4], b. in 1832.
Mary[1.1.1.5.4.3.1.5], b. in 1833, and d. in 1920. She m. Singleton Kimmel. He was b. in 1827, and d. in 1906.

George Dull

George[1.1.1.5.4.3.2] m. Catherine Walter. She was b. in 1805, and d. in 1865. George d. in 1880. They had the following children:

Daniel W.$^{1.1.1.5.4.3.2.1}$, b. in 1829, and m. Rebecca$^{1.1.8.5.4a}$, dau. of George and Eva$^{1.1.8.5a}$ (Putman) Barron. She was b. in 1827, and d. 1893. Daniel d. in 1891.

Uriah$^{1.1.1.5.4.3.2.2}$, b. in 1831, and m. Margaret Kooser.

Julia$^{1.1.1.5.4.3.2.3}$, b. in 1833, and d. in 1894. She m. David L. Colbern. He was b. in 1827, and d. in 1868.

Jacob$^{1.1.1.5.4.3.2.4}$, b. in 1835, and d. in 1902.

Harriet$^{1.1.1.5.4.3.2.5}$, b. in 1837.

Romanus$^{1.1.1.5.4.3.2.6}$, b. in 1839, and d. in 1865.

William$^{1.1.1.5.4.3.2.7}$, b. in 1841, and m. Louise Sipe.

Rebecca$^{1.1.1.5.4.3.2.8}$, b. in 1843, and m. Solomon Davis.

John$^{1.1.1.5.4.3.2.9}$, b. in 1846, and d. in 1917. He m. Jane Bailey.

Mary$^{1.1.1.5.4.3.2.10}$, b. in 1848, d. in 1891. She m. Hiram C. Sipe.

Lucinda$^{1.1.1.5.4.3.2.11}$, b. in 1850, and m. Alexander Brooks.

Elizabeth Dull

Elizabeth$^{1.1.1.5.4.3.3}$ m. Jonathan, son of Daniel Sechler, and d. on May 14, 1883. He was b. in Milford Twp. in 1800, and d. there in 1869 (70). They had the following children:

Harriet$^{1.1.1.5.4.3.3.1}$, m. John Mason.

Daniel$^{1.1.1.5.4.3.3.2}$.

Juliana$^{1.1.1.5.4.3.3.3}$, m. Joseph Siebert.

Barbara$^{1.1.1.5.4.3.3.4}$, b. June 20, 1837, m. George F., son of Samuel K. and Mary (Flich) Kimmel, on April 12, 1861. He was b. in Somerset Co., Milford Twp. on Dec. 30, 1837.

George$^{1.1.1.5.4.3.3.5}$, m. Minerva Boucher and Catherine (Knogey) Reese. George served in the Civil War. Minerva d. on May 23, 1891.

Elizabeth$^{1.1.1.5.4.3.3.6}$ m. Samuel Kuhlman and Herman Kreager.

Joseph$^{1.1.1.5.4.3.3.7}$.

Peter Dull

Peter$^{1.1.1.5.4.3.6}$ m. Catherine Weller. She was b. in 1823, and d. in 1907. Peter d. on March 31, 1885. They had the following children:
Martha$^{1.1.1.5.4.3.6.1}$, m. --- Critchfield; Samantha$^{1.1.1.5.4.3.6.2}$, m. --- Fritz; Susan$^{1.1.1.5.4.3.6.3}$, d. in 1884; Minerva$^{1.1.1.5.4.3.6.4}$, m. --- Reid; Albertha$^{1.1.1.5.4.3.6.5}$; Elmira$^{1.1.1.5.4.3.6.6}$; R. H.$^{1.1.1.5.4.3.6.7}$; I. P.$^{1.1.1.5.4.3.6.8}$; John W.$^{1.1.1.5.4.3.6.9}$, d. in 1884; William L.$^{1.1.1.5.4.3.6.10}$.

Elisabeth Dull

Elisabeth$^{1.1.1.5.4.4}$ m. Jacob Sipe. Elisabeth d. in Somerset Co., Pennsylvania in 1824. They had the following children in Somerset Co.: Christina$^{1.1.1.5.4.4.1}$, b. in Aug., 1815; Joseph$^{1.1.1.5.4.4.2}$, b. March 9, 1816; Michael$^{1.1.1.5.4.4.3}$, b. May 11, 1818; Jacob$^{1.1.1.5.4.4.4}$, b.

Aug. 21, 1820, and d. at New Centerville, Pennsylvania in 1887. He m. Sarah Chorpenning; Sarah$^{1.1.1.5.4.4.5}$, b. about 1822.

Christina Sipe

Christina$^{1.1.1.5.4.4.1}$ m. Jonas Shultz. He was b. in 1815, and d. in 1883. Christina d. in Somerset Co. on Aug. 16, 1905. They had the following children: Sarah$^{1.1.1.5.4.4.1.1}$, b. in 1837, and m. Daniel Barklay. He was b. in 1837, and d. in 1907. Sarah d. in 1927; Mary Anne$^{1.1.1.5.4.4.1.2}$, b. in 1838, and d. in 1851.

Joseph Sipe

Joseph$^{1.1.1.5.4.4.2}$ m. Mary Friedline in Somerset Co. on Sept. 9, 1836. She was b. in 1818. They had the following daus.: Joanna$^{1.1.1.5.4.4.2.1}$, b. in 1844; Elizabeth$^{1.1.1.5.4.4.2.2}$.

Frederick Dull

Frederick$^{1.1.1.5.4.7}$ resided in Somerset Co., Upper Turkeyfoot Twp., Pennsylvania. He had the following sons: Jacob$^{1.1.1.5.4.7.1}$, b. in Somerset Co., Pennsylvania in 1804, and d. in Preston Co., West Virginia in 1881; Abraham$^{1.1.1.5.4.7.2}$, b. in Somerset Co., Pennsylvania, and d. in Preston Co., West Virginia.

Magdalena Dull

Magdalena$^{1.1.1.5.4.8}$ m. Christian Speicher, and had the following children in Somerset Co., Pennsylvania: Sarah$^{1.1.1.5.4.8.1}$, b. Oct. 24, 1814, and d. on Feb. 28, 1831; John$^{1.1.1.5.4.8.2}$, b. Dec. 6, 1816; Joseph$^{1.1.1.5.4.8.3}$, b. May 18, 1817; Samuel$^{1.1.1.5.4.8.4}$, b. Feb. 11, 1823; Francis$^{1.1.1.5.4.8.5}$, b. Sept. 12, 1825; Aaron$^{1.1.1.5.4.8.6}$, b. May 7, 1827; Peter$^{1.1.1.5.4.8.7}$, b. April 5, 1829; Mary Ann$^{1.1.1.5.4.8.8}$, b. March 5, 1831, and d. on June 28, 1836; Christian$^{1.1.1.5.4.8.9}$, b. March 25, 1833, and d. on April 13, 1834.

George Dull

George$^{1.1.1.5.4.10}$ m. Christina, dau. of Frederick G. and Catherine (Patton) Younkin. She was b. in Milford Twp. on Aug. 15, 1795, bapt. at Sanner Lutheran Church on Feb. 23, 1797, and d. in Milford Twp. on July 9, 1881. George d. in Milford Twp. on March 27, 1852. They are buried in New Centerville cemetery. They had the following children in Milford Twp.:

Sabina$^{1.1.1.5.4.10.1}$, b. about 1814, and d. in 1896.
Elizabeth$^{1.1.1.5.4.10.2}$, b. April 9, 1815, and m. Jonathan Cable Dumbauld$^{1.1.1.3.5.2d}$.
Catherine$^{1.1.1.5.4.10.3}$, b. Oct. 6, 1817, and d. in Milford Twp. on Oct. 5, 1843.
Frederick$^{1.1.1.5.4.10.4}$, b. Jan. 29, 1819.

Mary Ann$^{1.1.1.5.4.10.5}$, b. about 1820.
Lucinda$^{1.1.1.5.4.10.6}$, b. about 1820, and m. Jacob Howenstein.
John Rhees$^{1.1.1.5.4.10.7}$, b. Feb. 1, 1821, and d. in Black Hawk
   Co., Waterloo, Iowa. He m. Caroline Howenstein on Sept. 16,
   1841.
Gertrude Junta$^{1.1.1.5.4.10.8}$, b. March 11, 1823.
William$^{1.1.1.5.4.10.9}$, b. May 20, 1825, and d. in Milford Twp. on
   Jan. 8, 1908. He m. Margaret Flick. She was b. in 1830.
Sarah Ann$^{1.1.1.5.4.10.10}$, b. Oct. 11, 1827, and m. Samuel Saylor.
Marion$^{1.1.1.5.4.10.11}$, b. June 3, 1830.
Juliana Christine$^{1.1.1.5.4.10.12}$, b. Sept. 8, 1833, and d. on Sept. 5,
   1889. She m. Jesse Sweitzer.
Josiah$^{1.1.1.5.4.10.13}$, b. Dec. 22, 1835.
Harriet$^{1.1.1.5.4.10.14}$, b. Aug. 18, 1837.

Frederick Dull

Frederick$^{1.1.1.5.4.10.4}$ d. in Somerset Co., Ursina, Pennsylvania on
May 10, 1896. He m. Margaret Fadley in Somerset Co. on Sept. 6,
1840. She was b. Oct. 13, 1822, and d. in Lower Turkeyfoot Twp. on
Feb. 27, 1899. They had the following children in Lower Turkeyfoot
Twp., Ursina:
   Sarah$^{1.1.1.5.4.10.4.1}$, b. in 1841, and m. Jacob J. Rush on June 12,
      1859.
   Freeman$^{1.1.1.5.4.10.4.2}$, b. about 1843.
   Christina$^{1.1.1.5.4.10.4.3}$, b. April 28, 1845, and m. Samuel Baley.
   Barbary$^{1.1.1.5.4.10.4.4}$, b. April 28, 1845, and d. before 1852.
   John$^{1.1.1.5.4.10.4.5}$, b. in 1847.
   Barbara Ellen$^{1.1.1.5.4.10.4.6}$, b. July 15, 1852, and m. Albert Ream
      about 1870, Samuel Brougher in Somerset Co. on Feb. 2, 1879,
      and --- Crosson about 1887. Barbara d. in Somerset Co., Upper
      Turkeyfoot Twp. on May 3, 1938. Samuel was b. in Upper
      Turkeyfoot Twp. on Sept. 2, 1937, and d. there on Jan. 29,
      1886.
   Ann$^{1.1.1.5.4.10.4.7}$, b. about 1854, and m. Bruce Harnett.
   George$^{1.1.1.5.4.10.4.8}$, b. about 1856.
   Frederick Wilson$^{1.1.1.5.4.10.4.9}$, b. about 1858, and m. Candace
      Conn.
   Mary M.$^{1.1.1.5.4.10.4.10}$, b. about 1860, and m. James Sanbour.
   Harris H.$^{1.1.1.5.4.10.4.11}$, b. about 1862.

Mary Ann Dull

Mary Ann$^{1.1.1.5.4.10.5}$ m. Jacob Critchfield, and d. in Somerset Co.,
Rockwood, Pennsylvania. He was b. in Milford Twp. on March 10, 1830.
They had the following children:
   Oliver$^{1.1.1.5.4.10.5.1}$, m. Rohama Knepper.

John M.$^{1.1.1.5.4.10.5.2}$, b. in Milford Twp. on July 29, 1851, and m. Anna, dau. of John and Martha (Lobe) Hay, in Somerset Co. on Feb. 2, 1875. She was b. in Milford Twp. on March 1, 1856.
Louisa$^{1.1.1.5.4.10.5.3}$, m. Jacob Critchfield.
Emma$^{1.1.1.5.4.10.5.4}$, m. Watson Schrock.
Minerva$^{1.1.1.5.4.10.5.5}$, m. Edward Hoover.
Anna M.$^{1.1.1.5.4.10.5.6}$, m. Edward Spangler.
Eleanora$^{1.1.1.5.4.10.5.7}$, b. March 22, 1871, and m. Charles, son of Lewis J. and Elizabeth (Walker) Knepper in Somerset Co., Pennsylvania on April 15, 1897. He was b. in Brother's Valley Twp. on Aug. 9, 1870, and d. in Somerset Co. on June 1, 1894. Eleanora d. in Somerest Co. on Aug. 1, 1889.
Edward S.$^{1.1.1.5.4.10.5.8}$, m. Kate Ferman.
William W.$^{1.1.1.5.4.10.5.9}$, m. Sadie Braham.

Josiah Dull

Josiah$^{1.1.1.5.4.10.13}$ m. Elizabeth Gilbert/Ross in 1857. Josiah d. in Cerro Gordo Co., Rockwell, Iowa in 1909. They had the following children: Emma$^{1.1.1.5.4.10.13.1}$, b. in Black Hawk Co., Waterloo, Iowa in 1859; Flora$^{1.1.1.5.4.10.13.2}$, b. in Waterloo, Iowa in 1861; Frederick$^{1.1.1.5.4.10.13.3}$, b. in Waterloo, Iowa in 1863, and d. in South Dakota in May, 1929; Louis Augusta$^{1.1.1.5.4.10.13.4}$, b. in Waterloo, Iowa in 1866; Charles Albert$^{1.1.1.5.4.10.13.5}$, b. in Waterloo, Iowa in 1872; Martha Mae$^{1.1.1.5.4.10.13.6}$, b. in Rockwell, Iowa on May 22, 1880; Guy Hornea$^{1.1.1.5.4.10.13.7}$, b. in Rockwell, Iowa in 1884.

Johan Jurg Doll

Johan Jurg "Georg"$^{1.1.1.5.7}$ m. Hannah, and bapt. the following children in Northampton Co., Pennsylvania: Elizabeth$^{1.1.1.5.7.1}$, bapt. on Aug. 7, 1775; John$^{1.1.1.5.7.2}$, bapt. on Dec. 24, 1775.

Martin Doll

Martin$^{1.1.1.5.9}$ m. Elisabeth. He resided in Northampton Co., Moore Twp., Pennsylvania in Aug., 1793, and York Co., Chanceford Twp., Pennsylvania in 1798. They had the following children:
John$^{1.1.1.5.9.1}$, b. in Moore Twp. on Feb. 12, 1788, bapt. at Kreidersville (Stone) Church on March 23, 1788, and sponsored by Gertrude Flick.
Susanna$^{1.1.1.5.9.2}$, b. Feb. 24, 1791, bapt. at Kreidersville on April 3, 1791, and sponsored by Christian Esch and Barbara Bartholemi.
Elisabeth$^{1.1.1.5.9.3}$, b. in York Co., Chanceford Twp. on Aug. 5, 1800, bapt. at Stehli's Union Church on Aug. 24, 1800, and sponsored by Jacob Arner.

Johan Caspar Doll

Johann Caspar$^{1.1.1.8}$ m. Margaret. She was b. in 1724, and d. in Northampton Co., Plainfield, Pennsylvania on April 26, 1790. Caspar was appointed guardian of Maria Margaretha, Susannah and Maria Elisabetha, daus. of Johan Nickel and Maria Margaretha Heil in Moore Twp. in Sept., 1762. Johann Caspar d. sometime after his wife. They had the following dau.:

Anna Catharina$^{1.1.1.8.1}$, b. in Bucks Co., Tohickon Twp., Pennsylvania on Jan. 1, 1757, bapt. at Tohickon Union Church on Feb. 22, 1757, and sponsored by Jost and Christina Edelman.

Johan Nickel Doll

Johan Nickel$^{1.1.1.9}$ m. Margaretha Sholtz, and had the following children:

Susanna Margaret$^{1.1.1.9.1}$, b. Sept. 24, 1759, and bapt. in Bucks Co., Tohickon Twp., Tohickon Union Church Oct. 26, 1759. She was sponsored by Peter Doll and wife.

Elizabeth$^{1.1.1.9.2}$, bapt. at Northampton Co., Plainfield, Pennsylvania on April 1, 1764.

Johan Frederick$^{1.1.1.9.3}$, bapt. at Plainfield on Aug. 31, 1766.

Anna Elisabetha Doll

Anna Elisabetha$^{1.1.2}$ m. Johan Christian, son of Adam Drum, at Ulmet Germany on Feb. 26, 1696/97. Johan Christian was b. at Ulmet on Oct. 14, 1665, and d. there on March 8, 1730/31. They had the following children at Ulmet:

Maria Margaretha$^{1.1.2.1}$, bapt. on April 7, 1700, and m. Johan Daniel Staudt.

Christina Barbara$^{1.1.2.2}$, bapt. on Sept. 8, 1703, and m. Johan Peter Klein.

Johannes Adam$^{1.1.2.3}$, bapt. on Dec. 9, 1705.

Maria Elisabetha$^{1.1.2.4}$, bapt. on May 17, 1708, and d. in 1714.

Johan Peter$^{1.1.2.5}$, bapt. on March 18, 1711, and d. in 1714.

Anna Maria$^{1.1.2.6}$, bapt. on June 13, 1713, and m. Johan Adam Albert on April 24, 1731.

Johann Georg$^{1.1.2.7}$, bapt. on Jan. 16, 1716.

Johann Abraham$^{1.1.2.8}$, bapt. on Sept. 1, 1718.

Johannes Adam Drum

Johannes Adam$^{1.1.2.3}$ arrived at Philadelphia on the ship *Samuel* in 1737 with his cousins, Peter and Christian Doll. Adam m. Maria Gertraud, dau. of Peter Bier, at Ulmet, Germeny on Jan. 22, 1732/33. She was b. at Ulmet on April 2, 1704, and d. sometime after 1757. Adam was killed by Indians in Berks Co., Albany Twp., Allemangel,

Pennsylvania on June 22, 1757. The Indians also took his wife, and their 19 year old son prisoner. When his wife escaped, one of the Indians threw a tomahawk, and cut her badly in the neck. They had the following children:

    Johan Christian$^{1.1.2.3.1}$, bapt. on April 17, 1735.

    George A.$^{1.1.2.3.2}$, b. in Albany Twp. in 1738, and m. Maria Catherine Strasser in Berks Co., Pennsylvania in 1759. George d. in Fairfield Co., Ohio on Oct. 19, 1808. Maria Catherine d. in Fairfield Co., about 1817.

****

Phillip Boudemont

Phillip^{1a} was b. in 1690. He m. Maria Magdalena Pusset. They were members of the Waldensian (French Protestant) faith. He d. in Bayern Pfalz Rohrbach Germany in 1762, and his will mentions two sons that had settled in the new world. They had the following children at Rhorbach:

    Andreas$^{1.1a}$, b. June 10, 1716.

    Philipp Jacob$^{1.2a}$, b. in 1720, and m. Ann Mary. He arrived at Philadelphia on Oct. 7, 1743, on the ship *St. Andrew*. He d. in Frederick Co., Middletown Valley, Maryland in Dec., 1792.

    Jean Philipp$^{1.3a}$, b. Aug. 4, 1722, and m. Anna Catharina Grebauer at Rohrbach on June 10, 1749.

Andreas Boudemont

Andreas$^{1.1a}$ m. Catharina Barbara, dau. of Nicholas Bourgey of Moehrfelden, at Steinweiler Church at Rohrbach on Jan. 10, 1746/7. They arrived at Philadelphia in the ship *Osgood* on Sept. 29, 1750. They settled in Frederick Co., Middletown Valley, Maryland. Andreas was naturalized on Sept. 24, 1762, after baptism on Sept. 5, 1762 by Reverend William Otterbein at the German Reformed Church of Frederick Town (witnessed by Thomas Schley and Peter Hergat). In 1770, they moved to Washington Co., Maryland, south of Eakles's Mills, on a 50 acre tract called Root's Hill, purchased from Joseph Chapline on Dec. 18, 1769. Andreas later purchased a 92 and one fourth acre tract called Partnership. Andreas was a farmer, and d. in June, 1777. Andreas's will was written on Feb. 4, 1777, and probated on June 14, 1777. Catharina d. sometime after 1793. They had the following children:

    John/Frantz$^{1.1.1a}$, b. Feb. 2, 1747/8.

    Peter$^{1.1.2a}$, b. in 1750.

    Elisabeth$^{1.1.3a}$, b. Dec. 22, 1751, and m. John Dull$^{1.1.1.5.4.1}$.

    Maria Magdalena$^{1.1.4a}$, b. in 1753.

    Mary Ann Amelia$^{1.1.5a}$, b. in 1755.

    Catharina$^{1.1.6a}$, b. about 1757.

Susanna$^{1.1.7a}$, b. about 1761.
Andreas$^{1.1.8a}$, b. in 1767.

John Buttmann

John$^{1.1.1a}$ m. Sarah Schneider. John was a distiller, farmer, and a Private in the Revolutionary War. He moved to Somerset Co., Pennsylvania about 1785. He d. in Somerset Co., Milford Twp., Pennsylvania in April, 1799. They had the following children:
Magdalena$^{1.1.1.1a}$, b. Sept. 30, 1775.
Henry$^{1.1.1.2a}$, b. June 18, 1783, and d. in Somerset Co., Pennsylvania in 1815.
John$^{1.1.1.3a}$, b. Jan. 1, 1787.
Elizabeth$^{1.1.1.4a}$, b. Feb. 22, 1789.
Peter$^{1.1.1.5a}$, b. about 1791.

Magdalena Putman

Magdalena$^{1.1.1.1a}$ m. George Ankeny in 1794. He was b. in 1772, and d. in 1850. She d. in Somerset Co., Milford Twp., Pennsylvania on Oct. 2, 1858. They had the following children: Christian$^{1.1.1.1.1a}$, b. in 1796; Sarah$^{1.1.1.1.2a}$, b. in 1796; Elizabeth$^{1.1.1.1.3a}$, b. about 1798; Regina$^{1.1.1.1.4a}$, b. about 1800; Margaret$^{1.1.1.1.5a}$, b. in 1803; Henry$^{1.1.1.1.6a}$, b. in 1805; Mary Magdalena$^{1.1.1.1.7a}$, b. in 1811; Mattie$^{1.1.1.1.8a}$, b. about 1813; Joanna$^{1.1.1.1.9a}$, b. in 1816.

Christian Ankeny

Christian$^{1.1.1.1.1a}$ m. Catherine$^{1.1.2.10a}$, dau. of Peter$^{1.1.2a}$ and Maria (Schneider) Putman. She was b. in 1805, and d. in Tazwell Co., Illinois on Jan. 3, 1890. Christian d. there on Sept. 15, 1872. They had the following children:
George$^{1.1.1.1.1.1a}$, b. May 19, 1823, and d. in Somerset Co., Pennsylvania on Dec. 12, 1824.
Magdalena Margaret$^{1.1.1.1.1.2a}$, b. in 1825, and d. in Waukegan, Wisconsin on Jan. 20, 1915. She m. Harrison Nelcher.
Joseph$^{1.1.1.1.1.3a}$, b. Feb. 24, 1827, and m. Mary Chamberlain in Peoria, Illinois on March 13, 1861. She was b. in 1843, and d. in 1920. Joseph d. in Saline Co., Tobias, Nebraska on Oct. 6, 1902.
Mary$^{1.1.1.1.1.4a}$, b. in 1829, and m. Louis Kopcha.
Catherine$^{1.1.1.1.1.5a}$, b. in 1831, and m. Conrad Yarger.

Sarah Ankeny

Sarah$^{1.1.1.1.2a}$ m. William Seibert. He d. in 1852, and Sarah d. in 1855. They had the following children:
George$^{1.1.1.1.2.1a}$; Joseph$^{1.1.1.1.2.2a}$; Mary$^{1.1.1.1.2.3a}$; Matty$^{1.1.1.1.2.4a}$, m. Baltzer Meese; Jonas$^{1.1.1.1.2.5a}$;

Harriet[1.1.1.1.2.6a]; Hannah[1.1.1.1.2.7a].

Elizabeth Ankeny

Elizabeth[1.1.1.1.3a] m. John Laub. He d. in 1836. They had the following children: Margaret[1.1.1.1.3.1a], m. Jonathan Hay; Jonathan[1.1.1.1.3.2a]; Emma Ann[1.1.1.1.3.3a]; Magdalena[1.1.1.1.3.4a]; Hannah[1.1.1.1.3.5a]; Mary[1.1.1.1.3.6a]; Rosanna[1.1.1.1.3.7a].

Regina Ankeny

Regina[1.1.1.1.4a] m. Samuel Flickinger, and had the following children: Mary[1.1.1.1.4.1a]; Sarah[1.1.1.1.4.2a], b. in 1833, and m. Isaac Levi Knupp; Jacob[1.1.1.1.4.3a]; Ankeny[1.1.1.1.4.4a]; Catherine[1.1.1.1.4.5a]; William[1.1.1.1.4.6a]; Carrie[1.1.1.1.4.7a]; Annie[1.1.1.1.4.8a].

Margaret Ankeny

Margaret[1.1.1.1.5a] m. George Humbert. He was b. in 1799. They had the following children: Hannah[1.1.1.1.5.1a], b. in 1823; Joseph[1.1.1.1.5.2a], b. in 1826; John Henry[1.1.1.1.5.3a], b. in 1831; David[1.1.1.1.5.4a], b. in 1831, and m. J.; William[1.1.1.1.5.5a], b. in 1836; Franklin[1.1.1.1.5.6a], b. in 1836.

Henry Ankeny

Henry[1.1.1.1.6a] m. Mary Magdalena Cunningham. She was b. in 1816, and d. in 1891. Henry d. in 1878. They had the following children: Joanna[1.1.1.1.6.1a], b. in 1834, and m. John H. Huston; George[1.1.1.1.6.2a], b. in 1838, and m. Mary Hay; Henry[1.1.1.1.6.3a], b. in 1840; John[1.1.1.1.6.4a], b. in 1842; Fred[1.1.1.1.6.5a], b. in 1845, and m. --- Wechtenheiser; Joseph[1.1.1.1.6.6a], b. in 1847, and m. --- Kring; Christian[1.1.1.1.6.7a], b. in 1849, and m. Elizabeth Bittner; Sarah[1.1.1.1.6.8a], b. in 1852, and m. Benjamin Dickey; William[1.1.1.1.6.9a], b. in 1854, and m. Lydia Dull. She was b. in 1859. William d. in 1942; Jacob[1.1.1.1.6.10a], b. in 1857; Mary[1.1.1.1.6.11a], b. in 1860, and m. --- Coleman.

Mary Magdalena Ankeny

Mary Magdalena[1.1.1.1.7a] m. Christian Ankeny. Mary d. in 1850. They had the following children: George[1.1.1.1.7.1a], b. in 1833; Hannah[1.1.1.1.7.2a]; Elizabeth[1.1.1.1.7.3a]; Magdalena[1.1.1.1.7.4a]; David[1.1.1.1.7.5a]; Adam[1.1.1.1.7.6a].

Mattie Ankeny

Mattie[1.1.1.1.8a] m. Joseph Scritchfield. Mattie d. in 1846. They had the following children: David[1.1.1.1.8.1a], b. about 1832; Jesse[1.1.1.1.8.2a], b. in 1834; William[1.1.1.1.8.3a], b. in 1838; Henry[1.1.1.1.8.4a], b. in 1842.

Joanna Ankeny

Joanna$^{1.1.1.1.9a}$ m. David Humbert. He was b. in 1816, and d. in 1896. She d. in 1894. They had the following children: George Franklin$^{1.1.1.1.9.1a}$, b. in 1837, and m. Elizabeth Long; Joseph D.$^{1.1.1.1.9.2a}$, b. in 1838, and m. Catherine Wilkie.

John Putman

John$^{1.1.1.3a}$ m. Catherine$^{1.1.4ca}$, dau. of John$^{1.1ca}$ and Elizabeth Lohr. Catherine m. --- McKlveene, and later d. on Feb. 20, 1855. They had the following dau.: Elizabeth$^{1.1.1.3.1a}$.

Peter Buttmann

Peter$^{1.1.2a}$ m. Maria Schneider. He had 597 acres in Milford Twp., Somerset Co., Pennsylvania, and served in the third Battalion, Cumberland Co., Pennsylvania Militia during the Revolutionary War. He moved to Somerset Co. about 1785. Peter d. in Feb., 1809 in Somerset Co., Milford Twp., Pennsylvania. She d. in 1814. They had the following children: John $^{1.1.2.1a}$, b. in 1785; Jacob$^{1.1.2.2a}$, b. May 24, 1787; Peter$^{1.1.2.3a}$, b. Feb. 25, 1789; Elizabeth$^{1.1.2.4a}$, b. in 1793; Henry$^{1.1.2.5a}$, b. in 1795; Michael$^{1.1.2.6a}$, b. in 1797; David$^{1.1.2.7a}$, b. Aug. 20, 1798; George$^{1.1.2.8a}$, b. in 1800; Andrew$^{1.1.2.9a}$, b. March 2, 1803; Catherine$^{1.1.2.10a}$, b. in 1805, and m. Christian Ankeny$^{1.1.1.1a}$; Joseph$^{1.1.2.11a}$, b. March 6, 1808.

Jacob Putman

Jacob$^{1.1.2.2a}$ m. Elizabeth Gross. She was b. in 1789. Jacob d. in Sandusky Co., Fremont, Ohio in 1869. They had the following children: Michael$^{1.1.2.2.1a}$, b. in 1815; Peter$^{1.1.2.2.2a}$, b. about 1816; Jacob$^{1.1.2.2.3a}$, b. about 1818; Joseph$^{1.1.2.2.4a}$, b. about 1820.

Michael Putman

Michael$^{1.1.2.2.1a}$ m. Elizabeth Bates. She was b. in 1816, and d. in 1886. They had the following children:

Alpheus$^{1.1.2.2.1.1a}$, b. in 1837, and m. --- Inman.
Mary Anne$^{1.1.2.2.1.2a}$, b. in 1839, and m. Samuel Earl.
Sarah Ann$^{1.1.2.2.1.3a}$, b. in 1841, and m. Jacob Shue.
Eliza Jane$^{1.1.2.2.1.4a}$, b. in 1842.
Jacob$^{1.1.2.2.1.5a}$, b. in 1844.
Andrew$^{1.1.2.2.1.6a}$, b. in 1847, and m. Charity Earl. She was b. in 1856, and d. in 1895. He d. in 1923.
Hannah$^{1.1.2.2.1.7a}$, b. in 1850, and m. Henry Dysinger.
Michael$^{1.1.2.2.1.8a}$, b. in 1851, and m. Melissa Inman.
Sophronia$^{1.1.2.2.1.9a}$, b. in 1854, and m. Daniel Vandersale.
Fanny$^{1.1.2.2.1.10a}$, b. in 1857, and m. Henry Rupert.
Amanda$^{1.1.2.2.1.11a}$, b. in 1859.

Joseph Putman

Joseph$^{1.1.2.2.4a}$ m. Elizabeth, and had the following children:
J. H.$^{1.1.2.2.4.1a}$, b. in 1855; M. E.$^{1.1.2.2.4.2a}$, b. in 1858; L. L.$^{1.1.2.2.4.3a}$, b. in 1859.

Peter Putman

Peter$^{1.1.2.3a}$ m. Elizabeth Kooser. She was b. in 1790, and d. in 1857. Peter d. in Somerset Co., Pennsylvania on June 17, 1857. They had the following children:
Joseph$^{1.1.2.3.1a}$, born about 1815.
John$^{1.1.2.3.2a}$, b. in 1817, and d. in 1850. He m. ---Keim.
Rebecca$^{1.1.2.3.3a}$, b. in 1822, and m. Peter Keim. He was b. in 1822, and d. in 1879. Rebecca d. in 1900.
David$^{1.1.2.3.4a}$, b. in 1826, and m. Barbara Keim. She was b. in 1828, and d. in 1913. David d. in 1855.
Amelia$^{1.1.2.3.5a}$, b. in 1828, and m. Henry Kiem. He was b. in 1822, and d. in 1900.
Peter$^{1.1.2.3.6a}$, b. in 1830, and m. Susan Catherine Walter. She was b. in 1835, and d. in 1907. Peter d. in 1902.

Elizabeth Putman

Elizabeth$^{1.1.2.4a}$ m. Wilhelm Shunck. He was b. Oct. 24, 1784. and d. in Somerset Co., Brother's Valley Twp., Pennsylvania in Dec., 1852. Elizabeth d. in 1852. They had the following children:
Phillippina$^{1.1.2.4.1a}$, b. in 1812, and m. Daniel Coleman in Somerset Co., Berlin, Pennsylvania on May 3, 1829. In 1850 they were residing in Somerset Twp.
Peter$^{1.1.2.4.2a}$.
Josiah$^{1.1.2.4.3a}$.
Alexander$^{1.1.2.4.4a}$.

Josiah Shunk

Josiah$^{1.1.2.4.3a}$ m. Christina$^{1.1.8.3.1a}$, dau. of Gabriel$^{1.1.8.3a}$ and Susanna (Weimer) Putman, and had the following son: Joseph L.$^{1.1.2.4.3.1a}$.

Michael Putman

Michael$^{1.1.2.6a}$ m. Esther Landis. She was b. in 1810, and d. in 1883. Michael d. in 1869. They had the following children: Michael$^{1.1.2.6.1a}$, b. in 1818.

David Putman

David$^{1.1.2.7a}$ m. Eva Barron. Eva was b. in 1801, and d. in 1891. David d. at Trent, Pennsylvania on Dec. 23, 1875. They had the following children: Rosanna$^{1.1.2.7.1a}$, b. in 1828, and d. in 1911;

Phoebe[1.1.2.7.2a], b. in 1831, and d. in 1898; Emma[1.1.2.7.3a], b. in 1849, and d. in 1872.

George Putman

George[1.1.2.8a] m. Julian Baker. George d. on March 9, 1834. They had the following children:

John[1.1.2.8.1a], b. in 1827, and m. Maria Kooser. She was b. in 1831. John d. in 1884.

William[1.1.2.8.2a], b. in 1829, and m. Julia Ann Barnes. She was b. in 1832, and d. in 1908. William d. in 1863.

Andrew Putman

Andrew[1.1.2.9a] m. Sarah Bitner about 1823, and Dartha Huldah Richter after 1843. Sarah d. in 1842. Dartha was b. in 1821, and d. in 1895. Andrew d. in Van Wert Co., Ohio in 1865. Andrew had the following children:

Joseph[1.1.2.9.1a], b. in 1823; Mary Ann[1.1.2.9.2a], b. in 1829. Phebe[1.1.2.9.3a], b. in 1832; Fanny[1.1.2.9.4a], b. in 1838, and m. Patrick Thomas Fox; Harriet[1.1.2.9.5a], b. in 1840; Sally[1.1.2.9.6a], b. in 1842, and m. Erlas Mitchell; Margaret[1.1.2.9.7a], b. in 1843, and m. John Morrison.

Joseph Putman

Joseph[1.1.2.11a] m. Elizabeth, dau. of Andreas and Anna Elisabetha (Lenhart) Putman, in Somerset Co., Pennsylvania in Oct., 1829. Elizabeth d. in Stark Co., Sugar Creek Twp., Ohio on Oct. 6, 1893. Joseph d. there on Nov. 23, 1892. In 1833, Joseph purchased 365 acres in Stark Co., Sugar Creek Twp., Ohio, and moved there. In the Spring of 1876, he moved to Wilmot. They had the following children:

John[1.1.2.11.1a].
Gabriel[1.1.2.11.2a].
Harriet[1.1.2.11.3a], m. Benjamin Bumgardiner, and d. in 1862.
Sevilla[1.1.2.11.4a], m. Henry Kreiling.
Mary[1.1.2.11.5a], resided in Columbiana Co., Ohio.
Catherine[1.1.2.11.6a], m. Frederick Nowman.
William J.[1.1.2.11.7a], and m. Caroline, dau. of D. and Elizabeth (Ricksicker) Olmstead, on May 23, 1871. She was b. in Tuscarwas Co., Ohio on Dec. 20, 1849.

Mary Magdalena Buttmann

Mary Magdalena[1.1.4a] m. Heinrich, son of George Michael and Elizabeth Bruner, and grandson of Ulrich and Veronica Bruner, in Washington Co., Maryland in 1775. He was b. in 1750, and d. in Jessamine Co., Kentucky in 1813. Henry was a Private in the Washington Co. Rangers from 1778 to 1783, during the Revolutionary

War. They moved to Somerset Co., Pennsylvania about 1772, and to Kentucky in 1798. Maria d. in Jessamine Co., Hickman Valley, Kentucky on Oct. 22, 1810. They had the following children in Washington Co., Maryland:

John$^{1.1.4.1a}$, b. in 1775.

Catherine$^{1.1.4.2a}$, b. March 24, 1777, and d. in Jessamine Co., Kentucky on April 5, 1850. She m. Frederick Safercer on Oct. 3, 1799. Frederick was b. in 1776, and d. in 1864.

Elizabeth$^{1.1.4.3a}$, b. Jan. 24, 1779, and m. Simeon Rowland in Jessamine Co., Kentucky on Feb. 21, 1823.

Jacob$^{1.1.4.4a}$, b. in Aug., 1780, and d. in Jessamine Co., Kentucky in 1826. He m. Mahala Crimes.

Martha$^{1.1.4.5a}$, b. in 1781, and d. in Davies Co., Indiana in 1881. She m. John Trentor in Jessamine Co., Kentucky on June 6, 1809.

Mary Magdalena$^{1.1.4.6a}$, b. Feb. 10, 1783, and d. in Murfreesboro, Tennessee in 1854. She m. Matthew Walker. He was b. in 1776, and d. in 1850.

Rosina Christine$^{1.1.4.7a}$, b. April 26, 1785, and m. George Bruner.

Henry$^{1.1.4.8a}$, b. in April, 1787, and d. in 1813.

John Bruner

John$^{1.1.4.1a}$ m. Catherine Binfert. She was b. in 1791, and d. in 1840. John d. in Somerset Co., Milford Twp., Pennsylvania in 1852. They had the following children:

Henry$^{1.1.4.1.1a}$, b. in 1809.

Elizabeth$^{1.1.4.1.2a}$, b. Aug. 22, 1811, and d. on Oct. 9, 1893. She m. Joseph, son of Andreas and Anna Elisabetha (Lenhart) Putman on Feb. 14, 1829.

John$^{1.1.4.1.3a}$, b. in 1814, and d. in 1894.

Jacob$^{1.1.4.1.4a}$, b. in 1816, and d. in 1898.

Joseph$^{1.1.4.1.5a}$, b. in 1818, and d. in 1887.

Moses$^{1.1.4.1.6a}$, b. in 1825, and d. in 1901.

Mary Anne$^{1.1.4.1.7a}$, b. in 1827, and d. in 1900.

Christine$^{1.1.4.1.8a}$, b. in 1831.

Henry Bruner

Henry$^{1.1.4.1.1a}$ m. Hannah, dau. of Andreas and Anna Elisabetha (Lenhart) Putman. Henry d. in Baskerville, Pennsylvania in 1851. Hannah d. there on Oct. 26, 1894. They had the following children:

Savila$^{1.1.4.1.1.1a}$, b. in 1831, and d. in 1909.

John Andrew$^{1.1.4.1.1.2a}$, b. in 1832, and m. Harriet Bowman. John d. in 1909.

Hiram$^{1.1.4.1.1.3a}$, b. in 1834, and d. in 1883.

Margaret$^{1.1.4.1.1.4a}$, b. in 1835, and d. in 1854.

George Washington$^{1.1.4.1.1.5a}$, b. in 1837, and d. in 1936.
Myria$^{1.1.4.1.1.6a}$, b. in 1839, and d. in 1929.
Harriet$^{1.1.4.1.1.7a}$, b. in 1840.
Louisa$^{1.1.4.1.1.8a}$, b. and d. in 1842.
Elizabeth$^{1.1.4.1.1.9a}$, b. in 1843, and d. in 1917.
Josophene$^{1.1.4.1.1.10a}$, b. in 1845, and d. in 1904.
Israel$^{1.1.4.1.1.11a}$, b. in 1847, and d. in 1939.
Noah$^{1.1.4.1.1.12a}$, b. in 1849, and d. in 1929.

Mary Ann Amelia Buttmann

Mary Ann Amelia$^{1.1.5a}$ m. Christian Wyandt in Washington Co., Maryland on March 12, 1778. He was b. in 1753, and d. in 1810. Christian was a winemaker, and served in the Revolutionary War. Mary Ann Amelia d. in Washington Co., Maryland on Nov. 6, 1853. They had the following children:

Jacob$^{1.1.5.1a}$, b. in 1779.
John$^{1.1.5.2a}$, b. in 1783.
Catherine$^{1.1.5.3a}$, b. in 1784, and m. Jacob Schneider$^{1.1.6.2a}$.
Henry$^{1.1.5.4a}$, b. in 1787.
Susan$^{1.1.5.5a}$, b. in 1790.
Elizabeth$^{1.1.5.6a}$, b. in 1793, and m. David Rohrer. They resided in Montgomery Co., Dayton, Ohio.
Mary$^{1.1.5.7a}$, b. in 1795.
Christina$^{1.1.5.8a}$, b. in 1797.
Christian$^{1.1.5.9a}$, b. in 1800.
Simon$^{1.1.5.10a}$, b. in 1804.

Jacob Wyandt

Jacob$^{1.1.5.1a}$ m. Magdalena Brubaker. She was b. in 1785, and d. in 1864. Jacob d. in Stark Co., Ohio in 1838. They had the following children:

Joseph$^{1.1.5.1.1a}$, b. in 1807, and d. in 1891.
Christian$^{1.1.5.1.2a}$, b. in 1809, and d. in 1891.
Lena$^{1.1.5.1.3a}$, b. about 1811.
Elizabeth$^{1.1.5.1.4a}$, b. in 1814, and d. in 1889.
Sarah$^{1.1.5.1.5a}$, b. in 1818, and d. in 1857. She m. Henry Grimes.
Daniel$^{1.1.5.1.6a}$, b. about 1820.
Mary$^{1.1.5.1.7a}$, b. about 1822.
Rachel$^{1.1.5.1.8a}$, b. about 1824.

John Wyandt

John$^{1.1.5.2a}$ m. Magdalena Warner. She was b. in 1795, and d. in 1868. John d. in Harrison Co., Monroe Twonship, Ohio in 1848. They had the following children: John$^{1.1.5.2.1a}$; Jacob$^{1.1.5.2.2a}$; Daniel$^{1.1.5.2.3a}$, b. in 1820, d. Sept. 18, 1867, and m. Hannah Shanks; Abraham$^{1.1.5.2.4a}$;

Christina$^{1.1.5.2.5a}$; Mary A.$^{1.1.5.2.6a}$.

Henry Wyandt

Henry$^{1.1.5.4a}$ m. Elizabeth Warner in Somerset Co., Pennsylvania. She d. in 1849. Henry d. in Stark Co., Wilmont, Ohio in 1859. They had the following children:

Simon$^{1.1.5.4.1a}$, b. May 25, 1812.
Sarah$^{1.1.5.4.2a}$, b. in 1814, and m. John Brubaker. He was b. in 1812, and d. in 1892.
Eva$^{1.1.5.4.3a}$, b. in 1816, and m. George W. Agler. He was b. in 1810, and d. in 1871.
Susan$^{1.1.5.4.4a}$, b. in 1818, and d. in 1885. She m. William Reed.
David$^{1.1.5.4.5a}$, b. in 1820, and m. Mary Fribley. She was b. in 1820, and d. in 1892. David d. in 1861.
Catherine$^{1.1.5.4.6a}$, b. in 1822.
Magdalena$^{1.1.5.4.7a}$, b. in 1824, and d. in 1889. She m. Jacob Hurrow.
Elizabeth$^{1.1.5.4.8a}$, b. in 1826, and m. --- Wilhelm.
Jacob$^{1.1.5.4.9a}$, b. in 1830, and d. in 1903. He m. Isabel Sager. She was b. in 1832, and d. in 1895.
Mary A.$^{1.1.5.4.10a}$, b. in 1833, and m. John Ball.
Annetta$^{1.1.5.4.11a}$, b. in 1837, and m. John Spidell.

Simon Wyandt

Simon$^{1.1.5.4.1a}$ m. Elizabeth$^{1.1.5.4.1.8}$, dau. of John$^{1.1.5.4.1}$ and Hannah (Lenhart) Dull in Stark Co., Ohio on Nov. 5, 1834. They moved to Van Wert Co., Harrison Twp., Ohio in 1839, and brought Elizabeth's sister Catherine. Simon d. in Harrison Twp. on Jan. 4, 1859, and Elizabeth d. in Van Wert Co., Convoy, Ohio on Oct. 9, 1900. They had the following children:

Henry$^{1.1.5.4.1.1a}$, b. in 1835.
John$^{1.1.5.4.1.2a}$, b. Jan. 30, 1837, and m. Harriet Gunsett in Van Wert Co., Ohio on Dec. 5, 1861. She was b. in 1839.
Hannah$^{1.1.5.4.1.3a}$, b. Dec. 19, 1838, and m. Josiah Gunsett in Van Wert Co., Ohio on March 3, 1860. He was b. in 1836. Hannah d. in 1929.
David S.$^{1.1.5.4.1.4a}$, b. about 1840, and d. about 1849.
Jacob$^{1.1.5.4.1.5a}$, b. Aug. 3, 1842, and m. Sarah E. North in Van Wert Co., Ohio on March 26, 1867. She was b. in Cumberland Co., Pennsylvania on May 11, 1846.
Catherine$^{1.1.5.4.1.6a}$, b. in 1844, and d. in 1860.
Franklin$^{1.1.5.4.1.7a}$, b. about 1846, and d. about 1849.
George W.$^{1.1.5.4.1.8a}$, b. in 1847.

Catherine Wyandt

Catherine[1.1.5.4.6a] m. John[1.1.8.4.2a], son of William and Catherine[1.1.8.4a] (Putman) Logan. He was b. in 1820. Catherine d. in 1864. They had the following children:
  infant[1.1.5.4.6.1a], b. in 1846.
  Sonora[1.1.5.4.6.2a], b. in 1857, and m. Harvey Ullom. He was b. in 1852, and d. in 1919. Sonora d. in 1938.

Susan Wyandt

Susan[1.1.5.5a] m. Jacob Snavely. Susan d. in Washington Co., Sharpsburg, Maryland in 1857. They had the following children:
  John[1.1.5.5.1a], b. in 1813.
  Catherine[1.1.5.5.2a], b. in 1815, and d. in 1896. She m. Martin Eakle.
  Betsey[1.1.5.5.3a], b. in 1817, and m. Jacob Miller.
  Washington C.[1.1.5.5.4a], b. in 1818, and d. in 1894. He m. Elizabeth Staubs.
  Mary E.[1.1.5.5.5a], b. in 1821, and m. John Key Fauver.

Mary Wyandt

Mary[1.1.5.7a] m. Benjamin Zimmerman. Mary d. in Washington Co., Sharpsburg, Maryland in 1838. They had the following children:
  Caroline[1.1.5.7.1a], b. in 1822, and d. in 1906. She m. Michael Flynn.
  Neil[1.1.5.7.2a], b. in 1835, and d. in 1909.
  Elias[1.1.5.7.3a].
  Nicodemus[1.1.5.7.4a], m. Rosanna Snyder.
  Amelia[1.1.5.7.5a].

Christina Wyandt

Christina[1.1.5.8a] m. Samuel Deaner. They resided in Washington Co., Kneedysburg, Maryland, and had the following children:
  Jonas[1.1.5.8.1a], d. in 1904, and m. Ann Marie Baker.
  Sophia[1.1.5.8.2a], m. George W. Rohrer.
  Catherine[1.1.5.8.3a], m. Joseph Thomas.

Christian Wyandt

Christian[1.1.5.9a] m. Polly Cost, and had the following children at Washington Co., Root's Hill, Maryland:
  Frederick[1.1.5.9.1a], b. in 1827, and m. Lydia Ecker.
  David Henry[1.1.5.9.2a], b. in 1830, and m. Kate E. Wilson:
  Hiram C.[1.1.5.9.3a], b. in 1833, and m. Susan Bovey.
  Mary[1.1.5.9.4a].

Simon Wyandt

Simon[1.1.5.10a] m. Rebecca Geeting. Simon d. in Maryland in 1872.

They had the following children:
Joshua$^{1.1.5.10.1a}$; Susan Catherine$^{1.1.5.10.2a}$, m. Ezra Wright; Caleb$^{1.1.5.10.3a}$; Barbara A.$^{1.1.5.10.4a}$; Daniel Webster$^{1.1.5.10.5a}$; Rose$^{1.1.5.10.6a}$; Aaron$^{1.1.5.10.7a}$.

Catharina Buttmann

Catharina$^{1.1.6a}$ m. Adam, son of Michael and Anna Barbara (Troutman) Schneider, in Frederick Co., Maryland on Nov. 1, 1775. He was b. in Gerhartsbrunn, Germany on Dec. 31, 1747, and d. in Washington Co., Maryland in 1826. Adam served as a Private in the Pennsylvania Line during the Revolutionary War. They had the following children:

Susan$^{1.1.6.1a}$, b. in 1777, and m. John Mong.
Jacob$^{1.1.6.2a}$, b. in 1779.
Adam$^{1.1.6.3a}$, b. in 1781, and d. in 1847, and m. Elizabeth Weimer and Anne Sparks (1800-1873).
Rosina$^{1.1.6.4a}$, b. in 1783, and m. George Maurer/Mowry.
Henry$^{1.1.6.5a}$, b. in 1784, and d. in Somerset Co., Stoney Creek Twp., Pennsylvania in 1856. He m. Christine Maurer/Mowry. She was b. in 1786.
Elizabeth$^{1.1.6.6a}$, b. in 1787, and d. in Tuscarwas Co., Ohio on March 25, 1845. She m. Christopher Neff and Adam Mueller.
John$^{1.1.6.7a}$, b. and d. in 1789.
Magdalena$^{1.1.6.8a}$, b. in 1790, d. in 1873. She m. John L. Leichtenberger.
John Adam$^{1.1.6.9a}$, b. in 1792.
Peter$^{1.1.6.10a}$, b. in 1794, and m. Elizabeth.
Catherine$^{1.1.6.11a}$, b. in 1795, d. in Somerset Co., Pennsylvania in 1874. She m. George Parker (1795-1870) and Joseph Keplinger.
Otilla Ailla$^{1.1.6.12a}$, b. in 1797, and d. in 1810.
Maria$^{1.1.6.13a}$, b. in 1799.
Joseph$^{1.1.6.14a}$, b. in 1802, and d. in Somerset Co., Pennsylvania in 1876. He m. Mary Walter. She was b. in 1812, and d. in 1880.

Jacob Schneider

Jacob$^{1.1.6.2a}$ m. Catherine$^{1.1.5.3a}$, dau. of Christian and Mary Ann Amelia$^{1.1.5a}$ (Putman) Wyandt. Jacob d. in Washington Co., Eakle's Mills, Maryland in 1869, and Catherine d. there in 1871. They had the following children: Christian$^{1.1.6.2.1a}$, b. in 1802; Rosanna$^{1.1.6.2.2a}$, b. in 1804; John$^{1.1.6.2.3a}$, b. in 1806; Elizabeth$^{1.1.6.2.4a}$, b. in 1809; Susanna$^{1.1.6.2.5a}$, b. in 1811; Ezra J.$^{1.1.6.2.6a}$, b. in 1813; Adam$^{1.1.6.2.7a}$, b. in 1815; Mary$^{1.1.6.2.8a}$, b. in 1817; Matilda$^{1.1.6.2.9a}$, b. in 1819, and d. in 1894; Jacob$^{1.1.6.2.10a}$, b. in 1821; Clarissa$^{1.1.6.2.11a}$, b. in 1823; Josiah$^{1.1.6.2.12a}$, b. in 1827; Jacob$^{1.1.6.2.13a}$, b. in 1832.

John Adam Schneider

John$^{1.1.6.9a}$ m. Elizabeth Shaffer. She was b. in 1802. John d. in Somerset Co., Pennsylvania in 1872. They had the following children: Mary Magdalena$^{1.1.6.9.1a}$, b. in 1833, and m. Absolem John Casebeer; Catherine$^{1.1.6.9.2a}$, b. in 1835; Rosanna$^{1.1.6.9.3a}$, b. in 1837; Charlotte$^{1.1.6.9.4a}$, b. in 1839; Amanda$^{1.1.6.9.5a}$, b. in 1843.

Susanna Buttmann

Susanna$^{1.1.7a}$ d. in Baltimore Co., Baltimore, Maryland sometime after 1790. She m. Henry Baker. He was b. in 1747, and d. in 1802. Henry was a Private in the Pennsylvania Line during the Revolutionary War. After Susanna's death Henry m. Charity Ault, and moved to Knoxville, Tennessee. Susanna and Henry had the following dau.: Catherine$^{1.1.7.1a}$, m. John Newman.

Andreas Buttmann

Andreas$^{1.1.8a}$ m. Anna Elisabetha$^{1.3.3.2n}$, dau. of Johan Georg and Anna Catharina Lenhart, in Bedford (now Somerset) Co., Berlin, Pennsylvania on May 4, 1790. Andreas d. in Somerset Co., Middle Creek Twp., Pennsylvania on Feb. 21, 1834. Anna Elisabetha d. in Somerset Co., Spring Creek Twp., Pennsylvania on Aug. 12, 1832. They had the following children:

John$^{1.1.8.1n}$, b. Feb. 9, 1791.
Mary$^{1.1.8.2n}$, b. in 1793.
Gabriel$^{1.1.8.3n}$, b. Jan. 24, 1794.
Catherine$^{1.1.8.4n}$, b. in 1797.
Eva$^{1.1.8.5n}$, b. March 15, 1799.
Salome$^{1.1.8.6n}$, b. March 6, 1800, and m. George Pile.
Peter$^{1.1.8.7n}$, b. March 2, 1802.
Rosina$^{1.1.8.8n}$, b. Dec. 18, 1804.
Joseph$^{1.1.8.9n}$, b. Jan. 25, 1807, and d. in Westmoreland Co., Cook Twp., Pennsylvania on March 3, 1880. He m. Elizabeth, dau. of John and Catharine (Binfert) Bruner on Feb. 14, 1829. She was b. Aug. 22, 1811, and d. on Oct. 9, 1893.
Elizabeth$^{1.1.8.10n}$, b. March 10, 1810, and m. Joseph, son of Peter and Maria (Schneider) Buttmann.
Hannah$^{1.1.8.11n}$, b. July 14, 1812, and m. Henry, son of John and Catherine (Binfert) Bruner.
Luiza$^{1.1.8.12n}$, b. in 1815.
Margaret$^{1.1.8.13n}$, b. Jan. 13, 1817.

John Putman

John$^{1.1.8.1n}$ m. Charlotte, dau. of Philip King, and Sarah Hall. Charlotte was b. in 1794, and d. in 1851. John d. in Stark Co., Wilmont, Ohio on May 3, 1872. John and Charlotte had the following

children:
   Mary$^{1.1.8.1.1n}$, b. in 1815.
   Andrew W. Justus$^{1.1.8.1.2n}$, b. Jan. 30, 1816.
   Elizabeth$^{1.1.8.1.3n}$, b. about 1818, m. Abraham Spidle, and resided in Wilmot.
   Phoebe$^{1.1.8.1.4n}$, b. Dec. 5, 1820, and m. William Robinson, son of Samuel and Elisabetha Barbara (Robinson) Schlater, in Stark Co., Ohio on Oct. 28, 1841. She d. in Mercer Co., Dublin Twp., Ohio on Feb. 18, 1891, and William d. there on April 17, 1884. William came to Mercer Co., Ohio with his brother, Peter, and his father, Samuel, in 1837. After Samuel's death, William returned to Stark Co., Ohio, briefly, but returned to Mercer Co. in 1841. He purchased 161 acres in section six of Dublin Twp. with his brother, Peter, from his brother-in-law, Peter Dull. William was b. in Fayette Co., Salt Lick Twp., Pennsylvania on June 3, 1820.
   Timothy C.$^{1.1.8.1.5n}$, b. Jan. 29, 1828.
   Anna$^{1.1.8.1.6n}$, d. at age 11.

Mary Putman

Mary$^{1.1.8.1.1n}$ m. Jeremiah Agler. He was b. in 1801, and d. in 1869. Mary d. in 1902. They had the following children:
   Timothy$^{1.1.8.1.1.1n}$, b. in 1834, and m. Elizabeth Brewer. She was b. in 1838, and d. in 1893. Timothy d. in 1924.
   Harmen$^{1.1.8.1.1.2n}$, b. in 1836.
   Wert$^{1.1.8.1.1.3a}$, b. in 1838, and m. Anna Krick. She was b. in 1842, and d. in 1921. Wert d. in 1924.
   Morris$^{1.1.8.1.1.4n}$, b. in 1841, and m. Mollie Sinder.
   Andrew$^{1.1.8.1.1.5n}$, b. in 1843, and m. Sarah Elizabeth$^{1.1.8.7.13n}$, dau. of Peter$^{1.1.8.7n}$ and Sarah E. (Neiferd) Putman. Sarah was b. in 1860, and d. in 1940. Andrew d. in 1905.
   Sarah$^{1.1.8.1.1.6n}$, b. in 1846, and d. in 1857.
   Charlotte$^{1.1.8.1.1.7n}$, b. in 1851, and m. Daniel Whitmore.
   John$^{1.1.8.1.3.3.2n}$, b. in 1855.

Andrew W. Justus Putman

Andrew$^{1.1.8.1.2n}$ m. Judith, dau. of Samuel and Elizabeth Barbara (Robinson) Schlater, in Stark/Tuscarwas Co., Ohio on Sept. 28, 1837. Andrew d. in Stark Co., Sugar Creek Twp., Ohio on Feb. 6, 1891, and Judith d. there on Feb. 16, 1898. She was b. in Fayette Co., Salt Lick Twp., Pennsylvania on July 23, 1818. They had the following children:
   Clarissa$^{1.1.8.1.2.1n}$, b. in 1838, and m. William Wert McClintock. He was b. in 1832, and d. in 1911. Clarissa d. in 1865.
   Harman$^{1.1.8.1.2.2n}$, b. March 12, 1843, and m. Mildred Samilda.

She was b. in 1853, and d. in 1903. Harman d. in Stark Co.,
Sugar Creek Twp., Ohio on Dec. 6, 1903.
Selecta$^{1.1.8.1.2.3n}$, b. in 1844, and d. in 1926. She m. Daniel
Hoffman. He was b. in 1838, and d. in 1895.
Winfield Clark$^{1.1.8.1.2.4n}$, b. in 1852, and m. Catherine P. Gardner.
She was b. in 1853.

Elizabeth Putman

Elizabeth$^{1.1.8.1.3n}$ m. Abraham Spidle, and had the following children:
Mary$^{1.1.8.1.3.1n}$, m. ___ Cole; John$^{1.1.8.1.3.2n}$; Clark$^{1.1.8.1.3.3n}$;
Lester$^{1.1.8.1.3.4n}$; Ida$^{1.1.8.1.3.5n}$; Phoebe$^{1.1.8.1.3.6n}$, m. ___ Stoner;
Charlotte$^{1.1.8.1.3.7n}$, m. ___ Clewell; Alice$^{1.1.8.1.3.8n}$, m. ___
Crossland; Charles E.$^{1.1.8.1.3.9n}$.

Timothy C. Putman

Timothy C.$^{1.1.8.1.5n}$ m. Elizabeth, dau. of Hezekiah and Arvilla
(Curtis) Griffith on Oct. 3, 1850. She was b. in 1833, and d. in 1903.
Timothy d. in 1898. He served in the Civil War in Co. K, 163rd O.N.G.,
and after the war was the Captain of Company F., of the State Militia.
He had 515 acres in Sugar Creek Twp. They had the following
children:
Alice$^{1.1.8.1.5.1n}$, m. Carrell B. Allman and ___ Bartruff.
John C. F.$^{1.1.8.1.5.2n}$, b. in 1856, and m. Clara Beidler. John d. in
1903.
Anne$^{1.1.8.1.5.3n}$.

Mary Putman

Mary$^{1.1.8.2n}$ m. John Shaffer. He was b. in 1793, and d. in 1848. Mary
d. in Stark Co., Massillon, Ohio in 1848. They had the following
children:
Sarah E.$^{1.1.8.2.1n}$, b. in 1817, and m. Ephraim Trout. Sarah d. in
1871.
George$^{1.1.8.2.2n}$, b. in 1818, and m. Margaret Carl/Gabriel and
Anna. Margaret was b. in 1820. George d. in 1906.
Gabriel$^{1.1.8.2.3n}$, b. in 1820, and m. Anna Warner.
child$^{1.1.8.2.4n}$, b. in 1820, and d. in 1840.
John Putman$^{1.1.8.2.5n}$, b. in 1826, and m. Maria Smith about 1850,
and Hilda Terrell McCoy about 1880. Maria was b. in 1829, and
d. in 1877. John d. in 1904.
Elizabeth$^{1.1.8.2.6n}$, b. in 1827, and m. Henry Clay Younkin.
Elizabeth d. in 1910.
William Samuel$^{1.1.8.2.7n}$, b. in 1829, and m. Jane Shaw. William d.
in 1904.
Catherine$^{1.1.8.2.8n}$, b. in 1832, and m. William C. Stewart.
Josiah$^{1.1.8.2.9n}$, b. in 1834, and m. Margaret Dick.

Gabriel Putman

Gabriel$^{1.1.8.3n}$ m. Susanna Weimer, Rebecca White, and Sarah Hite. Susan was b. in 1797, and d. in 1865. Gabriel d. in Stark Co., Wilmont, Ohio on Nov. 27, 1882. Gabriel and Susanna had the following children:

Christina$^{1.1.8.3.1n}$, b. in 1822, and m. Josiah Shunk, and ___ Kaylor.

Mary$^{1.1.8.3.2n}$, b. in 1823, and d. in 1841.

Harriet$^{1.1.8.3.3n}$, b. about 1825, and m. Alexander Shenk.

Sallie$^{1.1.8.3.4n}$, b. about 1826, and m. ___ Ash.

Joseph Weimer$^{1.1.8.3.5n}$, b. Oct. 16, 1828, and m. Hannah, dau. of Henry and Susan (Wallace) Stambaugh, in Aug., 1851. She was b. in Sugar Creek Twp. in Jan., 1834. Joseph had a custom mill in New Hope Twp., and was a member of the milling company, Putman and Bro., in Wilmot.

Hiram$^{1.1.8.3.4n}$, b. in 1831, and m. Mary Hobbs. She was b. in 1836.

Catherine Putman

Catherine$^{1.1.8.4n}$ m. William Logan. He was b. in 1781, and d. in 1883. She d. in Somerset Co., Pennsylvania on Sept. 23, 1837. They had the following children:

Andrew$^{1.1.8.4.1n}$.

John$^{1.1.8.4.2n}$, b. in 1820, and m. Catherine Wyandt$^{1.1.5.4.6n}$.

Malinda$^{1.1.8.4.3n}$, b. in 1845, and d. in 1930. She m. Benjamin Guise (1832-1913).

Eva$^{1.1.8.4.4n}$.

Canarissa$^{1.1.8.4.5n}$.

William$^{1.1.8.4.6n}$, b. in 1824, and d. in 1913.

Eva Putman

Eva$^{1.1.8.5n}$ m. George Barron. He was b. in 1795, and d. in 1861. Eva d. in Somerset Co., Middle Creek Twp., Pennsylvania on Jan. 15, 1868. They had the following children:

Sarah$^{1.1.8.5.1n}$, b. in 1819, an d. in 1903.

Harriet$^{1.1.8.5.2n}$, b. about 1821, and m. Daniel Dickey.

Elizabeth$^{1.1.8.5.3n}$, b. in 1825, and d. in 1888. She m. Jeremiah Weimer (1826-1883).

Rebecca$^{1.1.8.5.4n}$, b. in 1827, and m. Daniel W. Dull.

Moses$^{1.1.8.5.5n}$, b. in 1829, and d. in 1905. He m. Martha Critchfield (1833-1892).

John$^{1.1.8.5.6n}$, b. in 1833, and d. in 1895.

Simon$^{1.1.8.5.7n}$, b. in 1836, and d. in 1913. He m. Matilda Schlag (1840-1918).

Mary$^{1.1.8.5.8n}$, b. in 1836, and m. Jacob Lenhart. He was b. in 1835.

Amanda$^{1.1.8.5.9n}$, b. in 1840, and m. John Schlag.
Aaron$^{1.1.8.5.10n}$, b. about 1842, and m. Catherine Walker.

Peter Putman

Peter$^{1.1.8.7n}$ m. Margaret/Mary Ann Adams about 1826 and Sarah E. Neiferd in Van Wert Co., Liberty Twp., Ohio on May 26, 1853. Margaret/Mary Ann d. in 1844. Sarah was b. in 1823. Peter d. in Van Wert Co., Liberty Twp., Ohio on Jan. 13, 1885. He had the following children:

Alexander$^{1.1.8.7.1n}$, b. in 1827, and m. Mary Temple and Sarah A. Shaffer.
Isaac$^{1.1.8.7.2n}$, b. in 1829, and m. Sophia Mihm.
Rosanna$^{1.1.8.7.3n}$, b. in 1832, and m. Josiah Ickes.
John$^{1.1.8.7.4n}$, b. in 1833, and m. Martha Jane King.
Mary$^{1.1.8.7.5n}$, b. in 1839, and m. Mac Brewer.
Maria$^{1.1.8.7.6n}$, b. in 1841, and m. Marion B. Shaffer.
Catherine$^{1.1.8.7.7n}$, b. in 1844, and m. Crayton Brewer.
Winfield Scott$^{1.1.8.7.8n}$, b. in 1854.
Zachariah Taylor$^{1.1.8.7.9n}$, b. in 1855.
Jasper Newton$^{1.1.8.7.10n}$, b. in 1857, and m. Emma Frences Fortney.
Peter Farmer$^{1.1.8.7.11n}$, b. in 1858, and d. in 1900. He m. Anna E. McClure. She was b. in 1870.
Tanner$^{1.1.8.7.12n}$, b. in 1859.
Sarah Elizabeth$^{1.1.8.7.13n}$, b. in 1860, and m. Andrew Agler$^{1.1.8.1.1.5n}$.
Mary Ann$^{1.1.8.7.14n}$, b. in 1862.
Francis Marion$^{1.1.8.7.15n}$, b. in 1863.
Elder Willis$^{1.1.8.7.16n}$, b. in 1864, and m. Lena Gaier.
Arminta$^{1.1.8.7.17n}$, b. in 1866, and m. Frank King. He was b. in 1865.
William Clark$^{1.1.8.7.18n}$, b. in 1867.
Clara B.$^{1.1.8.7.19n}$, b. in 1872.
Andrew$^{1.1.8.7.20n}$, b. about 1874.

Rosina Putman

Rosina$^{1.1.8.9n}$ m. John P. Cover. He was b. in 1803, and d. in 1884. Rosina d. in Somerset Co., Brother's Valley Twp., Pennsylvania on June 2, 1879. They had the following children: Phoebe$^{1.1.8.9.1n}$, b. in 1826; Agnes$^{1.1.8.9.2n}$, b. in 1828; Silas$^{1.1.8.9.3n}$, b. in 1830; Amelia$^{1.1.8.9.4n}$, b. in 1832; David J.$^{1.1.8.9.5n}$, b. in 1834; Rosey Anne$^{1.1.8.9.6n}$, b. in 1843; Peter J.$^{1.1.8.9.7n}$, b. in 1845.

Philipp Jacob Boudemont

Philipp Jacob$^{1.2a}$ m. Ann Mary. He arrived at Philadelphia on Oct. 7,

1743, on the ship *St. Andrew*. He d. in Frederick Co., Middletown Valley, Maryland in Dec., 1792. His will was written on Feb. 10, 1792, and probated on Dec. 8, 1792. They had the following children: Peter$^{1.2.1a}$; John$^{1.2.2a}$; Magdalen$^{1.2.3a}$, m. James Dixon.

****

Heinrich Schlater

Heinrich^{1b} m. Catharina, and settled in the Ligonier Vally in the mid 1760s. He was a Yeoman, and made improvements on land in Westmoreland Co., Fairfield Twp., Pennsylvania, where he resided as early as 1768. In Nov., 1769, he is listed as a resident of Fort Ligonier. In the mid 1780s, he moved to Fayette Co., Bull Skin Twp., Pennsylvania. His land was called Schaffhusen, which indicates that he may have been an immigrant from Schaffhausen, Switzerland, where the name, Schlater, is prevalent. This area became Salt Lick Twp., where he d. in July, 1817.

Heinrich was a member of the Good Hope Lutheran Church. During the Revolutionary War, he was a Frontier Ranger (Ranger of the Forest)/Private in the 5th Battalion, 3rd Pennsylvania Regiment of the North Cumberland Co. Militia under Captain Mathew Duncan, from 1776 to 1777. He was taken prisoner at Fort Washington in 1776, and received pay on Sept. 1, 1776. He reenlisted on Feb. 15, 1777, and served until 1783, merging and transferring to different units. He served under Major General Wayne in the South Carolina Campaign. He served in Patterson's Company in 1781, and the 2nd Regiment of Walter Finley's Company in 1782. He also served under General Greene. He was paid for service on May 14, 1785, and received an $80 gratuity on April 20, 1792, and 100 acres of Military Bounty Land, which was issued to John Delabar (Delabarras), (assingee of Henry Schlater). Heinrich and Catharina had the following children: Barbara$^{1.1b}$, b. about 1760; Joseph$^{1.2b}$, b. about 1763; Isaac$^{1.3b}$, b. about 1766; Martin$^{1.4b}$, b. about 1769; Heinrich$^{1.5b}$, b. in 1772; Samuel$^{1.6b}$, b. in 1774; Elizabeth$^{1.7b}$, b. about 1778; Marie$^{1.8b}$, b. in Feb., 1781.

Barbara Schlater

Barbara$^{1.1b}$ m. Johannes Hasselton. He d. in Perry Co., Ohio on Oct. 6, 1834. Barbara d. sometime after 1834. They had the following children in Fayette Co., Salt Lick Twp., Pennsylvania: Sarah$^{1.1.1b}$, b. about 1781; William$^{1.1.2b}$, b. about 1783; Catherine$^{1.1.3b}$, b. Jan. 8, 1785, and m. ---Skinner; Samuel$^{1.1.4b}$, b. Dec. 19, 1787; Elizabeth$^{1.1.5b}$, b. about 1789, and m. ____ Skinner; Henrich$^{1.1.6b}$, b. Oct. 19, 1791; John$^{1.1.7b}$, b. about 1793; Joseph$^{1.1.8b}$, b. about 1795 on June 17, 1797, bapt. at Good Hope Lutheran Church on Aug. 6,

1797, sponsored by Joseph Schalter and wife; Mary$^{1.1.9b}$, b. about
1797, m. ____ Sain; Jacob$^{1.1.10b}$, b. Feb. 10, 1803, bapt. at Good Hope
Lutheran on April 1, 1803, sponsored by James Mitchel.

Joseph Schlater

Joseph$^{1.2b}$ m. Rosina$^{1.1.7d}$, dau. of Ernst Friderich and Elisabeth
Dumbauld, in Fayette Co., Pennsylvania on Jan. 17, 1784. Joseph
served in the Revolutionary War for an unspecified time, and was a 1st
Lt. in the Westmoreland Co., Militia, 3rd Company, 4th Regiment, on
June 6, 1793. Joseph d. in Fayette Co., Bull Skin Twp., Pennsylvania in
Jan., 1802. After his death, Rosina m. Mathias Lozier. Rosina d. in
Perry Co., Hopewell Twp., Ohio about 1832. Joseph and Rosina had
the following children in Bull Skin Twp.:

Christina$^{1.2.1b}$, b. Sept. 16, 1785, bapt. at Zion's Church in
Westmoreland Co., Hempfield Twp., and sponsored by
Frederick and Christina Dumbauld.

James$^{1.2.2b}$, b. about 1787, and d. in Bull Skin Twp. in Feb., 1814.
He m. Mary.

Heinrich$^{1.2.3b}$, b. Sept. 9, 1788, bapt. at Zion's Church, and
sponsored by Heinrich and Catharina Schlater. He m. Ann
Doty.

Elizabeth$^{1.2.4b}$, b. Feb. 27, 1790, and d. before 1832.

Anna Dorothea$^{1.2.5b}$, b. Dec. 4, 1792, bapt. at Mount Zion Lutheran
Church, and sponsored by Ludwig and Dorothea Bonsey/Banse.

Emanuel$^{1.2.6b}$, b. July 3, 1795, bapt. at Mount Zion, and d. in Salt
Lick Twp. on Dec. 13, 1825. He m. Julia Show.

Mariah$^{1.2.7b}$, b. about 1797, and was unm. in 1832.

John$^{1.2.8b}$, b. July 27, 1800, bapt. Sept. 28, 1800 at Good Hope
Lutheran Church, sponsored by Johannes Robinson and wife.
He was said to have m. Mary Neel in Perry Co., Ohio in 1814,
and d. there in May, 1833, but this has not been confirmed.

Christina Schlater

Christina$^{1.2.1b}$ m. Robert McMullin and George Albright (before 1832).
Christina and Robert had the following children: James$^{1.2.1.1b}$;
Rosina$^{1.2.1.2b}$; Mary$^{1.2.1.3b}$; Joseph$^{1.2.1.4b}$; infant$^{1.2.1.5b}$.

Anna Dorothea Schlater

Anna Dorothea$^{1.2.5b}$ m. George Baxter, and had the following children:
Peter$^{1.2.5.1b}$; William$^{1.2.5.2b}$; James$^{1.2.5.3b}$; Mary$^{1.2.5.4b}$;
son$^{1.2.5.5b}$.

Isaac Schlater

Isaac$^{1.3b}$ m. Appolonia Ulrey and Margareth ---. Appolonia was b. in

1762, and d. in Westmoreland Co., Donegal Twp., Pennsylvania on Oct. 29, 1855. Isaac d. there in July, 1838. His will was probated on July 10, 1838. They had the following children in Donegal Twp.:

infant[1.3.1b], b. Dec. 21, 1790, and bapt. at Good Hope Lutheran Church.

Anna Elizabeth[1.3.2b], b. July 27, 1792, bapt. at Mount Zion Lutheran Church, and m. Jacob Yetter.

Samuel[1.3.3b], b. Feb. 2, 1794, bapt. at Mount Zion, and d. in Westmoreland Co., Ligonier Twp., Pennsylvania on Jan. 30, 1882. He m. Mary Elizabeth Snow.

Joseph[1.3.4b], b. Feb. 2, 1794.

Eleanor[1.3.5b], b. Jan. 16, 1796, bapt. at the Good Hope Lutheran Church on Oct. 14, 1796, sponsored by her parents.

Sarah[1.3.6b], b. about 1798.

Mary[1.3.7b], b. about 1800, and m. Christian Kesler.

Sussana[1.3.8b], b. Oct. 28, 1800, bapt. at Good Hope Lutheran Church June 28, 1801, sponsored by her parents.

Catherine[1.3.9b], b. Feb. 16, 1806, bapt. at Good Hope Lutheran Church, sponsored by her parents.

Joseph Schlater

Joseph[1.3.3b] d. before 1838, and had the following children: Hannah[1.3.3.1b], b. about 1826, and m. John Thompson; Joseph[1.3.3.2b], b. in 1828, m. Elizabeth Brooks in 1852 and Elizabeth Porch in 1853, and d. on Jan. 31, 1894. Elizabeth Brooks d. in 1852. Elizabeth Porch was b. in 1834, and d. on March 24, 1921.

Martin Schlater

Martin[1.4b] m. Jane McMullin about 1791, and d. intestate before May 22, 1820, when the Orphans Court requested a partition in the records. They had the following children in Westmoreland Co., Donegal Twp., Pennsylvania:

Catherine[1.4.1a], b. Feb. 19, 1792, bapt. at Berlin Lutheran Church (Somerset Co.) on April 24, 1792, and sponsored by John and Anna Barbara Robinson.

Heinrich[1.4.2a], b. Aug. 15, 1794, bapt. at Mount Zion Lutheran Church, and d. before 1800.

Samuel[1.4.3a], b. March 21, 1796, and bapt. at Mount Zion. He resided in Indiana in May, 1820.

James[1.4.4b], b. about 1798.

Heinrich[1.4.5b], b. Feb. 13, 1800, bapt. at Good Hope Lutheran Church on May 10, 1801, sponsored by Daniel Meckendorf and wife. He d. in 1822.

Polly[1.4.6b], b. about 1800, and m. James Beatty.

Elizabeth[1.4.7b], b. about 1802.

Peter[1.4.8b], b. about 1802.
Barbara[1.4.9b], b. about 1804.
Martin[1.4.10b], b. about 1806.

Heinrich Schlater

Heinrich[1.5b] m. Martha, dau. of Daniel Morrison, before 1795. She was b. in Westmoreland Co., Hempfield Twp., Pennsylvania, and d. in Stark Co., Perry Twp., Massillon, Ohio sometime after 1840. Heinrich d. in Stark Co., Sugar Creek Twp., Ohio on Sept. 8, 1834. He is buried in Weimer cemetery. They may have had the following children in Fayette Co., Salt Lick Twp., Pennsylvania:

George[1.5.1b], b. about 1808, and d. in Stark Co., Sugar Creek Twp., Pennsylvania on Sept. 10, 1834. He is buried in Weimer cemetery.

Hannah[1.5.2b], b. about 1810, and d. in Stark Co., Sugar Creek Twp., Ohio on Sept. 13, 1834. She is buried in Weimer cemetery.

Mary[1.5.3b], b. about 1813, and m. Joseph Elliot in Stark Co., Ohio on Oct. 16, 1834.

Bathsheba[1.5.4a], b. about 1815, and m. Aaron/Adam Gruwell in Stark Co., Ohio on July 6, 1837.

Margaret[1.5.5a], b. about 1817, and m. Aaron Patterson in Tuscarwas Co., Ohio on Sept. 5, 1837.

John Schlater

John[1.6.1b] m. Phillipena "Phebe"[1.1.1.5.4.1.4], dau. of John[1.1.5.4.1] and Hannah (Lenhart) Dull, in Fayette Co., Pennsylvania about 1824. They moved to Stark Co., Ohio before 1831, and Van Wert Co., Ohio about 1836. John d. in Van Wert Co., Liberty Twp., Ohio on Sept. 22, 1845, and Phebe d. there on Aug. 11, 1887. They had the following children:

Joseph[1.6.1.1b], b. Nov. 27, 1824, bapt. in Good Hope Lutheran Church on March 18, 1827. He m. Maria. They resided in Van Wert Co., Liberty Twp., Ohio in 1850. He was Mayor of Van Wert from 1862 to 1866, and managed the America House Tavern.

Mary A.[1.6.1.2b], b. in 1826.

Nancy[1.6.1.3b], b. Feb. 11, 1828, bapt. at Good Hope Lutheran Church on May 11, 1828. She m. O. W. Rose in Van Wert Co., Ohio on Jan. 8, 1849.

Sarah[1.6.1.4b], b. Nov. 26, 1829, and m. Abraham Balyeat in Van Wert Co., Ohio on May 13, 1852. He was b. in 1823, and d. in 1881. Sarah d. in Van Wert Co., Pleasant Twp., Ohio on Jan. 19, 1894.

Polly[1.6.1.5b], b. Dec. 16, 18(30), and d. in Stark Co., Sugar Creek

Twp., Ohio on March 17, 18(33). She is buried in Weimer cemetery.

Catherine$^{1.6.1.6b}$, b. in 1830, and m. R. Conn.

Hannah$^{1.6.1.7b}$, b. in 1833, and m. Z. A. Smith. They resided in Kansas.

Judith$^{1.6.1.8b}$, b. in 1835, and m. Robert Bruce Encill. They resided in Kosciusco Co., Warsaw, Indiana.

Benjamin F.$^{1.6.1.9b}$, b. July 5, 1837, and m. Delilah Fortney in Van Wert Co., Ohio on April 21, 1861. She was b. in 1843, and d. in 1883.

Elizabeth$^{1.6.1.10b}$, b. Feb. 7, 1840, and m. George F. Edson in Van Wert Co., Ohio on March 29, 1857.

Jane$^{1.6.1.11b}$, b. in 1841, and m. William Henry McGough.

Samuel$^{1.6.1.12b}$, b. in 1844.

John$^{1.6.1.13b}$, b. in 1846.

Samuel Schlater

Samuel$^{1.6b}$ m. Elizabeth Barbara, dau. of John and Anna Barbara (Dumbauld) Robinson, about 1798. She was b. in d. in Tuscarwas Co., Wayne Twp., Ohio about 1834. Samuel moved to Carroll Co., Ohio in 1828, and after a short time moved to Tuscarwas Co., Ohio. In 1833, Samuel had 1 horse and 2 cattle in Wayne Twp. In 1837, Samuel and his sons, William and Peter, moved to Mercer Co., Dublin Twp., Ohio. Samuel d. in Mercer Co., Dublin Twp., Ohio in 1838. They had the following children in Fayette Co., Salt Lick Twp., Ohio:

Johannes$^{1.6.1b}$, b. Feb. 13, 1800, bapt. at Good Hope Lutheran Church on March 30, 1800, sponsored by John Robinson and wife.

Maria$^{1.6.2b}$, b. Sept. 18, 1801, bapt. at Good Hope Lutheran Church on Oct. 20, 1801, sponsored by Friedrich Dumball and Maria Robison.

Heinrich$^{1.6.3b}$, b. March 14, 1803, baptized at Good Hope Lutheran Church on May 15, 1830, sponsored by his parents.

Catherine$^{1.6.4D}$, b. Sept. 30, 1804, bapt. at Good Hope Lutheran Church on Oct. 21, 1804, sponsored by Abraham and Catharine Tumbald. She m. Peter Dull$^{1.1.1.5.4.1.1}$.

Barbara$^{1.6.5b}$, b. Sept. 30, 1804. bapt. at Good Hope on Oct. 21, 1804, sponsored by John and Babara Robison.

Samuel$^{1.6.6b}$, b. Oct. 15, 1806, bapt. by Good Hope Lutheran Church on Oct. 22, 1806, sponsored by parents.

Absalom$^{1.6.7b}$, b. May 3, 1809.

Elizabeth$^{1.6.8b}$, b. about 1811, and m. Samuel Kesler in Tuscarwas Co., Ohio on Sept. 13, 1834.

Nancy$^{1.6.9b}$, b. about 1813.

Jacob$^{1.6.10b}$, b. about 1815, and m. Rebecca Haney in Stark Co.,

Ohio on Oct. 7, 1834.
Jane$^{1.6.11b}$, b. May 20, 1816.
Sarah$^{1.6.12b}$, b. April 23, 1817.
Judith$^{1.6.13b}$, b. July 23, 1818, and m. Andrew W. Justus Putman$^{1.1.8.1.2a}$.
William Robinson$^{1.6.14b}$, b. June 3, 1820.
Peter$^{1.6.15b}$, b. in 1822.

Heinrich Schlater

Heinrich$^{1.6.2b}$ m. Anna Maria$^{1.1.1.5.4.1.2}$, dau. of John$^{1.1.1.5.4.1}$ and Hannah (Lenhart) Dull in Fayette Co., Pennsylvania in 1821. Henry d. in Tuscarwas Co., Wayne Twp., Ohio in 1847. Anna Maria d. in Davies Co., Indiana in 1882. In 1850, Anna Maria resided in Tuscarwas Co., Ohio. They had the following children:

Samuel $^{1.6.2.1b}$, b. Jan. 3, 1825, and bapt. at Good Hope Lutheran Church.

Catherine$^{1.6.2.1b}$, b. Dec. 9, 1826, bapt. at Good Hope Lutheran Curch on July 8, 1827, and m. Crawford Arford in Tuscarwas Co., Ohio on March 3, 1850.

Hanna$^{1.6.2.3b}$, b. Nov. 21, 1828, bapt. at Good Hope Lutheran Church on July 5, 1829, sponsored by Johannes and Hannah Dull.

Phebe Ann$^{1.6.2.2b}$, b. in 1835, and m. James M. Smith in Mercer Co., Ohio on Aug. 16, 1855.

Absalom Schlater

Absalom$^{1.6.7b}$ m. Sarah. She was b. in Pennsylvania in 1821. Apparently, Absalom returned to Pennsylvannia. He resided in Westmoreland Co., Hempfield Twp., Pennsylvania in 1850. In 1860, he resided in Stark Co., Sugar Creek Twp., Ohio. He d. in Stark Co. on May 15, 1863. Absalom and Sarah had the following children in Westmoreland Co., Pennsylvania: Robert$^{1.6.7.1b}$, b. in 1841; Cornelia$^{1.6.7.2b}$, b. in 1847; Judith$^{1.6.7.3b}$, b. in 1849.

Jane Schlater

Jane$^{1.6.11b}$ m. Ephraim Medaugh in Tuscarwas Co., Ohio on Feb. 5, 1835. He was b. in Westmoreland Co., Pennsylvania on May 25, 1814, and d. in Van Wert Co., Wilshire Twp., Ohio on Sept. 11, 1897. Jane d. in Wilshire Twp. on March 25, 1865. They moved to Van Wert Co., Ohio in 1836. They had the following children:

Sarah Ann$^{1.6.11.1b}$, b. Nov. 8, 1835, and d. in Van Wert Co., Liberty Twp., Ohio on Nov. 29, 1923. She m. George Shaffer$^{1.2.2bb}$.

Elmira$^{1.6.11.2b}$, b. Sept. 22, 1837, and m. Joshua Wagers in Van Wert Co., Ohio on Oct. 18, 1858. He was b. in Van Wert Co.,

Wilshire Twp. on Oct. 5, 1837. Elmira d. on Sept. 20, 1894.
Gordon Dwight[1.6.11.3b], b. and d. in 1838.
Mary[1.6.11.4b], b. in 1840, and m. Henry Smith in Van Wert Co., Ohio on Nov. 30, 1884.
John Glen[1.6.11.5b], b. March 2, 1842, and m. Emily Carter on Nov. 19, 1868. She was b. in Franklin Co., Ohio on Aug. 18, 1839, and d. in Van Wert Co., Wilshire Twp., Ohio on Aug. 16, 1919. John d. in Wilshire Twp. on May 17, 1918.
Andrew[1.6.11.6b], b. Jan. 9, 1844, and m. Sarah Jane Steen in Van Wert Co., Ohio on Nov. 10, 1863. She was b. in Pennsylvania, and d. in Wilshire Twp. on Aug. 27, 1927. Andrew d. in Wilshire Twp. on April 21, 1926.
Charity[1.6.11.7b], b. in 1846.
William Sylvania[1.6.11.8b], b. April 30, 1852, and m. Hannah Lucretia[1.1.1.5.4.1.1.12.2], dau. of Elias[1.1.1.5.4.1.1.1.12] and Jane (Walters) Dull, in Van Wert Co., Ohio on Aug. 7, 1873. She was b. in Wilshire Twp. on Sept. 4, 1854, and d. in Paulding Co., Paulding, Ohio on Sept. 11, 1882. William d. in Wilshire Twp. on June 6, 1882.

Sarah Schlater

Sarah[1.6.12b] m. Jacob King in Tuscarwas Co., Ohio on Feb. 25, 1836. He was b. in Pennsylvania on July 27, 1809, and d. in Van Wert Co., Liberty Twp., Ohio on June 9, 1881. Sarah d. in Liberty Twp. on July 5, 1870. They resided in Holmes Co., Paint Twp., Ohio until 1848, then they moved to Van Wert Co., Ohio. They had the following children:

Angeline[1.6.12.1b], b. in 1837.
Thomas Jefferson[1.6.12.2b], b. in 1838.
Tabitha[1.6.12.3b], b. in 1840.
William Henry Harrison[1.6.12.4b], b. May 28, 1841, and d. in Van Wert Co., Liberty Twp., Ohio on June 14, 1891. He m. Jemima Dague in Van Wert Co. in 1864.
Elizabeth[1.6.12.5b], b. in 1843.
Austin C.[1.6.12.6b], b. Jan. 24, 1845, and d. in Van Wert Co. on June 26, 1916. He m. Malissa Fortney.
Samantha J.[1.6.12.7b], b. May 5, 1847, and d. on Oct. 8, 1850.
Emma F.[1.6.12.8b], b. June 15, 1858, and d. on Oct. 22, 1872.

William Robinson Schlater

William Robinson[1.6.14b] m. Phebe[1.1.8.1.4a], dau. of John[1.1.8.1a] and Charlotte (King) Putman, in Stark Co., Ohio on Oct. 28, 1841. She d. in Mercer Co., Dublin Twp., Ohio on Feb. 18, 1891, and William d. there on April 17, 1884. William came to Mercer Co., Ohio with his brother, Peter, and his father, Samuel, in 1837. After Samuel's death, William returned to Stark Co., Ohio, but returned to Mercer Co. in

1841, and purchased 161 acres in section six of Dublin Twp. with his brother, Peter, from his brother-in-law, Peter Dull. William and Phebe had the following children:
- Charlotte$^{1.6.14.1b}$, b. April 27, 1843.
- Elizabeth$^{1.6.14.2b}$, b. Nov. 16, 1845.
- Melissa$^{1.6.14.3b}$, b. Feb. 12, 1848, and m. ___ Wagner.
- Clarissa$^{1.6.14.4b}$, b. Feb. 28, 1851, and m. George Clark Spidel in Mercer Co. on Nov. 14, 1869, Henry Bickel in Mercer Co. on Fenruary 27, 1876, and Martin Smith in Mercer Co. on June 2, 1881.
- Almyra$^{1.6.14.5b}$, b. Nov. 18, 1855, and m. William Moore in Mercer Co. on July 28, 1874.
- Willis$^{1.6.14.6b}$, b. April 10, 1857.
- Mary$^{1.6.14.7b}$, b. about 1859, and m. ___ Hardstock.

Peter Schlater

Peter$^{1.6.15b}$ m. Margaret Jane Wright in Mercer Co., Ohio on March 22, 1846. She was b. in 1828. Peter came to Mercer Co. in 1837, with his brother, William, and his father, Samuel. In 1841, Peter and William purchased 161 acres in section six of Dublin Twp. from their brother-in-law, Peter Dull. In 1849, Peter moved to Crawford Co., Prarie Du Chein Twp., Wisconsin, and resided there in 1850. In 1855, they resided in Bad Axe Co., Bad Axe, Wisconsin. They had a dau. in Mercer Co., Dublin Twp., Ohio: Elizabeth$^{1.6.15.1b}$, b. in 1848.

Elizabeth Schlater

Elizabeth$^{1.7b}$ m. Christopher Perkey, son of Christoph and Maria Magdalean Perkey, resided in Perry Co., Pike Twp., Ohio. They had the following children: Christoph$^{1.7.1b}$, b. March 5, 1799, bapt. at Good Hope Lutheran Church on April 27, 1799, sponsored by Christoph and Maria Magdalena Perky; Josep$^{1.7.2b}$, b. Dec. 23, 1800, bapt. at Good Hope Lutheran Church on May 10, 1801, sponsored by Josep Schlater and wife; Catharina$^{1.7.3b}$, b. Feb. 10, 1803, bapt. at Good Hope Lutheran Church on April 1, 1803, sponsored by her mother; Henrich$^{1.7.4b}$, b. April 17, 1805, bapt. at Good Hope Lutheran Church on June 16, 1805, sponsored by his parents; David$^{1.7.5b}$; Emylia "Amy"$^{1.7.6b}$, b. Feb. 5, 1809, bapt. at Good Hope Lutheran Church on July 16, 1809, sponsored by her parents.

Maria Schlater

Maria$^{1.8b}$ m. Peter Kessler. He was b. in Maryland on April 10, 1780, and d. in Westmoreland Co., Donegal Twp., Pennsylvania on July 2, 1860. Maria d. in Donegal Twp. in June, 1853. They had the following children in Donegal Twp.: Samuel$^{1.8.1b}$; Elias$^{1.8.2b}$; John$^{1.8.3b}$; Sahra$^{1.8.4b}$, b. Feb. 14, 1803, bapt. at Good Hope Lutheran Church on

April 1, 1803, sponsored by Daniel and Sahra Berkey; Nancy[1.8.5b]; William J.[1.8.6b], b. in 1818, and m. Barbara Eischelman.

****

John Robinson

John[1c], b. Oct. 20, 1755, m. Anna Barbara[1.1.4d], dau. of Ernst Friderich and Elisabeth Dumbauld, in Westmoreland Co., Pennsylvania in Aug. 1774. She was b. in Washington Co., Hagerstown, Maryland about 1754, and d. in Fayette Co., Salt Lick Twp., Champion Run, Pennsylvania on Oct. 8, 1814. John was a Frontier Ranger from Westmoreland Co. from 1778 to 1783, and took the Oath of Allegiance on Oct. 13, 1777. In 1773, John was in Westmoreland Co., Hempfield Twp. (an Andrew Robeson had unclaimed land in Hempfield Twp. in 1773, and served in the military in 1782, and served on a jury; on April 7, 1774, he resided in Pitt Twp.) in 1785, he had land in Bull Skin Twp. John d. at Champion Run on April 2, 1821. They are buried in Snyder Dumbauld cemetery. John served in the Revolutionary War. He and Anna Barbara had the following children in Westmoreland Co., Hempfield Twp., Pennsylvania:

Elisabeth Barbara[1.1c], b. about 1778, and m. Samuel Schlater.
Anna Maria[1.2c], b. Nov. 10, 1783, bapt. by Reverend John Wilhelm Weber, and sponsored by Peter and Anna Maria Dumbauld. She m. Jacob Lohr[1.1.2ca].
Johannes[1.3c], b. Oct. 30, 1785, bapt. by Reverend Lutge, and sponsored by Frederick and Christina Dumbauld.

Johannes Robinson

Johannes[1.3c] m. Catherine, presumed dau. of George and Catherine Weimer. She was b. in Somerset Co., Pennsylvania in 1785. They resided in Fayette Co., Salt Lick Twp., Pennsylvania in 1850. They had the following children in Salt Lick Twp.: John[1.3.1c], b. Oct. 20, 1804, bapt. 1804; Anna Barbara[1.3.2c], b. Dec. 3, 1806, bapt. 1807; Elizaeth[1.3.3c], b. May 13, 1809, bapt. July 16, 1809; Jacob W.[1.3.4c], b. in 1818; William[1.3.5c], b. in 1825.

Jacob W. Robinson

Jacob W.[1.3.4c] m. Mary (b.1816), and had the following children in Salt Lick Twp.: Barbara[1.3.4.1c], b. in 1842; Mary[1.3.4.2c], b. in 1844; William[1.3.4.3c], b. in 1846; Elizabeth[1.3.4.4c], b. in 1848; John[1.3.4.5c], b. in 1852.

William Robinson

William[1.3.5c] m. Sophia. She was b. in 1827. They had the following dau. in Salt Lick Twp.: Catherine[1.3.5.1c], b. in 1849.

****

Dumbauld

unknown[1d] had the following children (presumed to be brothers) in Canton Berne, Switzerland: Ernst Friderich[1.1d], b. in 1717; Abraham[1.2d], b. about 1719, and arrived in Philadelphia with Ernst Friderich on the ship *Brigantine* on Oct. 19, 1736.

Ernst Friderich Dumbauld

Ernst Friderich[1.1d] arrived at Philadelphia on the ship *Brigantine* on Oct. 19, 1736. He settled in Frederick Co., Pipe Creek, Maryland after his arrival, and m. Elisabeth. Some sources state her maiden name was Hager (histories say "he settled at Hagerstown, where in time he m. a dau. of the founder of the town"), but that belief is totally unsubstantiated. Friderich soon moved to Washington Co., Maryland, and settled in Hagerstown (Elizabethtown), where he remained until 1766, when he moved to the Ligonier Valley, in Pennsylvania. He laid claim by tomahawk to a large tract on Four Mile Run. This land was situated west of Chestnut Ridge, on the Champion and Indian Creeks in what is now Westmoreland Co., Donegal Twp., Pennsylvania. After some Indian trouble, Friderich returned to Hagerstown, but returned to Pennsylvania in 1769, and errected a block house on Four Mile Run (called Fort Dumbauld). The block house was constructed with logs, and located "on a beautiful eminence overlooking the upper reaches of Four Mile Run, on the Barron-Kalp farm" (Frontier Fort South Western, Pennsylvania). Friderich took the Oath of Allegiance on March 24, 1778, served as a Frontier Ranger (1778) in Captain Richard Williams Company, first Battalion, and a Private in the Westmoreland Co., Militia during the Revolutionary War. After Elisabeth's death, between 1779 and 1785, he m. Christina Magdalena Leonhard, widow of Christian Harmon (m. in Montgomery Co., Franconia Twp., Pennsylvania on Nov. 4, 1756). Friderich wrote his will on Dec. 15, 1790, and it was proven in Bedford Co., Milford Twp., Pennsylvania on March 5, 1791. Friderich and Elisabeth had the following children in Hagerstown, Maryland:

Elisabeth[1.1.1d], b. about 1749.
Nancy[1.1.2d], b. in 1751.
Abraham[1.1.3d], b. in 1753.
Anna Barbara[1.1.4d], b. about 1754, and m. John Robinson[1c].
Salome[1.1.5d], b. in 1755.
Peter[1.1.6d], b. about 1757, m. Anna Maria Boyer, and d. in Perry
    Co., Hopewell Twp., Ohio sometime after 1810. Peter served as
    a Frontier Ranger in 1778, and later that year was a
    Lieutenant in the first Battalion under Colonel Alexander Barr.
Rosina[1.1.7d], b. about 1762, and m. Joseph Schlater[1.2b].
Anna Maria[1.1.8d], b. about 1764, and m. Lodowick Bunsey/ Bonesy.
    Lodowick d. in Westmoreland Co., Pennsylvania in 1795.

Lodowick was a Frontier Ranger in 1778.

daughter$^{1.1.9d}$, b. about 1766, and d. in Fayette Co., Salt Lick Twp., Indian Creek, Pennsylvania about 1785.

Anna Elisabetha Dumbauld

Elisabeth$^{1.1.1d}$ m. Daniel Mackendorfer/McInturf. He d. in Fayette Co., Bull Skin Twp., Pennsylvania in 1816. After Daniel's death, Elizabeth moved to Perry Co., Hopewell Twp., Ohio. They had the following children in Bull Skin Twp.:

John$^{1.1.1.1d}$, b. in 1774, and m. Hannah Parr.
Susannah$^{1.1.1.2d}$, b. in 1775, and m. ____ Gooly.
Daniel$^{1.1.1.3d}$, b. about 1777.
Catherine$^{1.1.1.4d}$, b. about 1779, and m. Eldad Gooly.
Mary$^{1.1.1.5d}$, b. about 1781, and m. Henry Jennings.
Frederick$^{1.1.1.6d}$, b. Sept. 8, 1786, m. Anna Myers in Perry Co., Ohio on Aug. 18, 1814, and d. in Licking Co., Johnstown, Ohio before 1879. Anna was b. Feb. 4, 1795, and d. sometime after 1879.
Johann David$^{1.1.1.7d}$, b. Sept. 2, 1794, bapt. at Good Hope Lutheran Church Sept. 21, 1794, sponsotered by Johannes Martin and Apolonia.
Anna Maria$^{1.1.1.8d}$, b. Sept. 12, 1797, bapt. at Good Hope Jan. 8, 1798, sponsored by Maria Dumbalt.

Nancy Dumbauld

Nancy$^{1.1.2d}$ m. Michael Hay. He was b. Jan. 23, 1740/41, and d. in Westmoreland Co., Donegal Twp., Pennsylvania on Feb. 3, 1829. He was a Frontier Ranger in 1778. Nancy d. in Donegal Twp. on Feb. 20, 1829. They are buried in Porch cemetery. They had the following children in Donegal Twp.:

Lewis$^{1.1.2.1d}$, b. March 4, 1775.
Elizabeth$^{1.1.2.2d}$, b. Nov. 25, 1777.
Abraham$^{1.1.2.3d}$, b. about 1779, and m. ____ Arenfret.
Michael$^{1.1.2.4d}$, b. Aug. 10, 1780, m. Elizabeth Young on Aug. 27, 1802, and d. in Somerset Co., Pennsylvania in 1842. Elizabeth was b. March 15, 1786, and d. in Somerset Co. on April 20, 1868.
Christina$^{1.1.2.5d}$, b. in 1786, m. Michael Palmer, and d. in Donegal Twp. in 1855. Michael was b. in 1785, and d. in Donegal Twp. in 1860.

Lewis Hay

Lewis$^{1.1.2.1d}$ m. Mary Arenfret. He d. in Donegal Twp. on July 6, 1847, and is buried in Porch cemetery. They had the following children in Donegal Twp.:

John L.$^{1.1.2.1.1d}$, b. in 1800, and m. Margaret Hines on Nov. 1,

1838. He was a tanner on Four Mile Run.
Mary$^{1.1.2.1.2d}$, and m. Thomas Richardson.
Michael$^{1.1.2.1.3d}$.
Elizabeth$^{1.1.2.1.4d}$.
Lewis$^{1.1.2.1.5d}$.

Elizabeth Hay

Elizabeth$^{1.1.2.2d}$ m. Peter Gay. She d. in Donegal Twp. on April 28, 1862. Peter was b. in Franklin Co., Pennsylvania on Feb. 10, 1777, and d. in Donegal Twp. on Dec. 1, 1860. They are buried in Porch cemetery. They had the following children in Donegal Twp.:
> Ann$^{1.1.2.2.1d}$, b. Dec. 24, 1803, m. Morrison Underwood, and d. on Aug. 2, 1876. He was b. in Cumberland Co., Carlisle, Pennsylvania on Jan. 21, 1795, and d. on Feb. 25, 1885.
> William B.$^{1.1.2.2.2d}$, b. Sept. 3, 1815. m. Martha, dau. of William Speer, in March, 1835. She was b. around 1815, and d. in Westmoreland Co., Jones Mill on Jan. 6, 1883. William served as Justice of the Peace from age twenty-one till his death. William d. in Donegal Twp. on Jan. 6, 1883. They are buried in Porch cemetery.
> Catherine$^{1.1.2.2.3d}$, b. in Dec., 1817. m. Samuel, son of Robert and Catharine (Crawford) Mathews. He was b. in Donegal Twp. on Oct. 3, 1818, and d. on Jan. 8, 1901. Samuel was a farmer. Catharine d. on Jan. 26, 1888.

Abraham Hay

Abraham$^{1.1.2.3d}$ m. ____ Arenfert, and had the following children in Westmoreland Co., Mount Pleasant Twp., Pennsylvania:
> Peter$^{1.1.2.3.1d}$, m. Sohia Lint on Aug. 17, 1837.
> Samuel$^{1.1.2.3.2d}$. m. Catherine, dau. of Peter Bossert, on April 19, 1838.

Michael Hay

Michael$^{1.1.2.4d}$ m. Elizabeth Young on Aug. 27, 1802. She was b. March 15, 1786, and d. on April 20, 1868. Michael was a farmer in Somerset Co., and d. there in 1842. They had the following children in Somerset Co.:
> Jacob$^{1.1.2.4.1d}$, b. June 26, 1803.
> Daniel$^{1.1.2.4.2d}$, b. Nov. 15, 1807, m. Catherine Friedline on April 14, 1829, and Margaret Stairs. Catherine was b. April 14, 1829, and d. in Feb., 1856. Daniel d. in Dec., 1872.
> John$^{1.1.2.4.3d}$, b. March 12, 1809.
> Iva$^{1.1.2.4.4d}$, b. Nov. 19, 1810.
> Mary$^{1.1.2.4.5d}$, b. June 19, 1813, and m. John Switzer.
> George$^{1.1.2.4.6d}$, b. Dec. 25, 1816.

Simon$^{1.1.2.4.7d}$, b. Oct. 12, 1818.
Andrew$^{1.1.2.4.8d}$.
Aaron$^{1.1.2.4.9d}$.
Louisa$^{1.1.2.4.10d}$, m. Andrew Pisell.
Isabelle$^{1.1.2.4.11d}$.
Carolina$^{1.1.2.4.12d}$, m. Jacob Ankeny.

Christina Hay

Christina$^{1.1.2.5d}$ m. Michael Palmer. He was b. in 1785, and d. in 1860. Christina d. in 1855. They had the following son in Westmoreland Co., Donegal Twp.: Michael$^{1.1.2.5.1d}$, b. May 31, 1812, m. Mary Ann Henry in 1840 and Mary Alice Kuntz. Mary Ann d. in 1867. In 1879, he resided in Youngstown.

Abraham Dumbauld

Abraham$^{1.1.3d}$ m. Eva Catherina Boyer. She was b. in 1753, and d. in Fayette Co., Salt Lick Twp., Indian Creek, Pennsylvania in 1837. Abraham moved to Fayette Co., Salt Creek Twp., Indian Creek, Pennsylvania in 1777. He was a Frontier Ranger in 1778. Abraham d. in Salt Lick Twp. on March 28, 1825. They had the following children in Salt Lick Twp.:

Frederick$^{1.1.3.1d}$, b. Feb. 6, 1778.
Mary$^{1.1.3.2d}$, b. July 6, 1780, m. John Lohr, and d. in Salt Lick Twp. on March 10, 1861.
Philip$^{1.1.3.3d}$, b. June 10, 1783.
David W.$^{1.1.3.4d}$, b. June 18, 1785.
Peter$^{1.1.3.5d}$, b. Dec. 20, 1787.
Christina$^{1.1.3.6d}$, b. March 3, 1790, and m. Samuel Fulton.
Anna Barbara$^{1.1.3.7d}$, b. Sept. 16, 1792, bapt. at Mount Zion on Nov. 9, 1792, and sponsored by John and Anna Barbara Robinson.
Dolly$^{1.1.3.8d}$, b. March 24, 1795.
Abraham1.1.1.3.9d, b. March 20, 1796, bapt. at Good Hope Lutheran Church, May 17, 1796, and sponsored by Peter Klinn
Elizabeth$^{1.1.3.10d}$, b. Sept. 8, 1797, and m. Henry Phillippi. He was b. in Somerset Co., Pennsylvania n Feb. 2, 1793, and d. in Somerset Co. on April 13, 1843.

Frederick Dumbauld

Frederick$^{1.1.3.1d}$ m. Christina Wolfe about 1801, and Susanna Weimer$^{1.2.1.1p}$, widow of his brother, Philip about 1830. Christina was b. in Franklin Co., Pennsylvania on April 26, 1783, and d. in Fayette Co., Salt Lick Twp., Pennsylvania on July 15, 1826. Frederick d. in Licking Co., Liberty Twp., Ohio on March 4, 1858. Christina is buried in Dumbauld-Miller cemetery, and Frederick in buried in Stockberger cemetery. Frederick and Christina had the following children in Salt Lick Twp.:

Abraham$^{1.1.1.3.1.1d}$, b. Jan. 3, 1803, bapt. at Good Hope May 15, 1803, sponsored by Abraham Thambald, and d. in Licking Co., Liberty Twp., Ohio on May 23, 1878. He is buried in Stockberger cemetery.

Joseph Buchanan$^{1.1.1.3.1.2d}$, b. Nov. 7, 1804, bapt. at Good Hope March 22, 1825.

Elizabeth Isabell$^{1.1.1.3.1.3d}$, b. Oct. 30, 1807, and m. Joseph Dull$^{1.1.1.5.4.1.3}$.

Peter Wolfe$^{1.1.1.3.1.4d}$, b. April 1, 1810, bapt. at Good Hope Sept. 26, 1810.

Catherine$^{1.1.1.3.1.5d}$, b. June 13, 1814.

Mary Magdalena$^{1.1.1.3.1.6d}$, b. June 3, 1816.

David$^{1.1.1.3.1.7d}$, b. Nov. 18, 1818.

Mary$^{1.1.1.3.1.8d}$, b. about 1820, and m. ____ Young.

Henry$^{1.1.1.3.1.9d}$, b. April 21, 1821, and bapt. at Good Hope Lutheran Church June 26, 1822.

Nancy$^{1.1.1.3.1.10d}$, b. April 23, 1823, and m. John Walters.

Joseph Buchanan Dumbauld

Joseph Buchanan$^{1.1.1.3.1.2d}$ m. Elizabeth Harbaugh, and d. in Johnson Co., Iowa on Nov. 15, 1860. She was b. in Fayette Co., Pennsylvania on Oct. 30, 1807. They are buried in Solon cemetery. They had the following children in Fayette Co. (except the last):

Frederick H.$^{1.1.1.3.1.2.1d}$, b. Nov. 24, 1829, m. Theresa, dau. of Kasper and Mary Elizabeth Carver, near Keokuk, Iowa on April 8, 1852 and Amanda R. Hawkins in Crawford Co., Garard, Kansas on April 8, 1882. Theresa d. in Crawford Co., Kansas on June 6, 1879. Frederick d. on Jan. 17, 1910.

Franklin$^{1.1.1.3.1.2.2d}$, b. June 4, 1832, and d. on Oct. 13, 1853.

Sarah Catherine$^{1.1.1.3.1.2.3d}$, b. May 18, 1834, and m. Brandon Lytle at Johnson Co., Solon, Iowa and Robert Grimes. Robert was b. in 1816, and d. in 1890. Sarah d. in Keota, Iowa, in 1890.

Mary$^{1.1.1.3.1.2.4d}$, b. April 27, 1838, and m. Jerome Shurtleff on March 24, 1853.

James P.$^{1.1.1.3.1.2.5d}$, b. in Licking Co., Newark, Ohio on Aug. 10, 1842, and m. Kathryn Shea on March 8, 1863. She d. in 1898, and James d. in Guthrie Co., Iowa on Jan. 13, 1903.

Peter Wolfe Dumbauld

Peter Wolfe$^{1.1.1.3.1.4d}$ m. Margaret, dau. of Peter C. and Hannah (Mechling) Cooperider, in Perry Co., Ohio on Sept. 22, 1836. She was b. in Licking Co., Bowling Green Twp., Ohio on Aug. 17, 1819, and d. in

Licking Co. on Oct. 24, 1896. Peter d. in Licking Co., Hancock Corners, Ohio on April 3, 1896. They had the following children (in Perry Co., Hopewell Twp. before 1850, and Licking Co., Bennington Twp. after 1850):

Hannah$^{1.1.1.3.1.4.1d}$, b. Aug. 27, 1837, m. John B., son of Gideon and Delilah (Butcher) Hall, in Licking Co. on Aug. 16, 1855, and d. in Licking Co., Bennington Twp. on Dec. 25, 1905. John was b. in Bennington Twp. in 1834.

Harriet$^{1.1.1.3.1.4.2d}$, b. Sept. 1, 1839, m. Abraham, son of Henry and Sarah Beckenbaugh Crotinger, in Licking Co. on April 22, 1858, and d. in McClean Co., Illinois on Sept. 3, 1921. Abraham was b. in Pennsylvania in 1821.

Frederick$^{1.1.1.3.1.4.3d}$, b. Dec. 6, 1841, m. Alzena, dau. of Luke Runnels, in Licking Co. on Oct. 12, 1865, and d. in Lyon Co., Emporia, Kansas on Jan. 31, 1915. She was b. in Licking Co. on March 10, 1845, and d. in Lyon Co. on Feb. 2, 1907.

Levi$^{1.1.1.3.1.4.4d}$, b. Feb. 11, 1843, m. Sarah Ellen Myers in McClean Co., Bloomington, Illinois on Dec. 1, 1868 and Margaret Breiner, and d. in Bent Co., Las Anamas, Colorado on Dec. 11, 1930. Sarah was b. Nov. 6, 1847, and d. on Aug. 5, 1882. Margaret was b. Aug. 26, 1857, and d. on Oct. 3, 1848.

Peter$^{1.1.1.3.1.4.5d}$, b. Sept. 8, 1846, m. Mary H., dau. of Robert E. Patton, in Licking Co., Sylvania on March 11, 1875, and d. in Licking Co., Bennington Twp. on May 10, 1910. Mary was b. in Nov., 1856, and d. in Licking Co., Highwater on Nov. 29, 1941.

Mary$^{1.1.1.3.1.4.6d}$, b. Jan. 25, 1849, m. Jonathan Nelson, son of Gideon Hall, in Licking Co. on Dec. 3, 1868, and d. in Bennington Twp. on June 2, 1908. Nelson was b. in Bennington Twp. on Aug. 31, 1841, and d. there on May 24, 1912.

Noah$^{1.1.1.3.1.4.7d}$, b. Nov. 25, 1851, m. Emma A., dau. of Alexander and Martha (Milligan) Iles, in Licking Co. on Nov. 13, 1873, and d. in Bennington Twp. on July 14, 1896. She was b. in Bennington Twp. on Aug. 9, 1852, and d. on Sept. 29, 1920.

Anson$^{1.1.1.3.1.4.8d}$, b. and d. on April 20, 1854.

Joseph Marion$^{1.1.1.3.1.4.9d}$, b. Feb. 23, 1855, m. Lovina, dau. of Alfred Lemming, on March 31, 1881 and Harriet Row on April 2, 1890, and d. in Licking Co., Alexandria on Oct. 15, 1941. Lovina was b. in Monroe Co., Bloomington, Indiana on Feb. 15, 1860, and d. on Jan. 18, 1888. Harriet was b. Dec. 18, 1867, and d. in Bennington Twp. on March 2, 1893.

Orlando$^{1.1.1.3.1.4.10d}$, b. Sept. 26, 1859, m. Arvesta Jennie, dau. of Enoch George and Martha M. Rice, on Dec. 24, 1879, and d. in Alexandria on March 6, 1934. She was b. in Licking Co., Liberty Twp., Ohio on Dec. 6, 1856, and d. in Alexandria, Ohio

on June 20, 1848.
Sarah Elizabeth[1.1.1.3.1.4.11d], b. Nov. 27, 1861, m. Elmer
Ellsworth, son of Isaac and Elizabeth (Oldaker) Dixon, on Oct.
30, 1884. He was b. in Licking Co. on June 25, 1861, and d. in
Homer, Ohio on Sept. 4, 1936.

Catherine Dumbauld

Catherine[1.1.1.3.1.5d] m. Henry, son of Frederick and Polly (Meckling) Slife, in Perry Co., Ohio on May 28, 1837, and d. in Licking Co., Liberty Twp. on Oct. 2, 1885. He was b. in Westmoreland Co., Pennsylvania on July 4, 1816, and d. on Aug. 8, 1893. They had the following children in Liberty Twp.:

Charles[1.1.1.3.1.5.1d], b. Oct. 26, 1840, and m. Ella Myers on May 25, 1876. She was b. in Liberty Twp. on Jan. 29, 1851.

Lydia A.[1.1.1.3.1.5.2d], b. March 10, 1843, m. Herman Forry on Sept. 20, 1866, and d. on March 20, 1880. He d. on Sept. 20, 1896.

Frederick[1.1.1.3.1.5.3d], b. in March, 1845.

David[1.1.1.3.1.5.4d], b. June 19, 1848, and d. on July 20, 1892.

Samuel[1.1.1.3.1.5.5d], b. Jan. 10, 1853, and d. on Oct. 10, 1856.

Maria Magdalena Dumbauld

Maria Magdalena[1.1.1.3.1.6d] m. Mathias, son of Johan Jacob and Maria Magdalena (Shoup) Stockberger, in Perry Co., Ohio on Aug. 13, 1836. He was b. in Westmoreland Co., Unity Twp., Ohio on Sept. 17, 1808, and d. on May 7, 1875. Maria d. in Licking Co., Liberty Twp. on Nov. 28, 1891. They had the following children (in Perry Co. before 1842, and Licking Co. after 1842):

John Dumbauld[1.1.1.3.1.6.1d], b. April 6, 1838, m. Malinda Alma, dau. of Israel and Mary Baker, in Dec., 1859, and d. in Licking Co., Liberty Twp. on July 3, 1878. She d. on March 12, 1896.

Savilla Catherine[1.1.1.3.1.6.2d], b. Feb. 5, 1841, m. Truman Perfect, son of Mahlon M. and Mary Elizabeth (Ashbrook) Hoover, on Dec. 18, 1862, and d. in Licking Co., Johnstown, Ohio in 1925. Truman was b. in Licking Co. on Sept. 14, 1840, and d. on Feb. 5, 1912.

Eli Mathias[1.1.1.3.1.6.3d], b. March 16, 1844, m. Elizabeth Amanda, dau. of Samuel and Mary (Seymour) Montgomery, on Dec. 27, 1866 and Allie Lyon on March 9, 1882. Elizabeth was b. Feb. 14, 1846, and d. in Licking Co. on April 9, 1872. Elisa resided in Licking and Franklin Co. Ohio, and Fulton Co., Indiana.

Mary M.[1.1.1.3.1.6.4d], b. May 16, 1846, m. Aaron, son of Frederick and Elizabeth (Long) Packer, on May 30, 1871, and d. in Fulton Co., Indiana on April 16, 1876. He was b. in Perry Co., Ohio on March 28, 1848, and d. in Fulton Co. on June 5, 1911.

William Allen[1.1.1.3.1.6.5d], b. Aug. 16, 1848, m. Mary Catherine, dau. of Eluid and Lucy A. (Wise) Shrader, on Oct. 6, 1870, and d. in Licking Co., Newark on May 2, 1928. She was b. in Washington Co., Ohio on Aug. 24, 1851, and d. on Jan. 22, 1936.

Luther Maurice[1.1.1.3.1.6.6d], b. Oct. 16, 1851, m. Nora A., dau. of George and Hester (Critchett) Hancock, on March 8, 1877, and d. in Licking Co., Newark on Nov. 3, 1916. She was b. in Licking Co. on Aug. 11, 1855, and d. on Aug. 27, 1938.

Roena Caroline[1.1.1.3.1.6.7d], b. Feb. 4, 1854, m. Oscar Reed, son of Hector K. and Susannah Ellen (Reed) Pratt, on Nov. 1, 1877, and d. in Licking Co., Johnstown on March 7, 1908. He was b. in Licking Co. on Dec. 29, 1852, and d. on Sept. 29, 1914.

daughter[1.1.1.3.1.6.8d], d. on July 18, 1856.

Celeste Anna Belle[1.1.1.3.1.6.9d], b. Sept. 8, 1857, m. Perry M., son of Mahlon M. and Mary Elizabeth (Ashbrook) Hoover, on March 6, 1884, and d. in Licking Co., Johnstown on Feb. 6, 1930. He was b. in Licking Co. on June 22, 1863, and was residing in Johnstown in 1935.

Clement Edson[1.1.1.3.1.6.10d], b. Aug. 4, 1863, m. Carrie, dau. of Samuel and Matilda (Scribner) Duffield, in Licking Co. on Oct. 30, 1889 and Ethel Todd Raymond in Franklin Co., Columbus, Ohio, and d. in Marfa, Texas on Dec. 22, 1926. Carrie was b. in Licking Co., Appleton on March 29, 1871, and d. on March 29, 1915.

David Dumbauld

David[1.1.1.3.1.5d] m. Delilah, dau. of Phillip and Anna (Kreger) Poundstone in Perry Co., and d. in Coffey Co., Kansas on Nov. 29, 1888. Delilah was b. in Fayette Co., Uniontown, Pennsylvania on April 6, 1824, and d. in Coffey Co., Kansas on Sept. 26, 1884. David had a general store in Licking Co., Burlington Twp., Ohio, and moved to Kansas in 1880. They had the following children in Licking Co.:

Christina Ann[1.1.1.3.1.5.1d], b. March 7, 1843, m. Albert, son of Moses and Elizabeth (McCrackin) Cummins, in Licking Co. on Feb. 19, 1868, and d. in Coffey Co., California Twp., Strawn, Kansas on March 8, 1917. He was b. in Licking Co., Burlington Twp. on Aug. 29, 1842. Christina graduated from Oberlin College.

William Allen[1.1.1.3.1.5.2d], b. Sept. 7, 1846, m. Eliza Jennie, dau. of A. J. and Eliza (Burford) Walker, and d. in Jasper Co., Webb City, Missouri on July 9, 1917. She was b. in Martinsburg, Ohio on April 7, 1850, and d. on May 29, 1929.

Mary Catherine[1.1.1.3.1.5.3d], b. in 1850, m. Elias Fassett, son of Christopher and Sarah Ann (Belknap) Shoemaker. He was b.

in Licking Co. on Jan. 5, 1845. They resided in Franklin Co., Columbus, Ohio.

Ella Frances$^{1.1.1.3.1.5.4d}$, b. Sept. 9, 1855, m. James Searle, son of Edwin Catherine (Searle) Williams, in Licking Co., Homer on Jan. 7, 1874, and d. in Licking Co., Newark on Sept. 17, 1937. He was b. in Homer on Aug. 9, 1851, and d. near Homer on April 10, 1918.

David Franklin$^{1.1.1.3.1.5.5d}$, b. Feb. 16, 1860, m. Emma Daily on May 11, 1880, Georgia Painter on Aug. 4, 1894 and Anna Marion Shaffer on Nov. 22, 1905, and d. in Jasper Co., Carl Junction on Aug. 27, 1915. Emma was b. July 16, 1861, and d. in Coffey Co., Waverly, Kansas on Oct. 20, 1893. Georgia was b. Feb. 11, 1872, and d. on Nov. 4, 1904. Ann was b. March 31, 1884. David graduated from Ohio State Medical College, and was a Doctor.

Philip Dumbauld

Philip$^{1.1.1.3.3d}$ m. Susanna, dau. of Jacob and Catharina Weimer, and d. in Salt Lick Twp. in Jan., 1824. Susanna was b. in Somerset Co., Milford Twp., Pennsylvania in 1783, and d. in Licking Co., Liberty Twp., Ohio in 1866. After Philip's death, Susanna moved to Licking Co., Ohio, and m. Philip's brother, Frederick. Philip had 349 acres in Salt Lick Twp. His will was written on Oct. 2, 1823, and probated on Jan. 5, 1824. He had the following children in Salt Lick Twp.:

Catherine$^{1.1.1.3.3.1d}$, m. Robert Ramsey, and resided in Davies Co., Indiana.

Mary$^{1.1.1.3.3.2d}$.

Sarah$^{1.1.1.3.3.3d}$.

Elizabeth$^{1.1.1.3.3.4d}$, b. March 29, 1811, and m. John, son of Joseph and Sarah (Gaff) Brown, in Pennsylvania on July 1, 1830 and Gabriel, son of John and Susanna (Lenhart) Weimer, in Stark Co., Sugar Creek Twp., Ohio on March 28, 1840. John was b. July 11, 1809, and d. in Tuscarwas Co., Wayne Twp., Ohio in 1838.

John$^{1.1.1.3.3.5d}$, b. Aug. 7, 1813, and m. Elizabeth Vought and Mary Thorp.

David W. Dumbauld

David $^{1.1.1.3.4d}$ m. Elizabeth Fulton. She was b. about 1786, and d. in Huntingdon Co., Union Twp., Pennsylvania on Sept. 6, 1867. David d. in Fayette Co., Salt Lick Twp. on Jan. 28, 1863. They had the following children in Salt Lick Twp.:

Hugh$^{1.1.1.3.4.1d}$, b. Aug. 7, 1813.

Samuel Frederick$^{1.1.1.3.4.2d}$, b. May 15, 1815, and m. Saloma/Sarah Weimer in Perry Co., Ohio on April 14, 1838.

She was b. in Perry Co., Ohio on March 14, 1820, and d. in Huntington Co., Union Twp., Indiana on April 16, 1899. Samuel d. in Union Twp. on Aug. 5, 1870.

Magdalena$^{1.1.1.3.4.3d}$, b. about 1825, and m. Daniel Eisaman and Frederick Reinacaer.

Peter Dumbauld

Peter$^{1.1.1.3.5d}$ m. Sarah Cable in 1802, and d. in Westmoreland Co., Donegal Twp., Pennsylvania on April 13, 1874. Sally was b. in April 13, 1785, and d. in Donegal Twp. on March 23, 1862. They had the following children in Salt Lick Twp.:

son$^{1.1.1.3.5.1d}$.

Jonathan Cable$^{1.1.1.3.5.2d}$, b. July 30, 1809.

Samuel Cable$^{1.1.1.3.5.3d}$, b. Dec. 5, 1810.

Elizabeth Cable$^{1.1.1.3.5.4d}$, b. Nov. 26, 1812, and m.
   Samuel$^{1.1.1.5.4.2.7}$, son of John and Catherine (Dull) Pyle.

Peter Cable$^{1.1.1.3.5.5d}$, b. March 12, 1820.

Jonathan Cable Dumbauld

Jonathan William Cable$^{1.1.1.3.5.2d}$ m. Elizabeth$^{1.1.1.5.4.9.2}$, dau. of George and Christina (Younkin) Dull, on Dec. 13, 1833. Elizabeth d. in Somerset Co., New Centerville, Pennsylvania on Dec. 17, 1895. Jonathan was a farmer, drover, justice of the peace and county, commissioner. He d. in Somerset Co., Turkeyfoot Twp., Pennsylvania on Sept. 29, 1885. They had the following children:

George$^{1.1.1.3.5.2.1d}$, b. in Fayette Co., Pennsylvania on Janauary 27, 1834, m. Mary Ellen Faidley, and d. in Upper Turkeyfoot Twp. on July 19, 1928.

Susan Savannah$^{1.1.1.3.5.2.2d}$, b. in Somerset Co., Lower Turkeyfoot Twp. Dec. 4, 1835, bapt. at Good Hope Lutheran Church June 11, 1837, m. Eli S. Younkin and Silas Kreger after 1859, and d. in Donstant, Illinois about 1928. Eli was b. in Somerset Co., Turkeyfoot Twp. on May 15, 1828, and d. in Somerset Co., Milford Twp. on Feb. 7, 1858.

Frederick$^{1.1.1.3.5.2.3d}$, b. in Somerset Co., Upper Turkeyfoot Twp. on June 25, 1837, m. Jane McNeil on Nov. 19, 1887, and d. in Geary Co., Milford, Kansas on Oct. 20, 1917. She was b. in Pennsylvania on July 31, 1836, and d. in Milford, Kansas on Nov. 28, 1919.

Sally$^{1.1.1.3.5.2.4d}$, b. in Somerset Co. about 1839, and m. Kreger Rhodes.

Christina$^{1.1.1.3.5.2.5d}$, b. in Upper Turkeyfoot Twp. on Jan. 16, 1842, m. Perry Schrock on Aug. 13, 1865, and d. in Fayette Co., Confluence, Pennsylvania on June 24, 1924. He was b. in Upper Turkeyfoot Twp. on Dec. 11, 1846, and d. in Somerset

Co., Milford Twp. on Dec. 17, 1911.
Daniel$^{1.1.1.3.5.2.6d}$, b. in Upper Turkeyfoot Twp. on April 26, 1844, and d. in Somerset Co. on Feb. 4, 1915.
Mary$^{1.1.1.3.5.2.7d}$, b. in Upper Turkeyfoot Twp. in 1847, and m. William Romesberg.
Peter$^{1.1.1.3.5.2.8d}$, b. in Somerset Co., Milford Twp. in March, 1849, m. Ellen Gerhard (1860-1927), and d. in 1926.
William$^{1.1.1.3.5.2.9d}$, b. about 1851, and d. in Somerset Co. in 1884.
Louisa$^{1.1.1.3.5.2.10d}$, b. Jan. 27, 1854, m. Wilson Silas Kreger on Oct. 5, 1872, and d. in Clay Co., Wakefield, Kansas on April 27, 1901. He was b. in Somerset Co., Pennsylvania on Oct. 22, 1853, and d. in Clay Co., Wakefield, Kansas on May 18, 1895.
Samuel$^{1.1.1.3.5.2.11d}$, b. about 1856.
Jonathan B.$^{1.1.1.3.5.2.12d}$, b. about 1858.

Samuel Cable Dumbauld

Samuel Cable$^{1.1.1.3.5.3d}$ m. Elizabeth Whitney and Pamelia, widow of ____ Canfield, on Dec. 5, 1872. She was b. Nov. 21, 1812, d. in Fayette Co., Pennsylvania on Sept. 17, 1872, while on a visit to relatives. Samuel moved to Whiteside Co., Morrison, Illinois in 1860, and d. ther on Dec. 25, 1906. Samuel and Elizabeth had the following children:
David W.$^{1.1.1.3.5.3.1d}$, b. June 12, 1833, and m. Phoebe Miller.
Peter W.$^{1.1.1.3.5.3.2d}$, b. April 15, 1836, and m. Catherine Bodfield.
John W.$^{1.1.1.3.5.3.3d}$, b. in 1837.
Sarah$^{1.1.1.3.5.3.4d}$, b. in 1839.
Susanna W.$^{1.1.1.3.5.3.5d}$, b. Feb. 17, 1841, and m. George Cooper.

Peter Cable Dumbauld

Peter Cable$^{1.1.1.3.5.5d}$ m. Catherine, dau. of George and Christina (Boyer) Stockberger, on March 12, 1843, Susanna, dau. of George and Christina (Boyer) Stockberger on Feb. 12, 1853, and Syrena, dau. of Daniel and Saloma (Stockberger) Wagner, on Feb. 7, 1889. Catherine was b. in Perry Co., Hopewell Twp., Ohio on March 20, 1818, and d. in Fulton Co., Indiana on Feb. 7, 1852. Susanna was b. in Hopewell Twp. on Feb. 3, 1816, and d. in Fulton Co., Indiana on March 7, 1888. Syrena d. in Fulton Co., Richland Twp., Indiana on Feb. 24, 1908. Peter was a retail dry goods merchant, and d. in Fulton Co., Tioga on Feb. 25, 1892. Peter had the following children:
Lafayette$^{1.1.1.3.5.5.1d}$, b. Jan. 14, 1844.
Angeline$^{1.1.1.3.5.5.2d}$, b. July 10, 1845, and m. Michael Sullivan.
Sarah/Sally$^{1.1.1.3.5.5.3d}$.
Almanary$^{1.1.1.3.5.5.4d}$, b. Jan. 29, 1851, and m. Amos Gordon.
Cordelia$^{1.1.1.3.5.5.5d}$, b. Nov. 8, 1854, and m. Marshall Ralston.
Delilah$^{1.1.1.3.5.5.6d}$, b. April 25, 1857, and m. William Taylor.

Salome Dumbauld

Salome[1.1.1.4d] m. Mathias Stockberger. He was b. in Wurtemburg, Germany about 1752, and d. in Westmoreland Co., Unity Twp., Pennsylvania in Oct., 1822. Salome d. in Unity Twp. sometime before 1822. They had the following children in Unity Twp.:

Michael[1.1.1.4.1d], b. Sept. 4, 1774, and m. Catherine Crist. She was b. in 1783, and d. in 1857.
George[1.1.1.4.2d], b. Nov. 18, 1776, m. Christina Boyer/Clapper (b.1786), and d. in Glenford, Ohio in 1846.
Frederick[1.1.1.4.3d], b. Feb. 15, 1778, and m. Anna Maria Shoup.
Mathias[1.1.1.4.4d], b. about 1780, and m. Nancy.
Ludwick[1.1.1.4.5d], b. about 1784.
Johan Jacob[1.1.1.4.6d], b. Feb. 26, 1788, m. Mary Magdalena Shoup, and resided in Perry Co., Ohio in 1827.
Peter[1.1.1.4.7d], b. about 1789, and m. ___ Weaver.

****

Lohr

unknown[1e] had the following children, presumed to be brothers:

John[1.1e], b. about 1754; Georg[1.2e], b. about 1756; Peter[1.3e], b. about 1758.

John Lohr

John[1.1e] m. Elizabeth. She d. in Somerset Co., Milford Twp., Pennsylvania on Dec. 21, 1821. He d. in Jan., 1815, and his will was probated in Milford Twp. on Jan. 24, 1815. His will was executed by John Lohr and John Pritz. They had the following children in Milford Twp.:

John[1.1.1e], b. in 1777.
Jacob[1.1.2e], b. April 1, 1780.
Peter[1.1.3e], b. about 1782.
Catherine[1.1.4e], b. about 1784, and m. John Putman[1.1.1.3a].
Elizabeth[1.1.5e], b. about 1786, and m. John Bargman. He d. before 1815.
Sarah[1.1.6e], b. about 1788, and m. Frederick Weimer [1.2.10p].
Magdalene[1.1.7e], b. Oct. 18, 1791, bapt. at the Berlin Reformed Church, and sponsored by Julius and Magdalene Volter. She m. John Pritz. Magdalene d. on March 20, 1822.
Susanna[1.1.8e], b. about 1793, and m. David Crosson.

John Lohr

John[1.1.1e] m. Mary[1.1.1.3.2d], dau. of Abraham and Catherine (Boyer) Dumbauld, and d. in Salt Lick Twp. on Oct. 8, 1847. She d. in Salt Lick Twp. on March 10, 1861. They had the following children: John D.[1.1.1.1e], b. about 1800; David[1.1.1.2e], b. July 4, 1806, bapt. at Good

Hope Aug. 24, 1806, m. Catherine Baker; Samuel$^{1.1.1.3e}$, b. Dec. 22, 1808, bapt. at Good Hope Dec. 24, 1809, m. Ann Yard; Peter$^{1.1.1.4e}$; Lizzie$^{1.1.1.5e}$, m. ___ Patterson; Jacob$^{1.1.1.6e}$, b. May 4, 1813; Elizabeth$^{1.1.1.7e}$, b. April 7, 1817; Nancy$^{1.1.1.8e}$, b. in 1820; Henry$^{1.1.1.9e}$, b. May 18, 1820, and bapt. at Good Hope June 26, 1822; Mary$^{1.1.1.10e}$, b. in 1823.

John D. Lohr

John D.$^{1.1.1.1e}$ m. Rachel, and d. in Salt Lick Twp. on June 22, 1875. She was b. Jan. 14, 1800, and d. on June 17, 1865. They had the following children in Salt Lick Twp.: George$^{1.1.1.1.1.e}$, b. Nov. 15, 1822, and bapt. at Good Hope Oct. 5, 1823; Jeremias$^{1.1.1.2e}$, b. Dec. 18, 1826, bapt. at Good Hope Sept. 2, 1827; Ephraim$^{1.1.1.2e}$, b. in 1831; Jacob$^{1.1.1.4e}$, b. in 1834; Sarah A.$^{1.1.1.5e}$, b. in 1837; Rachel$^{1.1.1.6e}$, b. in 1841.

Jacob Lohr

Jacob$^{1.1.1.6e}$ m. Hannah, dau. of George Miller, on Nov. 2, 1834, and d. in Salt Lick Twp. on Nov. 19, 1887. Hannah was b. in Salt Lick Twp. on Aug. 28, 1812, and d. there on May 5, 1882. They had the following children:

Henry$^{1.1.1.6.1e}$; Sarah$^{1.1.1.6.2e}$; Mary$^{1.1.1.6.3e}$; David$^{1.1.1.6.4e}$; Harriet$^{1.1.1.6.5e}$; Ellen$^{1.1.1.6.6e}$; Nancy$^{1.1.1.6.7e}$; Emma$^{1.1.1.6.8e}$; Sophia$^{1.1.1.6.9e}$.

Nancy Lohr

Nancy$^{1.1.1.8e}$ m. William Kalp/Kalb on Nov. 26, 1837, and had the following children: John$^{1.1.1.8.1e}$; Susan$^{1.1.1.8.2e}$; Jemina$^{1.1.1.8.3e}$; Aaron$^{1.1.1.8.4e}$.

Mary Lohr

Mary$^{1.1.1.9e}$ m. George Kalp/Kalb (b. in 1818) on Dec. 29, 1839, and had the following children: Jacob$^{1.1.1.9.1e}$; Rebecca$^{1.1.1.9.2e}$; Lucy A.$^{1.1.1.9.3e}$; Amos$^{1.1.1.9.4e}$; James W.$^{1.1.1.9.5e}$.

Jacob Lohr

Jacob$^{1.1.2e}$ m. Anna Maria$^{1.2c}$, dau. of John^{1c} and Anna Barbara$^{1.4d}$ (Dumbauld) Robinson in Fayette Co., Pennsylvania on Aug. 17, 1802. She d. on Nov. 13, 1853. Jacob d. in Fayette Co., Salt Lick Twp., Pennsylvania on Jan. 8, 1826. They had the following children in Salt Lick Twp.:

John Robinson$^{1.1.2.1e}$, b. Oct. 19, 1802.
Samuel Robinson$^{1.1.2.2e}$, b. May 7, 1806.
Anna Catharina$^{1.1.2.3e}$, bapt. at St. John's Lutheran on Feb. 1, 1807.

Barbara$^{1.1.2.4e}$, b. June 2, 1809.
Jacob$^{1.1.2.5e}$, b. July 22, 1810.
Josiah$^{1.1.2.6e}$, b. Aug. 12, 1811, and d. on March 13, 1814.
Elizabeth$^{1.1.2.7e}$, b. April 1, 1813, and d. on Jan. 11, 1826.
Catherine$^{1.1.2.8e}$, b. December 30, 1814.
Mary$^{1.1.2.9e}$, b. June 22, 1816.
Robinson$^{1.1.2.10e}$, b. Sept. 22, 1818, m. Rebecca Palmer, and d. on Aug. 18, 1898.
Peter$^{1.1.2.11e}$, b. March 7, 1820.

John Robinson Lohr

John Robinson$^{1.1.2.1e}$ m. Agnes. She was b. April 8, 1802, and d. in Salt Lick Twp. on March 7, 1871. They had the following children in Salt Lick Twp.: John K.$^{1.1.2.1.1e}$, b. in 1832, and m. Susanna Poorman; Agnes$^{1.1.2.1.2e}$, b. in 1834; Esther Ann$^{1.1.2.1.3e}$, b. in 1836; Milton Sutton$^{1.1.2.1.4e}$, b. in 1840; Adonirah Gadson$^{1.1.2.1.5e}$, b. in 1845; Rebecca Slater$^{1.1.2.1.6e}$, b. in 1847.

Samuel Robinson Lohr

Samuel Robinson$^{1.1.2.2e}$ m. Nancy. She was b. May 6, 1812, and d. in Salt Lick Twp. on Sept. 21, 1888. Samuel d. in Salt Lick Twp. on Oct. 25, 1894. They had the following children in Salt Lick Twp.: Delilah$^{1.1.2.2.1e}$, b. in 1832; William$^{1.1.2.2.2e}$, b. in 1834; Jacob$^{1.1.2.2.3e}$, b. in 1838; Mary$^{1.1.2.2.4e}$, b. in 1845; Isaac$^{1.1.2.2.5e}$, b. in 1848; John Robinson$^{1.1.2.2.6e}$, b. in 1851.

Peter Lohr

Peter$^{1.1.2.11e}$ m. Sophia Murray. She was b. Aug. 17, 1828, and d. on Aug. 13, 1916. Peter d. on July 15, 1894. They had the following children:

Mary Amanda$^{1.1.2.11.1e}$, b. April 1, 1847, m. Jonathan Winnett Moss, and d. in Dec., 1932.
William$^{1.1.2.11.2e}$, b. April 1, 1849, m. Mary Ellen and Hannah, and d. on July 16, 1933.
Lydia$^{1.1.2.11.3e}$, b. Feb. 3, 1851, m. John C. Whipkey, and d. on April 25, 1918.
Susanna$^{1.1.2.11.4e}$, b. Jan. 24, 1853, m. W. S. Cochran, and d. in 1948.
Sarah$^{1.1.2.11.5e}$, b. Dec. 8, 1854.
Murray$^{1.1.2.11.6e}$, b. Sept. 14, 1856.
John$^{1.1.2.11.7e}$, b. July 8, 1858.
Rebecca Jane$^{1.1.2.11.8e}$, b. July 20, 1860, m. Peter Weaver, and d. on April 20, 1943.
Samuel J.$^{1.1.2.11.9e}$, b. June 1, 1862, m. Sadie J. Magilland about 1884, Mary E. Patterson about 1897, and Josphene Ewers after

1914. Mary d. in 1914. Samuel d. in Fayette Co., Pennsylvania on May 22, 1953.
Isaac Freeman$^{1.1.2.11.10e}$, b. Feb. 2, 1865, and d. on Feb. 12, 1916.
James M.$^{1.1.2.11.11e}$, b. Sept. 26, 1967, and d. in 1954.

Georg Lohr

Georg$^{1.2e}$ m. Barbara, dau. of Conrad Nagle, in the First Reformed Church of Lancaster, Pennsyvania on March 23, 1773. George moved to Somerset Co., Quemahoning Twp., Pennsylvania in 1775, and settled on the west bank of Stoney Creek. On Feb. 28, 1785, he purchased 149 acres north of his original purchase. George was a Captain in the Lancaster Co., Militia during the Revolutionary War, and d. in Somerset Co., Quemahoning Twp., Pennsylvania in 1788. After Georg's death, Barbara m. Helfrick Theil on Dec. 28, 1788. They bapt. the following children at Berlin:

Margaretha$^{1.2.1e}$, b. March 23, 1773 (?).
John George$^{1.2.2e}$, bapt. on Jan. 1, 1777, and sponsored by John Fry.
Frederick$^{1.2.3e}$, bapt. on Nov. 20, 1779, and sponsored by Magdalene Fry.
John$^{1.2.4e}$, bapt. on Feb. 3, 1781.
Jacob$^{1.2.5e}$, b. Nov. 13, 1784, bapt. on Dec. 29, 1788, and d. on Feb. 26, 1851.

John George Lohr

John George$^{1.2.2e}$ m. Barbara, dau. of Yost Miller, and had the following children: Henry$^{1.2.2.1e}$, bapt. at Stoyestown Lutheran Church on May 15, 1806; John$^{1.2.2.2e}$, bapt. at Stoyestown Lutheran on Oct. 7, 1807; George$^{1.2.2.3e}$, bapt. at Stoyestown Lutheran on April 3, 1809; Maria$^{1.2.2.4e}$, b. June 9, 1811.

Frederick Lohr

Frederick$^{1.2.3e}$ m. Catharina, dau. of Peter and Mary Shaffer, and had the following children: George$^{1.2.3.1e}$, bapt. at Stoyestown Lutheran Church on July 3, 1803; Elizabeth$^{1.2.3.2e}$, bapt. at Stoyestown Lutheran Church on Aug. 10, 1805; Barbara$^{1.2.3.3e}$, bapt. at Stoyestown Lutheran Church on April 23, 1807; Jacob$^{1.2.3.4e}$, b. Dec. 19, 1807; Margaretta$^{1.2.3.5e}$, bapt. at Stoyestown on Feb. 16, 1811; Hanna$^{1.2.3.6e}$, bapt. at Stoyestown Lutheran on July 27, 1815; Sally$^{1.2.3.7e}$, bapt. at Stoyestown Lutheran on Nov. 29, 1818; Solomon$^{1.2.3.8e}$, bapt. at Stoyestown Lutheran on May 2, 1824; Solomon$^{1.2.3.9e}$, bapt. at Stoyestown Lutheran on Sept. 3, 1826.

John Lohr

John$^{1.2.4e}$ m. Magdalena, dau. of Andrew Woy, in 1806. Magdalena d.

about 1833, and John m. Sarah Weigley. John was a grist miller, and d. in 1858. John had the following children:

Rebecca$^{1.2.4.1e}$, b. March 3, 1807, and m. Peter Short.
Sarah$^{1.2.4.2e}$, b. Aug. 12, 1811, and m. Abe Brubaker.
Jacob$^{1.2.4.3e}$, b. Aug. 27, 1812, bapt. at Stoyestown on May 16, 1813, and m. Catharine Gohn and Mary Gardner.
David$^{1.2.4.4e}$, b. in 1814, and m. Elizabeth Gohn and Sarah Peterson.
John$^{1.2.4.5e}$, b. in 1816.
Andreas$^{1.2.4.6e}$, b. in 1817, bapt. at Trinity Lutheran Church of Somerset on July 18, 1819, and m. Barbara Maurer on Jan. 19, 1840.
Michael$^{1.2.4.7e}$, b. in 1820, and m. Sybilla Gohn.
Henry$^{1.2.4.8e}$, b. about 1822, m. Sara, and d. in March, 1858.
Magdalena$^{1.2.4.9e}$, b. November 24, 1831, and m. David Barnhart.
Mary$^{1.2.4.10e}$, b. December 14, 1832, and m. Eli Bowman.
Josiahm$^{1.2.4.11e}$.
Jeremiah$^{1.2.4.12e}$, was killed in the Civil War.
Samuel$^{1.2.4.13e}$, d. at age 16.
Lavina$^{1.2.4.14e}$, m. Wes Horner, and resided in Johnstown, Pennsylvania.
Elizabeth$^{1.2.4.15e}$, m. John Horner.

Jacob Lohr

Jacob$^{1.2.5e}$ m. Christina, dau. of Michael Kocher, in 1806. She was b. July 10, 1786, and d. on Sept. 13, 1861. They had the following children: Rebecca$^{1.2.5.1e}$, bapt. at Stoyestown Lutheran on March 3, 1807; Jacob$^{1.2.5.2e}$, bapt. at Stoyestown Lutheran on Dec. 22, 1811; Samuel$^{1.2.5.3e}$, bapt. at Stoyestown Lutheran on Dec. 25, 1813.

Peter Lohr

Peter$^{1.3e}$ bapt. the following children at Berlin: John$^{1.3.1e}$, bapt. on May 8, 1779, and sponsored by Nicholas Fous; Nicholas$^{1.3.2e}$, bapt. on Oct. 14, 1780, and sponsored by John Nicholas Foust; John Jacob$^{1.3.3e}$, bapt. on Jan. 18, 1784, and sponsored by John Jacob Hoy.

****

Johan Christopffel Leonhard

Johan Christopffel^{1f} m. Anna Eva$^{1.4g}$, dau. of Hanss Peter and Anna Christina (Peters) Kessler, in Horn Hunsrueck, Rheinland, Preussen on Nov. 10, 1693. They had the following children in Horn Hunsrueck: Annam Margretam$^{1.1f}$, bapt. on Aug. 28, 1695; Johannes Georg$^{1.2f}$, bapt. on Nov. 15, 1705; Johannes Peter$^{1.3f}$, bapt. on May 27, 1708, and presumed to be the Johann Peter, b. May 4, 1708, that immigrated to America; Johann Christopffel$^{1.4f}$, b. March 22, 1710/11.

Johann Peter Leonhardt

Johann Peter$^{1.3f}$ m. Maria Margaretha, and resided in Zweibrucken, before immigrating to America (according to tradition). They arrived at Philadelphia on the ship *Two Brothers* on Sept. 15, 1748, and settled in Berks Co., Greenwich Twp., Pennsylvania. Peter was a cooper, and moved to York Co., Dover Twp., Pennsylvania. He was residing there on April 13, 1763. Maria Magdalena was b. Sept. 28, 1715, and d. on July 1, 1777. Peter d. on April 4, 1774. They are buried in Strayer's Lutheran cemetery. They had the following children:

Philip$^{1.3.1f}$, b. in 1734.
Johan Jacob$^{1.3.2f}$, b. Nov. 18, 1736.
Johann Georg$^{1.3.3f}$, b. in 1738.
Jon Christoph$^{1.3.4f}$, b. in 1740.
Heinrich$^{1.3.5f}$, b. in 1742, m. Catherine, and d. in Somerset Co., Pennsylvania on March 21, 1837. He moved to Bedford (now Somerset) Co. in 1785.
Wilhelm$^{1.3.6f}$, b. in 1745.
Johan Peter$^{1.3.7f}$, b. Jan. 30, 1749/50.
Frederick$^{1.3.8f}$, b. March 7, 1751/52, m. Catherine Kramer, and d. in York Co., Dover Twp., Pennsylvania in 1837.
Gottfried$^{1.3.9f}$, b. March 17, 1754.

Philip Lenhart

Philip$^{1.3.1f}$ m. Anna. Philip d. in Berks Co., Greenwich Twp., Pennsylvania in 1803. They had the following children in Greenwich Twp.:

Johannes$^{1.3.1.1f}$, b. about 1753, took the Oath of Allegiance in 1778, and received land in Windsor Twp. from Phillip in 1794.
Phillip$^{1.3.1.2f}$, b. in 1755, served in the Revolutionary War, and received a pension in 1833.
Johan Jacob$^{1.3.1.3f}$, bapt. on April 24, 1757.
Johan Peter$^{1.3.1.4f}$, bapt. on Oct. 8, 1758.
Johan Georg$^{1.3.1.5f}$, b. Aug. 16, 1770, bapt. on Sept. 11, 1770, and sponsored by Johan Georg and Rebekah.

Johan Jacob Lenhart

Johan Jacob$^{1.3.2f}$ m. Anna Maria (Feb., 1738-Dec., 1791), dau. of Johannes Kuhl/Keel, in Berks Co., Pennsylvania on Jan. 21, 1760, and Barbara sometime after 1791. Jacob d. in Greenwich Twp. on Aug. 3, 1793, and is buried in Jerusalem Church cemetery. Barbara d. in 1793. Jacob had the following children in Greenwich Twp.:

Jacob$^{1.3.2.1f}$, b. about 1762.
Catharina$^{1.3.2.2f}$, m. Frederick Moyer.

Christina[1.3.2.3f], m. Jacob Homberger.
Johannes[1.3.2.4f], b. in 1770, m. Catherine, and d. in 1839.
Heinrich[1.3.2.5f], b. Aug. 13, 1773.
Sebastian[1.3.2.6f], b. about 1775, m. Catherine Eliza Miller, and d. in 1856.

Heinrich Lenhart

Heinrich[1.3.2.5f] m. Christina. She was b. Aug. 30, 1773, and d. in Berks Co. on Jan. 18, 1825. Heinrich founded Lenhartsville, and d. there on May 21, 1837. They had the following children:
Jacob[1.3.2.5.1f], b. Oct. 6, 1792.
Johannes[1.3.2.5.2f].
Rebecca[1.3.2.5.3f], m. Jacob Reichelederfer.
Samuel[1.3.2.5.4f], b. Feb. 28, 1798, m. Lydia Hamen (April 1, 1802-Feb. 1, 1872), and d. in Lenhartsville on Aug. 1, 1869.
Isaac[1.3.2.5.5f].
Daniel[1.3.2.5.6f].
Benjamin[1.3.2.5.7f], b. Oct. 13, 1802.
Henry[1.3.2.5.8f], b. July 21, 1804.
Frederick[1.3.2.5.9f].
Lydia[1.3.2.5.10f], m. Jonathan Losher.
Reuben[1.3.2.5.12f].

Jacob Lenhart

Jacob[1.3.2.5.1f] m. Esther Hahl, d. in Berks Co., Albany Twp. on July 9, 1825, and had the following dau.:
Lydia[1.3.2.5.1.1f], b. in 1818, and d. in 1825.

Johannes Lenhart

Johannes[1.3.2.5.2f] m. Hannah Heinly (Sept. 13, 1792-May 6, 1878), d. in Berks Co., Greenwich Twp. on Feb. 22, 1839, and had the following children: Jacob[1.3.2.5.2.1f]; daughter[1.3.2.5.2.2f], m. John Fister; daughter[1.3.2.5.2.3f], m. John Reber.

Isaac Lenhart

Isaac[1.3.2.5.5f] m. Elizabeth Leiby (b.1801), and had the following dau.:
Catherine[1.3.2.5.5.1f], b. Nov. 15, 1830.

Benjamin Lenhart

Benjamin[1.3.2.5.7f] m. Esther Hahl, widow of Jacob Lenhart, and d. in Albany Twp. on Jan. 8, 1858. She was b. Nov. 6, 1801, and d. on Feb. 6, 1849. They had the following children: James[1.3.2.5.7.1f]; dau.[1.3.2.5.7.2f], m. Daniel Grim; dau.[1.3.2.5.7.3f], m. John B. Hammerly.

Henry Lenhart

Henry$^{1.3.2.5.8f}$ m. Salome Leiby, d. in Greenwich Twp. on Aug. 9, 1840, and had the following children: Augustus$^{1.3.2.5.8.1f}$; Alfred$^{1.3.2.5.8.2f}$.

Johann Georg Lenhart

Johann Georg$^{1.3.3f}$ m. Anna Catharina in York Co., Pennsylvania about 1767. They moved from Dover Twp. to Newberry Twp. between 1777 and 1779, and to Monaghan Twp. between 1779 and 1783. Georg served as a Private in the Revolutionary War. Between 1783 and 1784, he moved to Somerset Co., Pennsylvania, and settled in Milford Twp., and in 1784, he purchased 390 acres on Coxes and Middle Creek. Georg d. there in 1797. Georg and Anna Catharina had the following children:

- Johan Peter$^{1.3.3.1f}$, bapt. at Strayer's on March 31, 1768, and sponsored by Johan Peter and Maria Margaretha Lenhart.
- Anna Elisabetha$^{1.3.3.2f}$, bapt. at Strayer's on March 10, 1770, and sponsored by Johan Adam and Anna Elisabetha Kramer. She m. Andreas Boudemont/Buttman.
- Anna Maria$^{1.3.3.3f}$, b. about 1772, m. Abraham Whipkey in Somerset Co. on Dec. 25, 1792, and d. in Milford Twp. in 1832. Abraham d. in Milford Twp. in June, 1820.
- Catharina$^{1.3.3.4f}$, bapt. in the First Reformed Church of York on June 5, 1774, and sponsored by Frederick and Catharine Lenhart. She m. John Whipkey in Somerset Co. on Oct. 22, 1793.
- Susanna$^{1.3.3.5f}$, b. in 1776, and m. John, son of John and Susanna Weimer.
- Maria Barbara$^{1.3.3.6f}$, b. Nov. 5, 1777, and bapt. at Strayer's on June 7, 1778, and sponsored by Michael and Margetha Gross.
- Hannah$^{1.3.3.7f}$, b. in 1780, m. John, son of John and Elisabetha (Boudemont) Dull, in Milford Twp. about 1799, and d. of Cholera in Stark Co., Sugar Creek Twp., Ohio on Sept. 27, 1834. She m. John Dull.
- Eva$^{1.3.3.8f}$, b. in 1782.
- Rebecca$^{1.3.3.9f}$, b. Nov. 1, 1785, bapt. at Samuel's Church, and m. Adam Harrah.
- Johan Georg$^{1.3.3.10f}$, b. Jan. 3, 1789, and bapt. at Samuel's Church.
- Joseph$^{1.3.3.11f}$, b. Oct. 15, 1792.

Johan Peter Lenhart

Johan Peter$^{1.3.3.1f}$ m. Elizabeth, dau. of Yost Miller, in Bedford Co., Berlin, Pennsylvania on Aug. 13, 1793. They resided in Ohio in 1825, and had the following children: Peter$^{1.3.3.1.1f}$, m. Catherine Yorty and Nancy; Eve[1.3.3.1.2f], m. Jonathan Friedline; Samuel[1.3.3.1.3f], was blind and unm.; George[1.3.3.1.4f]; Mary[1.3.3.1.5f], m. Phillip Zimmerman; Elizabeth[1.3.3.1.6f]; Sarah[1.3.3.1.7f], m. ____ Grady.

Maria Barbara Lenhart

Maria Barbara[1.3.3.6f] m. Samuel, son of John and Susannah (Whipkey) Berkey, in Somerset Co., Pennsylvania on June 13, 1797, and had the following children in Somerset Co.: Samuel[1.3.3.6.1f], b. in 1798; son[1.3.3.6.2f], b. in 1800.

Johan Georg Lenhart

Johan Georg[1.3.3.10f] m. Mary (possibly Berkey). She was b. in 1799, and d. in 1875. Georg d. in Somerset Co., Milford Twp., Pennsylvania in 1842. They had the following children in Milford Twp.:

George[1.3.3.10.1f], b. about 1819, and resided in Short Creek, West Virginia.
Benjamin[1.3.3.10.2f], b. in 1820, and m. Elizabeth Ann Faust in 1847.
Hannah[1.3.3.10.3f], b. in 1823, and m. Baltzer Walter (b.1824).
Monroe[1.3.3.10.4f], b. in 1825, and m. Rose Ann Coleman. She was b. in 1831, and d. in 1900. Monroe d. in 1907.
Victorian[1.3.3.10.5f], b. about 1827.
Mary[1.3.3.10.6f], b. about 1829, and m. ____ Kiem.
Useba[1.3.3.10.7f], b. in 1833, and m. ____ Shumaker.
Elizabeth Ann[1.3.3.10.8f], b. in 1837.
Anna E.[1.3.3.10.9f], b. in 1838.

Jon Christoph Lenhart

Jon Christoph[1.3.4f] m. Anna Maria. In 1780, he served as a Private in the Revolutionary War, and resided in York Co., Dover Twp., Pennsylvania. By 1790, he resided in Westmoreland Co., Unity Twp., Pennsylvania, and d. there about 1813. Christoph and Anna Maria had the following children:

Johan Christoffel[1.3.4.1f], bapt. at Strayer's Lutheran Church on July 31, 1768, and sponsored by Hans Georg and Christina Stauch.
Johan Adam[1.3.4.2f], b. Sept. 6, 1770, bapt. at Strayer's on Dec. 25, 1770, and sponsored by Adam and Anna Margaretha Diehl.
Peter[1.3.4.3f], b. about 1775.
Johannes[1.3.4.4f], b. Sept. 30, 1779, bapt. at Strayer's on March 26, 1780, and sponsored by George and Barbara Richter.
Frederick[1.3.4.5f], b. in 1781.
Heinrich[1.3.4.6f], b. about 1788.

Johan Christoffel Lenhart

Christoffel$^{1.3.4.1f}$ m. Catherine. Christoffel moved to Tuscarwas Co., Ohio with his brother Peter around 1809, in 1810, he was in Goshen Twp., and later settled in Muskingum Co., Newton Twp., Ohio, before 1816, where he d. in June, 1848 (in 1819/20 he is on the census of Perry Co., Madison Twp., Ohio). Christoffel and Catherine had the following children:

John$^{1.3.4.1.1f}$, b. in Unity Twp. in 1795, and m. Eliza Fluke in Perry Co., Ohio on April 29, 1824. He resided in Perry Co., Ohio in 1830, 40, 50.

Mary$^{1.3.4.1.2f}$, b. in Westmoreland Co., Unity Twp., Pennsylvania about 1798, m. Adam Ramer, and resided in Tuscarwas Co., Wayne Twp., Ohio in 1820.

Elizabeth$^{1.3.4.1.3f}$, b. in Unity Twp. in 1801, and m. James Oatley in Muskingum Co., Ohio on Feb. 19, 1824.

Joseph$^{1.3.4.1.4f}$, b. in Unity Twp. about 1804, and m. Nancy Vickers in Muskingum Co., Ohio on Aug. 18, 1825. He resided in Perry Co. in 1830, and d. before 1840.

David$^{1.3.4.1.5f}$, b. about 1806, and m. Harriet Fluke in Perry Co., Ohio on Feb. 28, 1828. He d. in Perry Co., Ohio in 1850. His will was written on June 18, 1850, and probated on Sept. 30, 1850. He resided in Muskingum Co. in 1830 and 1840.

Isaac P.$^{1.3.4.1.6f}$, b. in 1808, and m. Ellen Rutledge in Perry Co. on Dec. 28, 1848, and Sarah (b.1808) before 1850.

William M.$^{1.3.4.1.7f}$, b. about 1810, m. Mary Ann Emrey in Muskingum Co., Ohio on July 29, 1830, Rachel Rambo in Muskingum Co. on Oct. 2, 1834, Mary Ann Sylvester in Muskingum Co. on Nov. 20, 1844, and Naomi J. Roberts in Muskingum Co. on Sept. 15, 1859. He resided in Muskingum Co., Ohio in 1840.

Jacob$^{1.3.4.1.8f}$, b. about 1812, m. Hannah Griffith in Muskingum Co., Ohio on May 27, 1834, and Polly (?Mary Ann Treesch in Stark Co., Ohio on May 27, 1838), and d. before 1848.

Peter Lenhart

Peter$^{1.3.4.3f}$ was in Tuscarwas Co., Dover Twp., Ohio from 1810-23. He is presumed to have d. about 1823. (A William Lenhart payed tax on a Dover Town Lot on Nov. 7, 1814) He came to Ohio with his brother, Christoffel about 1809/10. Peter had the following children:

Daniel$^{1.3.4.3.1f}$, b. in Westmoreland Co., Unity Twp., Pennsylvania about 1795, and m. Elizabeth Shanks in Tuscarwas Co., Ohio on Jan. 12, 1817.

John$^{1.3.4.3.2f}$, b. in Unity Twp. on Feb. 24, 1797.

David$^{1.3.4.3.3f}$, b. in Unity Twp. in 1804.

Margaret$^{1.3.4.3.4f}$, b. in Unity Twp. about 1806, and m. Anthony

Fabra in Tuscarwas Co. on Oct. 1, 1826.

Peter$^{1.3.4.3.5f}$, b. in Unity Twp. in 1807, m. Nancy Thomas in Tuscarwas Co. on Sept. 18, 1823, and d. in 1872.

Joseph$^{1.3.4.3.6f}$, b. in Unity Twp. in 1809.

Dalena$^{1.3.4.3.7f}$, b. in Tuscarwas Co., Dover Twp., Ohio in 1812.

John Lenhart

John$^{1.3.4.3.2f}$ m. Rebecca, dau. of John Burrell, in Tuscarwas Co., Ohio about 1819. She was b. in Washington Co., Maryland on Sept. 22, 1801, and d. in Adams Co., Root Twp., Indiana on May 20, 1873. They resided in Tuscarwas Co., Wayne Twp., Ohio from 1820 to the fall of 1839, and then moved to Adams Co., Indiana. From 1831-33, he had 60 acres in Section 23, and 4 cattle. From 1842-43, John served as the Adams Co. Commissioner. He was a farmer in Section 34 of Root Twp., and d. there on May 18, 1877. John and Rebecca are buried in Alpha/Valley United Brethern cemetery. John's family also went by the spelling Linhard. They had the following children:

- Lawson$^{1.3.4.3.2.1f}$, b. March 18, 1820, and m. Lois, dau. of Josiah and Sarah (Warner) Brown, in Adams Co., Indiana on May 3, 1847. She d. in Root Twp. on March 28, 1912. Lawson was a farmer, and d. in Root Twp. on Dec. 18, 1894. They are buried in Alpha cemetery. Lawson had 54 acres in Section 40 of Root Twp.

- Sarah$^{1.3.4.3.2.2f}$, b. June 9, 1822, and m. John King in Adams Co., Indiana on Jan. 31, 1841. He was b. March 26, 1820, and d. in Root Twp. on Nov. 17, 1891. Sarah d. in Adams Co., Decatur, Indiana on Jan. 9, 1903.

- Peter$^{1.3.4.3.2.3f}$, b. Aug. 14, 1824, and m. Huldah, dau. of Josiah and Sarah (Warner) Brown, in Adams Co., Indiana on March 25, 1849. About 1881, Hudah was committed to the Co. Home, and d. there on April 13, 1888. She is buried in the Co. Home cemetery. Peter was a farmer in Root Twp., until 1893, when he moved to Allen Co., Madison Twp., Indiana. He d. in Madison Twp. on Feb. 19, 1902, and was buried in Alpha cemetery in Adams Co.

- Catharine$^{1.3.4.3.2.4f}$, b. Dec. 14, 1826, and m. Conrad Chronister in Adams Co., Indiana on Nov. 28, 1850. He was b. in Cumberland Co., Pennsylvania in 1827, and d. in Adams Co., Saint Mary's Twp., Indiana in 1905. Catherine d. in Saint Mary's Twp. on Oct. 6, 1917.

- Elizabeth$^{1.3.4.3.2.5f}$, b. Oct. 24, 1830, and m. Daniel Battenburg in Adams Co., Indiana on Aug. 19, 1858. He was b. in Butler Co., Ohio on April 19, 1835, and d. in Allen Co., Monroe Twp., Indiana on March 12, 1917. Elizabeth d. in Monroe Twp. on Feb. 5, 1922.

Mary[1.3.4.3.2.6f], b. Oct. 24, 1830, m. James Peterson in Adams Co., Indiana on Jan. 1, 1852, and d. about 1911.

John[1.3.4.3.2.7f], b. Sept. 8, 1832, and d. in Adams Co., Root Twp., Indiana on July 28, 1872. He is buried in Alpha cemetery.

Joseph[1.3.4.3.2.8f], b. Dec. 31, 1835, and m. Emma Bradley in Montgomery Co., Kansas on Oct. 17, 1875, an unknown individual about 1881 (born in Missouri, and d. before 1900), and Samantha D. before 1900. Emma was b. in Illinois in 1857, and d. about 1881. Joseph served in the Civil War from Adams Co., Indiana. He founded the town of Tyro, Kansas, had a general store there, and d. there in 1923 (Montgomery Co., Fawn Creek Twp.).

Susannah[1.3.4.3.2.9f], b. Aug. 29, 1838, and m. Phineas Shackley in Adams Co., Indiana on Dec. 15, 1868. He was b. in Massachusetts in 1829, and d. in Adams Co., Washington Twp., Indiana before 1880. Susannah d. in Washington Twp. in 1917.

Rebecca[1.3.4.3.2.10f], b. in 1841. She resided with her father until his death, and then remained on his farm.

William H.[1.3.4.3.2.11f], b. Jan. 20, 1844, and d. in Adams Co., Root Twp., Indiana on May 24, 1904. He is buried in Alpha cemetery.

George Clinton[1.3.4.3.2.12f], b. June 1, 1849, and d. in Adams Co., Root Twp., Indiana in Feb., 1850. He is buried in Alpha cemetery.

David Lenhart

David[1.3.4.3.3.3f] m. Sarah Shoup in Tuscarwas Co., Ohio on Sept. 3, 1823. She was b. in Pennsylvania in 1805. They had the following children in Dover Twp.: Peter[1.3.4.3.3.1f], b. in 1823. He has not been confirmed as a son of David; Jacob[1.3.4.3.3.2f], b. in 1832; Isaac[1.3.4.3.2.3.2.3.3.3f], b. in 1833; William[1.3.4.3.3.4f], b. in 1836; Susanna[1.3.4.3.3.5f], b. in 1838; Sarah A.[1.3.4.3.3.6f], b. in 1842; Elias[1.3.4.3.3.7f], b. in 1844; Emily[1.3.4.3.3.8f], b. in 1849.

Peter Lenhart

Peter[1.3.4.3.3.1f] m. Elizabeth (b. in Ohio in 1827). He was a shoemaker in Sugar Creek Twp. in 1850. They had the following children: Catherine[1.3.4.3.3.1.1f], b. in 1846; William[1.3.4.3.3.1.2f], b. in 1847; Mary M.[1.3.4.3.3.1.3f], b. in 1849.

Joseph Lenhart

Joseph[1.3.4.3.6f] m. July Ann Stone in Tuscarwas Co., Ohio on Dec. 17, 1829. She was b. in Pennsylvania in 1813. They had the following children in Tuscarwas Co., Sugar Creek Twp.: Mahala[1.3.4.3.6.1f], b. in 1832; Prudence[1.3.4.3.6.2f], b. in 1834; John[1.3.4.3.6.3f], b. in 1836;

Peter$^{1.3.4.3.6.4f}$, b. in 1838; Elizabeth$^{1.3.4.3.6.5f}$, b. in 1840;
William$^{1.3.4.3.6.6f}$, b. in 1842; Hannah$^{1.3.4.3.2.3.6.7f}$, b. in 1844;
Hester A.$^{1.3.4.3.6.8f}$, b. in 1846; Rebecca$^{1.3.4.3.3.6.9f}$, b. in 1848.

Dalena Lenhart

Dalena$^{1.3.4.3.7f}$ m. Elijah Hawk in Tuscarwas Co., Ohio on Nov. 16, 1834. He was b. in Pennsylvania in 1806. They had the following children in Dover Twp.: Rebecca$^{1.3.4.3.7.1f}$, b. in 1836; Elizabeth$^{1.3.4.3.7.2f}$, b. in 1842; Edward$^{1.3.4.3.7.3f}$, b. in 1848.

Johannes Lenhart

Johannes$^{1.3.4.4f}$ is presumed to have m. Anna, about 1793, and Eliza Morgan in Muskingum Co., Ohio on May 11, 1809. He d. in Muskingum Co., Ohio in 1822. Johannes had the following children in Westmoreland Co.:
    Johann Nichlaus$^{1.3.4.4.1f}$, b. Sept. 10, 1793, and bapt. at Mount Zion Lutheran Church in Donegal Twp.
    David$^{1.3.4.4.2f}$, b. in Mount Pleasant on Aug. 17, 1795, bapt. at St. John's Lutheran Church on Dec. 13, 1795, and sponsored by Frederick Mayer and Catharina Lavengeyer.

Frederick Lenhart

Frederick$^{1.3.4.5f}$ m. Mary M. (b. in Virginia in 1787), and resided in Tuscarwas Co., New Comer Twp., Ohio in 1850. They had the following son in Ohio: Isaac$^{1.3.4.5.1f}$, b. in 1822.

Heinrich Lenhart

Heinrich$^{1.3.4.6f}$ m. Catherine Munch in Muskingum Co., Ohio on Feb. 20, 1816, and d. in Muskingum Co., Newton Twp., Ohio in 1840. He had the following son: Frederick$^{1.3.4.6.1f}$, b. Feb. 19, 1819.

Wilhelm Lenhart

Wilhelm$^{1.3.6f}$ m. Anna Maria Rush. She was b. in 1751, and d. in 1822. Wilhelm d. in York Co., Dover Twp., Pennsylvania on Oct. 27, 1819. They had the following children in Dover Twp.:
    Susanna$^{1.3.6.1f}$, b. about 1775, and m. Samuel Close. She was a sponsor to a baptism in 1795.
    Wilhelm$^{1.3.6.2f}$, b. March 3, 1777, bapt. at Strayer's on April 20, 1777, and sponsored by Lorentz and Catharine Peitzel.
    Frederick$^{1.3.6.3f}$, b. in 177(8), and d. in 1803.
    Catherine$^{1.3.6.4f}$, b. about 1780.
    John$^{1.3.6.5f}$, b. in 1782, and d. in 1802.
    Johan George$^{1.3.6.5f}$, b. Sept. 26, 1784, bapt. at Strayer's on Dec. 12, 1784, and sponsored by George and Barbara Stauch.
    Peter$^{1.3.6.6f}$, b. in 1788.

Lisabeth[1.3.6.7f], b. April 28, 1790, bapt. at Strayer's on Aug. 2, 1790, and sponsored by Jonathan Beitzelin. She m. Henry Miller.

Heinrich[1.3.6.8f], b. about 1793.

Johan George Lenhart

Johan George[1.3.6.5f] m. Margareth (1783-1847), and Mary (1794-1864). George and Margareth bapt. the following children at Strayer's in Dover Twp.:

Elisabeth[1.3.6.5.1f], bapt. on April 5, 1807.
Lidia[1.3.6.5.2f], bapt. on May 1, 1808.
Magdalena[1.3.6.5.3f], bapt. on Aug. 11, 1816.

Peter Lenhart

Peter[1.3.6.6f] m. Elisabeth (1790-1859), d. in 1868, and bapt. the following children at Strayer's in Dover Twp.: Catharina[1.3.6.6.1f], bapt. on May 21, 1815; Elisabetha[1.3.6.6.2f], bapt. on June 16, 1817; David[1.3.6.6.3f], bapt. on April 27, 1819; Peter[1.3.6.6.4f], bapt. on Nov. 4, 1821; Hanna[1.3.6.6.5f], bapt. on March 21, 1824.

Heinrich Lenhart

Heinrich[1.3.6.6f] m. Christina, d. in 1867, and bapt. the following children at Strayer's in Dover Twp.: Louisa[1.3.6.6.1f], bapt. on Jan. 9, 1821.

Johan Peter Lenhart

Johan Peter[1.3.7f] m. Catherina Ogg about 1771. Peter d. in Somerset Co., Addison Twp., Pennsylvania in May, 1814. Catharina was b. in 1755, and d. in 1818. They moved to Bedford (now Somerset) Co., Pennsylvania in 1794. They had the following children:

Anna Maria[1.3.7.1f], bapt. at Strayer's in York Co., Dover Twp. on Sept. 3, 1772, and sponsored by Christophel and Charlotha Kauffman.
Johan Peter[1.3.7.2f], b. Oct. 26, 1776, bapt. at Harold's Zion Church in Westmoreland Co., Pennsylvania on Feb. 2, 1777, and sponsored by Peter and Catherine Klingensmith. He d. before 1813.
John[1.3.7.3f], b. about 1780.
Henry[1.3.7.4f], b. about 1782.
Eve[1.3.7.5f], b. about 1784.
Susannah[1.3.7.6f], b. Nov. 4, 1786.
Barabra[1.3.7.7f], b. about 1788, and m. Thomas McMillan.
William F.[1.3.7.8f], b. in 1793.
Jacob[1.3.7.9f], b. Jan. 2, 1793.
George[1.3.7.10f], b. April 10, 1794, and d. in Somerset Co., Lower

Turkeyfoot Twp., Pennsylvania on April 7, 1853.
Mary$^{1.3.7.11f}$, b. in Somerset Co., Lower Turkeyfoot Twp., Pennsylvania in 1802.
Sarah$^{1.3.7.12f}$, b. in Lower Turkeyfoot Twp. in 1803.

Susannah Lenhart

Susannah$^{1.3.7.6f}$ m. Jacob, son of Michael Schultz, and d. on Aug. 4, 1843. He was b. May 8, 1794, and d. on March 5, 1836. They had the following children in Somerset Co., New Centerville, Pennsylvania: Peter$^{1.3.7.6.1f}$, b. in 1806; John$^{1.3.7.6.2f}$, b. in 1807; Catherine$^{1.3.7.6.3f}$, b. in 1808; Elizabeth$^{1.3.7.6.4f}$, b. in 1810; Barbara$^{1.3.7.6.5f}$, b. in 1812, and m. Levi Knable on June 18, 1833; Jacob$^{1.3.7.6.6f}$, b. in 1814; Jonas$^{1.3.7.6.7f}$, b. July 13, 1815; Susannah$^{1.3.7.6.8f}$, b. in 1817; Maria$^{1.3.7.6.9f}$, b. July 2, 1818; Michael$^{1.3.7.6.10f}$, b. Oct. 12, 1819; Phebe$^{1.3.7.6.11f}$, b. Aug. 10, 1821; Lenhart$^{1.3.7.6.12f}$, b. in 1823; Eva$^{1.3.7.6.13f}$, b. April 17, 1824, and d. on Aug. 24, 1899.

William F. Lenhart

William F.$^{1.3.7.8f}$ m. Hulda, and had the following children in Lower
  Turkeyfoot Twp.: Zora$^{1.3.7.8.1f}$, b. in 1830; George$^{1.3.7.8.2f}$, b. in 1833; Jackson$^{1.3.7.8.3f}$, b. in 1836; Millie$^{1.3.7.8.4f}$, b. in 1839; Hiram$^{1.3.7.8.5f}$, b. in 1843; Sarah$^{1.3.7.8.6f}$, b. in 1844.

Jacob Lenhart

Jacob$^{1.3.7.9f}$ m. Diannah Christina Bowser. Jacob d. on April 2, 1855. They had the following children:
  Elizabeth$^{1.3.7.9.1f}$, b. Sept. 4, 1818.
  Catherine A.$^{1.3.7.9.2f}$, b. about 1820, m. George W. Turney, and d. in Somerset Co., Addison Twp. on March 14, 1885.
  Kiziah$^{1.3.7.9.3f}$, b. July 2, 1822, m. William Michael Wills, and d. Somerset Co., Ursina on Sept. 20, 1896.
  Susannah$^{1.3.7.9.4f}$, b. March 25, 1824, and d. in Addison Twp. on Jan. 28, 1905.
  Peter J.$^{1.3.7.9.5f}$, b. in Addison Twp. in 1828, and m. Almira Hyatt in Lower Turkeyfoot Twp. on Dec. 1, 1853.
  Sarah M.$^{1.3.7.9.6f}$, b. Nov. 29, 1828, m. Daniel Herring, and d. on Jan. 12, 1908.
  Barbara$^{1.3.7.9.7f}$, b. Jan. 15, 1831, m. Samuel C. Wilhelm, and d. on Jan. 21, 1909.
  Levinia$^{1.3.7.9.8f}$, b. Feb. 13, 1833, and d. in Addison Twp. on May 29, 1910.
  Diannah Christina$^{1.3.7.9.9f}$, b. July 22, 1834, m. William H. Bowser, and d. on May 17, 1879.
  Jacob Elogius$^{1.3.7.9.10f}$, b. June 25, 1838, and m. Catherine Fike.

William[1.3.7.9.11f], b. Jan. 29, 1845, and d. on Dec. 15, 1866.

Gottfried Lenhart

Gottfried[1.3.9f] m. Elizabeth Holtzinger in the First Reformed Church of York on Nov. 14, 1778. She was b. in 1753, and d. in 1824. Some sources say that he m. Maria Elisabetha, dau. of Yost and Maria Elisabetha Harbaugh, who was b. Good Friday, 1753, and d. on June 18, 1835. Possibly, Elizabeth Holtzinger was a widow, or Gottfried was m. twice. Gottfried was a clockmaker in York, and d. there on Aug. 15, 1819. They bapt. the following children in the First Reformed Church of York:

Margreda[1.3.9.1f], b. Sept. 5, 1779, bapt. on Dec. 19, 1779, and sponsored by her parents. She m. Georg Adam Euntz (1777-1815), and d. in 1860.

Elizabeth[1.3.9.2f], b. Oct. 3, 1781, and bapt. on Dec. 27, 1781.Heinrich[1.3.9.3f], b. July 22, 1784, bapt. on Aug. 30, 1784, and sponsored by his parents.

William Jost[1.3.9.4f], b. Jan. 19, 1787, and d. on July 10, 1840. He was a distinguished mathamatition.

Catharina[1.3.9.5f], b. Oct. 10, 1791, bapt. on Nov. 27, 1791, and sponsored by her parents.

Elizabeth Lenhart

Elizabeth[1.3.9.2f] m. John Bayley in York on April 30, 1803, d. in 1845, and had the following dau.: Catherine[1.3.9.2.1f], m. Samuel Tyler.

Catharina Lenhart

Catharina[1.3.9.5f] m. John Bayard McPhearson on April 25, 1811, d. on Jan. 25, 1859, and had the following son: Edward[1.3.9.5.1f], resided in Gettysburg, Pennsylvania.

****

Hanss Peter Kessler

Hanss Peter[1g] m. Anna Christina Peters in Horn Hunsrueck on Oct. 13, 1663, and had the following children there:

Anna Catharina[1.1g], bapt. on Aug. 28, 1664.

Anna Gertraud[1.2g], bapt. on Oct. 18, 1666, and m. Michael Schmidt in Horn Hunsrueck on Oct. 31, 1683.

Christophel[1.3g], bapt. on Feb. 25, 1671/72, and m. Maria Gertruda Weutler in Horn Hunsrueck on Nov. 10, 1693.

Anna Eva[1.4g], b. March 21, 1674/74, and m. Johan Christopffel Leonhard[1n].

Elisabeth Catharina[1.5g], b. July 14, 1678.

Jacob Schock

Jacob[1h] was taxed in Lebanon Co., Lebanon Twp. in 1755, and although it has not been confirmed, he is believed to have been the father of the following children:
   Johan Georg[1.1h], b. about 1743; Jacob[1.2h], b. in 1745.

If he moved to Frederick Co., Maryland, he may have been the father to these additional children:
   Johannes[1.3h], b. about 1752, and m. Barbara Botzin in Frederick
      Co., Middletown, Maryland on December 14, 1773.
   Catharine[1.4h], b. about 1765, and m. George Bossert in Frederick
      Co., Middletown, Maryland on Feb. 21, 1786.
   Eva Margreth[1.5h], b. about 1767, and m. Heinrich Reich in
      Frederick Co., Middletown, Maryland on Jan. 27, 1788.

Georg Schock

Georg[1h] was b. in the Shana River Valley, Germany about 1743. He is probably the Johan Georg Schock that m. Anna Catarina[1.1.2a], dau. of Johann Michael and Maria Christina (Schwingel) Maurer, in Lebanon Co., Lebanon, Pennsylvania on June 25, 1765, by Johan Casper Stover(he was of Lebanon, and she of Heidelberg). Georg Shock was taxed in Bedford Co., Hopewell Twp., Pennsylvania from 1774 to 1776, and 1779 to 1783. In 1779, he had 30 acres, 2 horses, and 2 cattle, and in 1783, he had 2 horses. It was possible that he was visiting relatives in Washington Co., Maryland as he was not taxed in Bedford Co. in 1777 and 1778, and a Susanna was b. to Georg and Catharina Schuck in Conococheague in 1778. In 1784, and from 1788 to 1791, he was taxed in Bedford (now Somerset) Co., Quemahoning Twp. In 1784, he was listed with three whites; in 1787, he had a warrentee of 200 acres; in 1788, he had 2 horses and 2 cattle; in 1789, he had 100 acres, 2 horses, and 2 cattle; in 1790, he had 300 acres, 2 horses, and 3 cattle; and in 1791, he had 2 horses and 4 cattle. In these records, his name appears as Schock, Shock, Shook, Sheck, Shick, Shake, Shuck, and Sheek, Shuk, and Shooke. In 1789, he is listed in the Quemahoning Twp. Militia. In 1792, the part of Quemahoning Twp. that he was residing in became Stoney Creek Twp.,where he d. sometime after Feb., 1802. He was taxed there from 1792 to 1798. In 1792, and 1796, he is listed as a weaver. In 1797, he had 200 acres, 2 horses, and 4 cattle. In 1798, he had a 15'x25' house and a 25'x25' barn adjacent to Michael Peterman. He appears on the 1800 census of Stoney Creek Twp., and was sued there by Gudleip Nitts in May, 1801. In Feb., 1802, a jury was called in the suit. On June 7, 1806, he was certified 206 acres located on the east side of Stoney Creek in Stoney Creek Twp., adjacent to Michael Peterson, John Wells, land said to belong to Dr. Smith, and Stoney Creek. Pursuant to a warrant dated May 31, 1787 for 200 acres. That is the last refrence found regarding Georg. He had the following children:

George[1.1h], b. about 1766.
Eve[1.2h], b. in 1775, and m. Phillip Shultz[1.5k].
Anna Maria[1.3h], b. about 1777.
Susanna[1.4h], dau. of Georg and Catharina Schuck, b. March 30, 1778, bapt. in Washington Co., Conococheague District, Salem German Reformed Church on July 26, 1778, and sponsored by Michael and Susanna Wetzstein. She has not been confirmed as a dau. of George Shock of Somerset Co., Pennsylvania.
Elizabeth[1.5h], b. about 1780. She sponsored her nephew, George Weimer, at his baptism in 1798.

George Shock

George[1.1h] m. Elizabeth[1.4k], dau. of Johann Nicholas and Catharina Shultz, about 1795 in Bedford Co., Brother's Valley Twp., Pennsylvania. George was a linen weaver. He is presumed to be the George taxed in Quemahoning Twp. with 2 horses and 2 cattle in 1790, and in 1793. In 1798, he was taxed in Somerset Co., Londonderry Twp., Pennsylvania on Savage Mountain, and appeared there in the 1800 census. In 1800, he had a 18'x20' house and a 18'x25' barn. In Sept., 1802, he may have been in Elk Lick Twp., where he was a tenant in possession, sued for ejectment by Michael Simpson. In May, 1805, Michael Simpson sued him again for Capias Trespass Quare Clausum Fregit. He appears on the 1810, 1820, and 1830 census' of Elk Lick Twp. According to family tradition, George and Elizabeth were residing in Coshocton Co., Mill Creek Twp., Ohio in 1836, and d. there. They had the following children:

Jacob[1.1.1h], b. in Stoney Creek Twp. about 1796.
George[1.1.2h], b. in Londonderry Twp., in 1798, m. Elizabeth (b. 1786), and resided in Elk Lick Twp. in 1840, and Milford Twp. in 1850.
daughter[1.1.3h], b. about 1799.
Peter[1.1.4h], b. Feb. 5, 1800.
Henry[1.1.5h], b. in Elk Lick Twp. about 1803, and resided in Elk Lick Twp. in 1830.
daughter[1.1.6h], b. about 1805 (note: an Elizabeth was b. April 12, 1808, and bapt. to a George and Elizabeth Schueck in Westmoreland Co., Greensburg First Lutheran Church on Oct. 26, 1808).
Joseph[1.1.7h], b. about 1807, and resided in Elk Lick Twp. in 1830.
Adam[1.1.8h], b. Jan. 20, 1809, bapt. at Sailsbury German Reformed Church on April 30, 1809, and d. in Elk Lick Twp. before 1820.
Samuel George Washington[1.1.9h], b. in 1810.
daughter[1.1.10h], b. about 1812.

son$^{1.1.11h}$, b. about 1814.
son$^{1.1.12h}$, b. about 1816.

Jacob Shock

Jacob$^{1.1.1h}$ m. Catherine Miller about 1816, and d. in Elk Lick Twp. before 1850. She was residing in Allegheny Co., Maryland in 1850. They had the following children in Elk Lick Twp.:

Elizabeth$^{1.1.1.1h}$, b. about 1817, m. Eli Engle in Somerset Co., Pennsylvania on May 5, 1837, and resided in Allegheny Co., Maryland in 1850.
Jeremiah$^{1.1.1.2h}$, b. in 1818, and d. in 1834.
John$^{1.1.1.3h}$, b. Nov. 25, 1822.
Samuel$^{1.1.1.4h}$, b. Jan. 21, 1823.
William Urias$^{1.1.1.5h}$, b. Jan. 7, 1826.
Eliza$^{1.1.1.6h}$, b. in 1831, m. Elias Lint in Somerset Co. on July 31, 1851, and resided in Greenville Twp. in 1850.
Jeffery$^{1.1.1.7h}$, b. in 1833, and resided in Greeneville Twp. in 1850.
Amos$^{1.1.1.8h}$, b. in 1835, and resided in Summit Twp. in 1850.

John Shock

John$^{1.1.1.3h}$ m. Susanna, dau. of Peter and Barbara (Garletts) Engle, and resided in Greenville Twp. in 1850. They had the following children: Lydia$^{1.1.1.3.1h}$, b. in 1842; Emily$^{1.1.1.3.2h}$, b. in 1843; James$^{1.1.1.3.3h}$, b. in 1845; Margaret$^{1.1.1.3.4h}$, b. in 1846; Mary F.$^{1.1.1.3.5h}$, b. Feb. 17, 1848; Elia Noah Webster$^{1.1.1.3.6h}$, b. April 28, 1855.

Samuel Shock

Samuel$^{1.1.1.4h}$ m. Catherine Barkley (b. 1825) in Somerset Co. in 1845, and resided in Elk Lick Twp. in 1850. They had the following children: Eliza$^{1.1.1.4h}$, b. in 1847; Zacheriah$^{1.1.1.4h}$, b. in 1848.

William Urias Shock

William Urias$^{1.1.1.5h}$ m. Mary Ann Patton (b. 1827) in Somerset Co. on Dec. 25, 1846, and resided in Elk Lick Twp. in 1850. They had the following children: Catherine$^{1.1.1.5.1h}$, b. April 20, 1848; Eli$^{1.1.1.5.2h}$, b. in 1850; Amanda$^{1.1.1.5.2.1h}$, b. July 7, 1853; Maggie A.$^{1.1.1.5.2.2h}$, b. Aug. 5, 1861; William Urias$^{1.1.1.5.2.2h}$, b. Jan. 13, 1862, and m. Rachel Jane Myers/May on Oct. 7, 1880.

Peter Shock

Peter$^{1.1.4h}$ m. Mary Ann$^{1.1.81}$, dau. of James and Anna Maria (Jauler) Boyd, in Somerset Co., Pennsylvania on April 22, 1827. About 1829, Peter moved from Elk Lick/Greeneville Twp. to Addison Twp., where he farmed 40 acres of government land. In April, 1832, he and Mary

Ann sold their land in Greenville Twp. (probably Mary Ann's inheritance) to their brother-in-law, Solomon Hutzell, and in Nov., 1835, sold the remainder to John Walker. On June 6, 1837, Peter purchased land in Coshocton Co., Ohio, but did not make the move to Ohio until 1840. In 1846, he moved to Allen Co., Amanda Twp., where he farmed 50 acres in section 34. In 1886, he moved to Mercer Co., Black Creek Twp., Ohio, and purchased 80 acres. While They resided in Black Creek Twp., Peter and Mary lived with their son, Levi, and in 1892, moved in with their dau., Sarah. Peter and Mary were members of the Dunkard Church until 1855, when they converted to the United Brethren Church. In their old age, both lost their sight. Peter d. in Mercer Co., Black Creek Twp., Ohio on Nov. 13, 1895, and Mary Ann on Oct. 1, 1895. They are buried in Fountain Chapel cemetery. They had the following children:

Levi$^{1.1.4.1h}$, b. May 9, 1828, and m. Mary Jane Carr in Allen Co., Ohio on Feb. 8, 1851 and Mary Albert in Coshocton Co., Ohio on March 30, 1869. Mary Carr was b. in Ohio in 1831, and d. in Mercer Co., Black Creek Twp., Ohio on Dec. 31, 1868. Mary Albert was b. in Coshocton Co., Ohio on Nov. 27, 1822, and d. in Black Creek Twp. on July 30, 1905. Levi d. in Mercer Co., Rockford, Ohio on July 3, 1912.

Elizabeth$^{1.1.4.2h}$, b. Dec. 25, 1829, m. David Eaton Baxter in Allen Co., Ohio on Jan. 30, 1848, and d. in Allen Co. on July 4, 1927. He was b. in Ross Co., Ohio on April 28, 1828.

Huldah Ann$^{1.1.4.3h}$, b. Sept. 1, 1832, m. Reuben R. Carr in Allen Co., Ohio on Dec. 4, 1852, and d. in Lucas Co., Toledo, Ohio on July 2, 1909. He was b. in Ohio on May 2, 1832, and d. in Mercer Co., Black Creek Twp., Ohio on June 16, 1909.

Carlisle$^{1.1.4.4h}$, b. Jan. 1, 1835, m. Amos Crites in Allen Co., Ohio on Aug. 17, 1854, and d. in Allen Co. on May 18, 1918. He was b. in Fairfield Co., Ohio on Nov. 18, 1832, and d. in Buckland, Ohio on March 4, 1919.

Catherine$^{1.1.4.5h}$, b. May 21, 1837, m. Joseph Daniel Allen in Allen Co., Ohio on Dec. 31, 1859, and d. in Allen Co., Allentown, Ohio on July 4, 1927. He was b. Dec. 6, 1838, and d. in Allen Co. on Oct. 29, 1918.

George$^{1.1.4.6h}$, b. Oct. 14, 1839, m. Nancy, dau. of Lewis and Elizabeth (Shope) Herring, in Allen Co., Ohio on Oct. 7, 1862, and d. in Mercer Co., Black Creek Twp., Ohio on Nov. 28, 1892. George farmed 20 acres in section 34 in Allen Co., Amanda Twp., Ohio until 1886, when he moved to Mercer Co., Black Creek Twp., Ohio where he took up 20 acres in section 24. George did from a heart attack suffered while clearing this land. Nancy d. in Paulding Co., Payne, Ohio about 1894, while residing with her sons, that were clearing trees. George is buried in Fountain Chapel cemetery, and Nancy's grave has not been located.

Sarah[1.1.4.7h], b. March 16, 1842, m. Hiram Baxter in Allen Co., Ohio on Dec. 10, 1863 and William C. Wagoner in Allen Co. on July 29, 1866. She d. in Mercer Co., Rockford, Ohio on March 19, 1913. William was b. in Allen Co., Ohio on April 26, 1845, and d. in Mercer Co., Black Creek Twp., Ohio on Aug. 11, 1926.

Mary Ann[1.1.4.8h], b. Aug. 17, 1845, had a illegitimate son by Louis McBride, and m. William T. Rumple in Allen Co., Ohio on April 11, 1877. Mary Ann d. in Mercer Co., Ohio on June 13, 1922. William was b. in Carroll Co., Ohio n Jan. 18, 1839, and d. in Mercer Co. on Dec. 6, 1912.

Elvina[1.1.4.9h], b. Dec. 11, 1847, m. Asa Binkley in Allen Co., Ohio on Dec. 24, 1871, and d. in Van Wert Co., Jackson Twp., Ohio on Aug. 10, 1914. He was b. in Allen Co., Ohio on Dec. 8, 1850, and d. in Van Wert Co., Jackson Twp., Ohio.

William[1.1.4.10h], b. Aug. 22, 1850, m. Margaret Elizabeth Kiracoff in Allen Co., Ohio on April 25, 1872, and d. in Allen Co., Amanda Twp., Ohio on Nov. 26, 1933. She was b. in Augusta Co., Virginia on April 22, 1951, and d. in Van Wert Co., Van Wert, Ohio on Feb. 1, 1919.

Peter[1.1.4.11h], b. May 12, 1852, m. Melinda Shope in Allen Co., Ohio on Dec. 7, 1876, and d. in Isabella Co., Blanchard, Michigan on March 5, 1932. She d. in Defiance Co., Ney, Ohio on Oct. 17, 1918.

Samuel George Washington Shock

Samuel George Washington[1.1.9h] m. Sarah, dau. of Johan Adam and Anna Maria (Glatfelter) Fadley, in Somerset Co., Bushtown, Pennsylvania on April 15, 1824, and d. while serving in the Civil War in Alcorn Co., Corinth, Mississippi on March 12, 1863. She was b. in Somerset Co., Elk Lick Twp., Pennsylvania in 1808, and d. in Indiana on Sept. 15, 1876. They had the following children:

infant[1.1.9.1h], b. in Somerset Co., Elk Lick Twp. on Jan. 31, 1825, and d. in 1827.

infant[1.1.9.2h], b. in Elk Lick Twp. on Jan. 31, 1825, and d. in 1827.

Elizabeth[1.1.9.3h], b. in Elk Lick Twp. on Feb. 4, 1826, and d. in Aug., 1826.

Catherine[1.1.9.4h], b. in Elk Lick Twp. on Feb. 4, 1826, and d. in Aug., 1826.

Azariah R.[1.1.9.5h], b. in Elk Lick Twp. on Jan. 13, 1828.

Minerva Jane[1.1.9.6h], b. in Elk Lick Twp. on June 5, 1830, and m. Joseph Miller in Allen Co., Ohio on May 6, 1852.

Lucretia[1.1.9.7h], b. in Elk Lick Twp. on June 5, 1833, and m.

Caspar Smith in Allen Co., Ohio on Aug. 5, 1855.

Marietta$^{1.1.9.8h}$, b. in Washington Co., Marietta, Ohio on March 26, 1835.

infant$^{1.1.9.9h}$, b. and d. in Coshocton Co., Mill Creek Twp., Ohio on April 23, 1836.

infant$^{1.1.9.10h}$, b. and d. in Coshocton Co., Mill Creek Twp., Ohio on April 23, 1836.

Elisha$^{1.1.9.11h}$, b. in Mill Creek Twp. on July 25, 1840, and d. in Indiana.

Mary Magdalene$^{1.1.9.12h}$, b. in Mill Creek Twp. on July 22, 1843, m. David W. Frock in Clay Co., Indiana on April 11, 1869, and d. in Indiana.

George$^{1.1.9.13h}$, b. in Mill Creek Twp. in 1846, and resided in Clay Co., Harrison Twp., Indiana in 1880. He has not been confirmed as a son.

Amanda$^{1.1.9.14h}$, b. in Mill Creek Twp. on Aug. 6, 1847, and m. Tobias Wallrick in Allen Co., Ohio on Jan. 1, 1872.

Caroline$^{1.1.9.15h}$, b. in Mill Creek Twp. on Aug. 6, 1847, and d. before 1850.

John$^{1.1.9.16h}$, b. in Mill Creek Twp. about 1848, and m. Mary Berger in Clay Co., Indiana on May 9, 1868. He has not been confirmed as a son.

Azariah R. Shock

Azariah R.$^{1.1.9.5h}$ m. Elizabeth Van Horn in Coshocton Co., Ohio on Nov. 25, 1853 and Nancy Cherryholmes in Clay Co., Indiana on Nov. 2, 1873. Azariah resided in Clay Co., Harrison Twp., Indiana in 1880. Nancy was b. in Ohio in 1850. Azariah and Elizabeth had the following children: Ettie$^{1.1.9.5.1h}$, b. in Ohio in 1862; Josophene$^{1.1.9.5.2h}$, b. in Ohio in 1864; Mercy$^{1.1.9.5.3h}$, b. in Ohio in 1866; Amanda$^{1.1.9.5.4h}$, b. in Indiana in 1868; Wakefield$^{1.1.9.5.5h}$, b. in Indiana in 1870.

Jacob Shock

Jacob$^{1.2h}$ m. Anna (Maria) Elisabetha, dau. of Daniel and Maria Elisabetha (Stroeher) Angst, in Lebanon Co.,Lebanon, Pennsylvania on May 14, 1765 by Johan Casper Stover (he was from Lebanon and she from Hanover). Daniel, son of Daniel and Maria (Junker) Angst, was b. in Enkirch, in the Moselle Valley on April 26, 1723, m. Maria Elisabeth, dau. of Johan Nicholas and Eva Maria Stroeher, in Germany on July 3, 1744, and d. in Lebanon Co., Annville Twp. on Nov. 22, 1803. This Jacob is presumed to be the Jacob Shock that resided in Bedford Co., Pennsylvania. Jacob was said to be from Frederick Co., Maryland, when he purchased 83 acres in Bedford Co., Bethel Twp., Pennsylvania on May 26, 1773. He resided in Bethel Twp. from 1773 to 1784. In 1785, he resided in Belfast Twp. Jacob d. in Bedford Co., Dublin Twp.,

Pennsylvania on June 14, 1813. He was an innkeeper, and served in the Revolutionary War as a Private from Bedford Co. Jacob had the following children: Esther$^{1.2.1h}$, m. Jacob Ambrosher, and d. before 1808; Jacob$^{1.2.2h}$, b. about 1789.

Jacob Shock

Jacob$^{1.2.2h}$ is presumed to be the Jacob that m. Esther Smith (b. 1789) in Bedford Co., Pennsylvania on March 28, 1811, d. in Koscuisko Co., Indiana in 1863, and had the following sons: David$^{1.2.2.1h}$, b. about 1813, and m. Sally/Sarah in Ohio in 1834; John$^{1.2.2.2h}$, b. in Montgomery Co., German Twp., Ohio on Aug. 18, 1815.

****

Maurer

This list of Maurers have not been confirmed as siblings, but it is quite possible that they were (it is believed that at least Michael and Georg were). They are placed here to add some clarity to the Maurer families in the region.

Johan Phillip^{1i}, b. about 1719.
Johann Michael^{2i}, b. about 1721.
Georg^{3i}, b. about 1725.
Peter^{4i}, b. about 1736.
Henrich^{5i}, m. Anna Elisabetha, and they were sponsors for the baptism of Anna Elisabetha, dau. of Jacob and Maria E. Kuhborts, at Trinity Lutheran Church in 1751. He d. in Lancaster Co. in 1767.
Johann^{6i}, confirmed at Trinity Lutheran Church in 1748.
Thomas^{7i}, confirmed at Trinity Lutheran Church in 1748.

Johan Phillip Maurer

Johan Phillip^{1i} m. Catarina, dau. of Leonhardt and Margareth Ramler, in Berks Co., Tulpehocken Twp., Pennsylvania on May 27, 1740. He received a 500 acre land warrant in Lebanon Co., Heidelberg Twp. on June 14, 1765. In 1754, he was in East Hanover/Lebanon Twp., and in 1770, was in Heidelberg Twp. On Nov. 16, 1755, he was one of the people in East Hanover Twp. when Indians crossed the Susquehanna and attacked settlers. They had the following children: Catarina Margaretha$^{1.1i}$, b. May 30, 1744; Johan Phillip$^{1.2i}$, b. Nov. 15, 1746; Johan Jacob$^{1.3i}$, b. June 9, 1748; Eva Margaretha$^{1.4i}$, b. Oct. 30, 1749; Johan Georg$^{1.5i}$, b. April 23, 1751; Maria Elisabetha$^{1.6i}$, b. July 25, 1754; Georg Michael$^{1.7i}$, b. Jan. 13, 1756.

Johan Phillip Maurer

Johan Philip$^{1.2i}$ m. Anna C. His will was written on Feb. 10, 1778, and probated on May 23, 1786. the executers were his wife Anna C. and

Wendle Bartholomew. They had the following children: Simon[1.2.1i]; Eva[1.2.2i]; Margaret[1.2.3i]; Catharine[1.2.4i]; Anna[1.2.5i], m. Christopher Brown; George[1.2.6i].

Johann Michael Maurer

Johann Michael[21] m. Maria Christina[1.1.1.1.8.3.2j], dau. of Johann Nickel and Maria Barbara (Anschuetz) Schwingel, in Trinity Lutheran Church of Lancaster, Lancaster Co., Pennsylvania on June 14, 1743, and had the following children:

Hans Georg[2.1i], b. April 1, 1744, bapt. at Trinity Lutheran Church on April 9, 1744, and sponsored by Paul and Rosine Reuter.
Anna Caterina[2.2i], b. about 1745, and m. Johan Georg Schock[1.1h].
Rosina Barbara[2.3i], b. Jan. 29, 1745/46.
Nicholas[2.4i], b. about 1748.
Anna Margaretha[2.5i], b. about 1750, and m. Johan Christoph Frank in Lebanon Co., Lebanon, Pennsylvania on Aug. 30, 1774.

Hans Georg Maurer

Hans Georg[2.1i] m. Maria Magdalena, dau. of Peter and Salome (Frey) Heylmann, in Lebanon Co., Lebanon, Pennsylvania on April 8, 1766. She was b. in Lebanon/North Annville Twp. on June 24, 1746. They moved to Washington Co., Hagerstown, Maryland, where the bapt. the following children at St. John's Lutheran Church (the Evangelical Lutheran Church at Elizabethtown (Hagerstown)): Johan Henrich[2.1.1i], b. April 3, 1774, and bapt. on April 24, 1774; Margarethe[2.1.2i], b. April 3, 1774, and bapt. on April 24, 1774.

Rosina Barbara Maurer

Rosina Barbara[2.3i] m. Anastasius, son of Peter and Salome (Frey) Heylmann, in Lebanon Co., Lebanon on April 8, 1766 by Joahn Casper Stover (he was from Lebanon, and she from Heidelberg). Rosina d. in Lebanon Co. on April 11, 1799. Anastasius was b. in Lebanon/North Annville Twp. on March 30, 1742, and d. in Lebanon Co. on March 18, 1815. They had the following children: Frederic[2.3.1i], b. Dec. 25, 1766; Anna Catharina[2.3.2i], b. Dec. 3, 1768; Johan Adam[2.3.3i], b. Oct. 12, 1771; Maria Christina[2.3.4i], b. Sept. 21, 1773; Rosina Barbara[2.3.5i], b. April 18, 1776; Johan[2.3.6i], b. Oct. 20, 1778; Johan Georg[2.3.7i], b. June 16, 1780.

Nicholas Maurer

Nicholas[2.4i] m. Maria Catarina, and was taxed in Lebanon Twp. in 1769. They had the following dau. in Lebanon: Rosina Barbara[2.4.1i], b. Dec. 2, 1769, bapt. in North Annville Twp., and sponsored by Anastasius and Rosina Heilman.

Georg Maurer

Georg^{31} m. Anna Maria. He may be the George Mauerer, who was killed and scalped in Lebanon Co. on Aug. 11, 1757, and the George Mowerer who's will was probated in Lancaster Co. in 1759. They bapt. a dau. in Trinity Lutheran Church of Lancaster: Anna Maria$^{3 \cdot 1 1}$, b. Oct. 25, 1748, bapt. on Oct. 30, 1748, and sponsored by Benjamin and Barbara Spieker.

Peter Maurer

Peter^{41} m. Catarina Elisabeth Kniesz in Lebanon Bethel on April 20, 1756. He d. in Bethel Twp. between Aug. 4, 1780 and Sept. 10, 1781, and had the following children: Magdalena$^{4 \cdot 1 1}$; Anna$^{4 \cdot 2 1}$; Barbara$^{4 \cdot 3 1}$; Elizabeth$^{4 \cdot 4 1}$; John$^{4 \cdot 5 1}$; Ernestina$^{4 \cdot 6 1}$; Henry$^{4 \cdot 7 1}$.

****

Jacob Schwingell

Jacob^{1j} resided in Remmesweiler in 1537 and 1542. He had the following son: Mathis$^{1 \cdot 1j}$.

Mathis Schwingel

Mathis$^{1 \cdot 1j}$ was a farmer in Remmesweiler in 1572, and had the following son: Georg$^{1 \cdot 1 \cdot 1j}$.

Georg Schwingel

Georg$^{1 \cdot 1 \cdot 1j}$ was the richest farmer in Remmesweiler in 1625, and had the following son: Michael$^{1 \cdot 1 \cdot 1 \cdot 1j}$, b. about 1627/28.

Michael Schwingel

Michael$^{1 \cdot 1 \cdot 1 \cdot 1j}$ m. Anna, dau. of Hans and Marg. N. Heitz, in Ottweiler on April 23, 1650, and d. on June 5, 1694. He was the mayor of Remmesweiler, Oberlinxweiler, and Niederlinxweiler, and church edler. They had the following children (bapt. at the Evangelical Lutheran Church in Ottweiler):

Hans Nickel$^{1 \cdot 1 \cdot 1 \cdot 1 \cdot 1j}$, b. Feb. 21, 1651, m. Anna Katharina Neunkirchen, and d. on Sept. 28, 1674.
Hans Velten$^{1 \cdot 1 \cdot 1 \cdot 1 \cdot 2j}$, b. Sept. 25, 1653.
Eva Margaretha$^{1 \cdot 1 \cdot 1 \cdot 1 \cdot 3j}$, b. March 8, 1655, and m. Hans Mikke Hell.
Georg$^{1 \cdot 1 \cdot 1 \cdot 1 \cdot 4j}$, b. about 1657, and m. Barbara, dau. of Simon Konig, in Ottweiler on Oct. 19, 1680.
Hans Jakob$^{1 \cdot 1 \cdot 1 \cdot 1 \cdot 5j}$, b. June 3, 1660, and m. Anna Leib, dau. of Caspar Schneider on Nov. 16, 1685.
Barbara$^{1 \cdot 1 \cdot 1 \cdot 1 \cdot 6j}$, b. March 1, 1664, and m. Hans Stefan Schiffler of Niederlinxweiler on Nov. 16, 1685.
Susanne Elisabeth$^{1 \cdot 1 \cdot 1 \cdot 1 \cdot 7j}$, b. April 22, 1666.
Nikolaus$^{1 \cdot 1 \cdot 1 \cdot 1 \cdot 8j}$, b. Dec. 12, 1667.

Nikolaus Schwingel

Nikolaus$^{1.1.1.1.8j}$ m. Katharina, dau. of Paulus Henrici, in Neunkirchen on July 17, 1691, and d. in Neunkirchen on May 31, 1713. Paulus was an ordnance blacksmith, and in 1711, he and his wife commited their household (a half house) to Nikolaus because he had "helped them both truely and childly in good and bad times during 23 years". On March 9, 1717, the inheritance of Paulus's grandchildren (children of Nikolaus and Katharina) was calculated, indicating he was deceased. Nikolaus was an ordnance blacksmith and church elder in Neunkirchen. After Nikolaus's death, Katharina m. Hanss Velten Kurtz on November 17, 1716. Hanss Velten became mayor of Neunkirchen. Nikolaus and Katharina had the following children in Neunkirchen, Sarrland (bapt. at the Neunkirchen Evangelical Lutheran Church):

Anna Barbara$^{1.1.1.1.8.1j}$, b. Nov. 9, 1692, and d. on Jan. 19, 1697.
Hanss Michael$^{1.1.1.1.8.2j}$, b. July 31, 1695, confirmed in 1708, and d. before April 15, 1719.
Hanns Nikolaus/Johan Nickel$^{1.1.1.1.8.3j}$, b. Jan. 26, 1698, and confirmed in 1711.
Johann Georg$^{1.1.1.1.8.4j}$, b. June 19, 1701, and confirmed in 1714.
Johann Jacob$^{1.1.1.1.8.5j}$, b. Aug. 17, 1704, and d. on Sept. 5, 1704.
Maria Christina$^{1.1.1.1.8.6j}$, b. Aug. 24, 1705, confirmed in 1719, and m. Hanss Adam Linxweiler.
Susanna Catharina$^{1.1.1.1.8.7j}$, b. Dec. 16, 1708, confirmed in 1721, and d. in Steinbach bei Ottweiler on May 10, 1764. She m. Johann Casper Mueller and Johan Peter Bleymehl in Doerrenbach on Jan. 2, 1749. Johan Peter was b. Dec. 24, 1719, and d. in Steinbach on Feb. 21, 1783.
Eva Catharina$^{1.1.1.1.8.8j}$, b. Feb. 25, 1712, and d. on Jan. 30, 1714.

Johan Nickel Schwingel

Johann Nickel$^{1.1.1.1.8.3j}$ m. Maria Barbara, dau. of Michael Anschuetz, on May 31, 1718 and Anna Margaretha Haas, widow of Ludwig (and possibly a dau. of Leonard Hoy), about 1742. Michael Anschuetz was a citizen, joiner, glass-blower, and the bellows-maker of Gelnhausen. Michael d. there on July 30, 1730. Barbara was b. about 1700, and moved to Neunkirchen with her brothers, Johann Andreas and Johann Jacob, about 1713. Johann Andreas Anschuetz was a master joiner, and glass blower, and m. Luise Katharina, dau. of Georg Bernhard and Eva Katharina (Werner) Meyer, on May 25, 1723. Johann Jacob Anschuetz was b. Feb. 2, 1685, was a master joiner and glass-blower, and m. Maria Elisabeth, dau. of Johann Michael and Maria Katharina (Lippin) Meyer, on May 16, 1713. Nickel, Barbara, and their four children left Germany on June 21, 1740, and arrived in Philadelphia on the ship *Samuel*, on Dec. 3, 1740. It is not certain if Barbara d. enroute or soon after arrival. Nickel was a blacksmith, and settled in the Tulpehocken region of Pennsylvania (then Lancaster Co., now Lebanon Co., Heidelberg Twp.). He was church councilman and reader of Christ's Lutheran Church in Stouchsburg in 1752. In Aug., 1758, Margaret and Nickel made a grant of 149 acres near Tulpehocken Creek, that had been patented to Margaret in 1741, and transferred the land to their two sons, and her four daus. by her first marriage. Soon after, Nickel moved to Washington Co., Maryland, where he died, and his estate was administered by his widow Margaret, and Garrard Stonebreaker on April 3, 1786. He had the following children (the first four in Neunkirchen and the rest in Berks Co.):

- Johann Michael$^{1.1.1.1.8.3j}$, b. April 9, 1719, and d. soon after his arrival in America.
- Maria Christina$^{1.1.1.1.8.3.2j}$, b. Aug. 10, 1721, and m. Johann Michael Maurer$^{1.1a}$.
- Georg Martin$^{1.1.1.1.8.3.3j}$, b. Feb. 2, 1724.
- Johann Nicolaus$^{1.1.1.1.8.3.4j}$, b. Feb. 23, 1730.
- Johann Michael$^{1.1.1.1.8.3.5j}$, b. Aug. 23, 1743, bapt. at Berks Co., Stouchsburg, Pennsylvania, and sponsored by Michael and Anna Maria Mueller.
- Johann Peter$^{1.1.1.1.8.3.6j}$, b. April 26, 1750, bapt. at Stouchsburg on May 10, 1750, and sponsored by Peter Hallstein and John Feg.

Georg Martin Schwingel

Georg Martin$^{1.1.1.1.8.3.3j}$ m. Anna Margaretta, dau. of Martin Thoma, about 1747. George received a land warrant for 150 acres in Lancaster Co., Warwick Twp., and on Jan. 8, 1752, 50 acres in Lancaster Co., Lebanon Twp. On Feb. 4, 1761, he purchased 224 acres in Lancaster Co., Heidelberg Twp. In 1752 and 1758, Nicholas and George Swingle were taxed in Heidelberg Twp. Georg was naturalized on April 8, 1761. He was overseer of roads in 1762 and overseer of the poor in Heidelberg Twp. in 1764. In 1771, Georg was taxed in Heidelberg Twp., and was presumed to have taken his family to Frederick Co., Maryland before Feb. 21, 1771, when he recorded a mortgage paid to him in the Conococheague settlement in Maryland. He purchased 614 acres called *Marsh Head, Resurvey on Addition to Marsh Head, Addition to Laferty's Lott, Resurvey on part of Shippen's Neglect*, and *Addition to Gook Luck* on March 18, 1772. On March 22, 1773, he bought 100 acres called *John's Lott* and *Resurvey on Dickson's Pleasure*, located on Antietam Creek, with intentions of building a mill or mills. During the Revolutionary War, he was a member of the committee to raise money for arms and ammunition for Marsh Hundred in Frederick Co., and was a member of that Co.'s Committee of Observation (elected on Sept. 12, 1775). About 1783, He moved to Baltimore, Maryland, and in 1786, he sold part of his 1772 purchase to his sons, George and Nicholas. About 1800, George and his wife moved to Jefferson Co., Tennessee. On March 15, 1802, Georg sold the land from his 1773 purchase, and he and his wife were presumed to have d. soon after that date. Georg and Margaretta had the following children:

Nicholas$^{1.1.1.1.8.3.3.1j}$, b. Oct. 12, 1748, m. Elisabeth, and d. in Washington Co., Hagerstown, Maryland on March 16, 1842. He served in the Revolutionary War from Maryland.

Anna Maria$^{1.1.1.1.8.3.3.2j}$, b. May 18, 1752, and m. Gerard Stonebreaker.

Leonhard$^{1.1.1.1.8.3.3.3j}$, b. Feb. 5, 1755, bapt. on March 9, 1755, and sponsored by Leonard and Eva Mueller. He served in the Revolutionary War from Pennsylvania and Maryland, and d. in Tennessee sometime after 1838. In late 1777, early 1778, he moved to Frederick Co., Maryland, and in all likelyhood, operated the grist and saw mill his father established on Antietam Creek. In 1788, he moved to Baltimore Co., Maryland. After becoming bankrupt in 1794, he moved to Washington Co., Conococheague Hundred, Maryland, to reside on his father-in-law's land. Sometime after April, 1804, he moved to Washington Co., Tennessee. He m. Eva, dau. of Michael Theiss.

George$^{1.1.1.1.8.3.3.4j}$, b. Dec. 11, 1757, m. Christina Householder in Washington Co., Maryland on April 23, 1778, Mary Householder in Baltimore Co., Maryland on April 1, 1793, and Mary Phillips, widow of John Savage, in Lewis Co., Kentucky on Jan. 2, 1812. George d. on Nov. 15, 1840. Hew served in the Revolutionary War from Pennsylvania and Maryland. About 1783, he moved to Baltimore, Maryland. George eventually lost all of his property in Maryland, and applied for, and was granted 300 acres on the north side of the French River in the Area of North Carolina that became Jefferson Co., Tennessee. In 1802, the Co. sold George's land for nonpayment of taxes, and George moved to Montgomery Co., Kentucky, and soon after, Lewis Co., Kentucky. He applied for pension in Lewis Co. in 1833. In 1838, he was residing in Greenup Co., Greenupsburg, Kentucky, and in 1842, resided in Franklin Co., Kentucky, where he died.

Michael$^{1.1.1.1.8.3.3.5j}$, b. Feb. 25, 1759, m. Mary, dau. of Charles Cummings in Washington Co., Virginia on Sept. 6, 1791, and d. in Washington Co., Virginia on Oct. 18, 1827. She was b. in Lancaster Co., Virginia on Dec. 15, 1771, and d. in Washington Co., Virginia on Dec. 6, 1847. Michael served in the Revolutionary War from Maryland. In 1783, he moved to Baltimore Co., Maryland, andpurchased land with his brother

George, and engaged in milling. By 1789, Michael left this partnership to form a new one in the retail goods, wares, and merchandise business with his brother, John in Washington Co., Virginia. On Oct. 1, 1791, he moved to the Lead Mines in Wythe Co., Virginia, and about the same time leased lead mines on the French Broad in Tennessee with his brother, John. In March, 1792, this venture failed, and in April, he, John, and Garret Fitzgerald purchased land in Jefferson Co., Tennessee. Garret dissolved the partnership in Sept., 1792, and Michael returned to Washington Co., Virginia in Nov., 1792. On Oct. 10, 1798, he moved to the Beaver Creek Iron Works in Sullivan Co., Bristol, Tennessee, and on Nov. 21, 1799, he moved to the Investry Iron Works. Later, he and John worked as iron moulders at Embreesville, in Unicoi Co., Tennessee. On July 1, 1806, Michael sold his 21 acres on Indian Creek to his nephew, George Swingle, and by April, 1813, was residing in Washington Co., Virginia

John$^{1.1.1.1.8.3.3.6j}$, b. May 1, 1761. In 1789, he and his brother, Michael had established a partnership in Washington Co., Virginia, and over the next 15 years worked with Michael in Virginia and Tennessee (see Michael's entry). In 1810, John resided in Montgomery Co., Kentucky, and on Sept. 2, 1816, was residing in Estill Co., Ravenna Twp., Kentucky. He served in the Revolutionary War as a Private in the 3rd Class, 4th Battallion, Lancaster Co., Militia on July 6, 1781. In 1820, he and his son, John, were in Estill Co., Kentucky. In 1830, one of them was in Estill Co., and the other in Franklin Co., Kentucky. In 1840, one was in Franklin Co., and the other in Jefferson Co., Kentucky.

Maria Barbara$^{1.1.1.1.8.3.3.7j}$, b. Oct. 23, 1763, bapt. in Berks Co., Tulpehocken Twp., Stouchsburg, Pennsylvania on Nov. 9, 1763, and sponsored by Maria Barbara, wife of John Schaeffer.

Magdalena$^{1.1.1.1.8.3.3.8j}$, b. about 1765, and m. Jacob Tice in Baltimore, Maryland on Oct. 23, 1784.

Johann Nicolaus Schwingel

Johann Nicolaus$^{1.1.1.1.8.3.4j}$ m. Maria Barbara, dau. of Michael and Maria Barbara (Feg) Reidt, in Berks Co., Tulpehocken Twp., Stouchsburg, Pennsylvania on May 26, 1752, and d. in Washington Co., Maryland before April 9, 1785, when his will was proved. Maria Barbara was b. in Tulpehocken on March 13, 1732, bapt. at Reed's Church, and sponsored by Johan Georg Reidt and her mother. She was confirmed at Tulpehocken on June 3, 1750, and d. in Washington Co., Maryland before Sept. 15, 1805, when her will was proven. On Dec. 23, 1752, Nicholas purchased 81 acres in Plumton Manor in Tulpehocken (now Marion) Twp. In 1759, he was taxed in Berks Co., Tulpehocken Twp. On May 29, 1777, he purchased 138 acres on the Conococheague Creek in Washington Co., Maryland, known as *Dutch Folly*, where he operated a mill. In 1778, he took the Oath of Fidelity. They had the following children in Tulpehocken Twp. (bapt. at Stouchsburg):

Margaretha Elisabeth$^{1.1.1.1.8.3.4.1j}$, b. March 5, 1753, bapt. on March 11, 1753, and sponsored by Michael and Margaretha Elisabeth Theiss. She m. Jacob, son of Abraham, Weitmann in Stouchsburg on Dec. 28, 1775, and d. in Washington Co., Williamsport, Maryland between 1800 and 1805.

Johan Georg$^{1.1.1.1.8.3.4.2j}$, b. April 9, 1754, bapt. on April 28, 1754, and sponsored by Johan Georg Schwengel and wife. On July 18, 1799, he bought 200 acres on the south side of the Cumberland River in Wilson Co., Tennessee. He bought 640 acres on Barton's Creek in Wilson Co. on Dec. 28, 1807, where he d. in 1842. He m. Catharine, dau. of Jacob Albert in Stouchsburg on June 9, 1778.

Maria Barbara$^{1.1.1.1.8.3.4.3j}$, b. March 15, 1756, bapt. on April 4, 1756, and sponsored by Johann Nicholas and Maria Barbara Reidt. She m. John, son of Johann Frederick and Anna Dorothea (Mueller) Roemer, Michael Weir before 1789 (he left her), and Henry Kindle before 1805. John was b. in York Co., Pennsylvania on March 1, 1753, and bapt. by Reverend Meuer on March 5, 1753. He served in the Revolutionary War from York Co. in 1778, and d. in Washington Co., Conococheague, Maryland between Sept. 20, 1784, and Oct. 3, 1784. Barbara and Henry were alive and residing in Washington Co., Maryland on Sept. 2, 1806.

Anna Maria$^{1.1.1.1.8.3.4.4j}$, b. Jan. 11, 1761, bapt. on Jan. 18, 1761, and sponsored by Frederick Weiser and wife. She m. George, son of Martin and Margaretha Kershner, in Washington Co., Maryland about 1782. George d. in Washington Co., Maryland before April 11, 1801, when letters of administration were grated to Anna Maria.

Catharina$^{1.1.1.1.8.3.4.5j}$, b. in March, 1763, bapt. on April 26, 1763, and sponsored by Michael and Anna Catharina Reidt. She m. Henry Seister, and d. in Washington Co., Williamsport, Maryland before July 25, 1805. He served in the Revolutionary War.

Benjamin$^{1.1.1.1.8.3.4.6j}$, b. about Nov. 1, 1764, bapt. at 3 years of age on Nov. 16, 1767, and sponsored by Benjamin and Margaret Barbara Spyker. He d. in Berkley Co., Gerrardstown, Virginia on Dec. 10, 1848. He m. Anna Eva, dau. of Nicholas and Barbara Smith in Hagerstown Lutheran Church, Washington Co., Maryland on Oct. 6, 1794. She was b. in 1769, and d. on May 22, 1856. Benjamin lead a group of German families from the Conococheague Settlement in Maryland to Berkley Co., Virginia.

Johannes$^{1.1.1.1.8.3.4.7j}$, b. Aug. 24, 1765, bapt. on Sept. 5, 1765, and sponsored by Johan Ramler and wife. He was not mentioned in his parents will.

Elizabeth$^{1.1.1.1.8.3.4.8j}$, b. about 1769, and m. George Gittinger/Kissinger. He was b. May 6, 1764, and d. in Washington Co., Hagerstown, Maryland on Nov. 9, 1844.

Christina$^{1.1.1.1.8.3.4.9j}$, b. Jan. 1, 1773, bapt. on Jan. 6, 1773, and sponsored by Henrich and Christina Koppenhefer. She was living with her mother in 1800, and was unm. in 1805.

Johann Phillip$^{1.1.1.1.8.3.4.10j}$, b. Nov. 24, 1774, bapt. on Dec. 12, 1774, and sponsored by Peter and Etel DeHaas. He m. Sarah, dau. of Jacob and Eleanor Friend, and d. in Washington Co., Maryland between Nov. 25 and Dec. 11, 1802.

Johann Michael Schwingel

Johann Michael$^{1.1.1.1.8.3.5j}$ m. Elizabeth, dau. of Johann Henrich, and Maria Margaretha (Reidt) Zeller, and d. in Northumberland (now Snyder) Co., Pennsylvania in 1794. An inventory of his estate was taken on Dec. 26, 1794. He was a blacksmith. Elizabeth was b. Nov. 28, 1744, and d. in Northumberland Co., Pennsylvania on Oct. 26, 1823. On April 24, 1769, Michael was a blacksmith in Lancaster Co., Heidelberg Twp., when he purchased 200 acres on Middle Creek in Northumberland Co., Penn Twp. It is believed that Michael may have worked on his land in Northumberland Co. during the summer months, and returned to his family in the Tulpehocken settlement in the winter months like other settlers during that time. He was taxed in Penn Twp. in 1771, and on Nov. 11, 1772, purchased 50 more acres in the twp. On April 23, 1773, he purchased an additional 50 acres, and sold the first two purchases on May 12, 1778. Michael may have returned to the Tulpehocken region during the Revolution to aid his family in the manufacture of arms (he appeared on the effective supply tax list of Lancaster Co., Newman's Town in 1779. On Sept. 12, 1792, he purchased 60 acres in the area that became Union Co., and finally Snyder Co. They had the following children (the first two and the sixth bapt. in Berks Co., Tulpehocken Twp., Stouchsburg, Pennsylvania):

Johannes$^{1.1.1.1.8.3.5.1j}$, b. Sept. 5, 1766, bapt. on Oct. 9, 1766, and sponsored by Henrich Zeller and wife.

Barbara$^{1.1.1.1.8.3.5.2j}$, b. April 12, 1768, bapt. on April 17, 1768, and sponsored by Peter Schutz and wife. She m. Mathias Spotz of Selinsgrove, Pennsylvania.

Eva Margaret$^{1.1.1.1.8.3.5.3j}$, b. Jan. 15, 1770, bapt. at Millbach Reformed Church, Lebanon Co. on June 4, 1770, and sponsored by Margaret Elizabeth Haas. She m. Anthony Gift.

Michael$^{1.1.1.1.8.3.5.4j}$, b. Jan. 13, 1773, m. Esther, dau. of George and Elizabeth (Dreiner/Breimer) Hassinger, and d. in Union Co., Penn Twp. on April 6, 1851. She was b. May 28, 1777, and d. on March 3, 1858.

Benjamin$^{1.1.1.1.8.3.5.5j}$, b. in Union Co., Harleton, Pennsylvania on Aug. 9, 1774, bapt. at Rau (Ray) Evangelical Church, and sponsored by Melcher and Orphla Stock.

Johann Peter$^{1.1.1.1.8.3.5.6j}$, b. May 18, 1779, bapt. on May 23, 1779, and sponsored by Johannes and Catharine Salzgeber.

Kate$^{1.1.1.1.8.3.5.7j}$.

Charles Phillip$^{1.1.1.1.8.3.5.8j}$, m. Regina, dau. of William and Anna Maria Gentzel/Gentzler, and moved to Pickaway Co., Washington Twp., Ohio about 1831. She was b. July 12, 1786, and d. in Jackson Co., Indiana on Jan. 10, 1875. Charles served as a Drum Major in the War of 1812.

Johann Peter Schwingel

Johann Peter$^{1.1.1.1.8.3.6j}$ d. intestate in Berkley Co. Virginia in 1796. An inventory of his estate was made on Jan. 22, 1798. He was a blacksmith, and served as a Captain in the Maryland Militia during the Revolutionary War. He was residing in Berkley Co., Virginia as early as Oct. 9, 1780. He m. Catherine, dau. of Barnett Bashore. On Aug. 24, 1799, Catherine m. John Kindar. Peter and Catherine had the following son:

Michael$^{1.1.1.1.8.3.6.1j}$, b. in Berkley Co., Virginia on April 26, 1785, m. Nancy, dau. of Henry Riner in Berkley Co. on Dec. 16, 1809, and d. in Clinton Co., Green Twp., New Antioch, Ohio on Oct. 16, 1850. She d. in Berkley Co., Virginia in 1822. Michael moved to Ohio about 1826.

****

Johann Nicholas Shultz

Johann Nicholas^{1k} m. Catharina. They immigrated to America from Germany between 1774 and 1777. In 1779, he had 100 acres in Brother's Valley, and, in 1798, he had 170 acres in Brother's Valley Twp. They resided in Somerset Co., Brother's Valley Twp., Pennsylvania in 1800, and had the following children:

Jacob$^{1.1k}$, b. in Germany about 1764.

Nicholas$^{1.2k}$, b. in Germany in 1766.

Mathias$^{1.3k}$, b. about 1768.

Elizabeth$^{1.4k}$, b. in Germany about 1771, and m. George Shock$^{1.1.1h}$.

Phillip$^{1.5k}$, b. in Germany about 1774.

Johan Georg$^{1.6k}$, b. in Bedford Co., Brother's Valley Twp.,

Pennsylvania on Feb. 2, 1777, and bapt. at Berlin Lutheran Church on Oct. 17, 1779, and sponsored by Johan Nikolas and John Coleman.

Catherine Elisabeth$^{1.7k}$, b. in Brother's Valley Twp. on November 17, 1780, bapt. at Berlin Lutheran Church on November 29, 1786, and sponsored by her parents.

Anna Barbara$^{1.8k}$, b. in Brother's Valley Twp. on April 22, 1783, bapt. at Berlin Lutheran Church, and sponsored by Anna Barbara Miller.

Mary$^{1.9k}$, b. in Brother's Valley Twp. in 1784.

Jacob Shultz

Jacob$^{1.1k}$ m. Margaret about 1784. In 1790, he resided in Brother's Valley Twp., in 1800, Londonderry Twp., and in 1810, Elk Lick Twp. They had the following children:

John$^{1.2.1k}$, b. about 1784, and resided in Elk Lick Twp. in 1810.

Johan Peter$^{1.2.2k}$, b. April 30, 1786, bapt. at Berlin Lutheran Church on Sept. 17, 1786, and sponsored by Arndt and Catharina Gressinger. He resided in Elk Lick Twp. in 1810.

Susanna$^{1.2.3k}$, b. Dec. 25, 1787, bapt. at Berlin Lutheran on Aug. 10, 1788, and sponsored by Jacob and Maria Kissinger.

Hannah$^{1.2.4k}$, b. Aug. 4, 1790, bapt. at Berlin Lutheran on Oct. 3, 1790, and sponsored by Arndt and Catharina Gressinger.

daughter$^{1.2.5k}$, b. about 1792.

Margaret$^{1.2.6k}$, b. May 16, 1794, and d. in Elik Lick Twp. on Sept. 16, 1818. She is buried in Sailsbury cemetery. She has not been confirmed as a dau.

George$^{1.2.7k}$, b. about 1798, and m. Elizabeth Boyd. He has not been confirmed as a son. daughter$^{1.2.8k}$, b. about 1800.

Henry$^{1.2.9k}$, b. in 1805. He has not been confirmed as a son.

Henry Shultz

Henry$^{1.2.9k}$ m. Catherine (b. 1811), resided in Greenville Twp. in 1850, and had the following children: Benjamin$^{1.2.9.1k}$, b. in 1831; Margaret$^{1.2.9.2k}$, b. in 1832; Michael$^{1.2.9.3k}$, b. in 1834; Samuel$^{1.2.9.4k}$, b. in 1834; Jacob$^{1.2.9.5k}$, b. in 1838; Catherine$^{1.2.9.6k}$, b. in 1840; John$^{1.2.9.7k}$, b. in 1842; Peter$^{1.2.9.8k}$, b. in 1844; Ezekiel$^{1.2.9.9k}$, b. in 1847; Amanda$^{1.2.9.10k}$, b. in 1848; Zacheus$^{1.2.9.11k}$, b. in 1850.

Nicholas Shultz

Nicholas$^{1.2k}$ m. Sarah after 1789, and resided in Somerset Co., Milford Twp., Pennsylvania in 1850. He was taxed in Brother's Valley Twp. in 1796 and resided there in 1800. Sarah was b. in Pennsylvania in 1768. They had the following children: dau.$^{1.2.1k}$, b. about 1790; son$^{1.2.2k}$, b.

about 1792; dau.$^{1.2.3k}$, b. about 1794; dau.$^{1.2.4k}$, b. about 1796.

Mathias Shultz

Mathias$^{1.3k}$ m. Elizabeth, and had the following dau.:Anna Maria$^{1.3.1k}$, b. Sept. 25, 1792, bapt. at Berlin Lutheran Church on July 30, 1793, and sponsored by Arndt and Catharina Gressinger.

Phillip Shultz

Phillip$^{1.5k}$ m. Eve$^{1.1.2h}$, dau. of George Shock, in Bedford Co., Pennsylvania on June 9, 1795, and d. in Stark Co., Ohio on Oct. 2, 1829. He was taxed in Brother's Valley Twp. in 1796, resided in Londonderry Twp. in 1800, and Elk Lick Twp. in 1810. After Phillip's death, Eve may have m. David Baker in Stark Co., Ohio on Feb. 24, 1831. Phillip and Eve had the following children: Anna Marie$^{1.5.1k}$, b. in 1795; Johan Henry$^{1.5.2k}$, b. in 1797; Catherine$^{1.5.3k}$, b. in 1798; Maria Eva$^{1.5.4k}$, b. in 1800; Julie$^{1.5.5k}$, b. in 1806; Elizabeth$^{1.5.6k}$, b. about 1809; Phillip$^{1.5.7k}$, b. about 1812.

Johan Georg Shultz

Johan Georg$^{1.6k}$ m. Elizabeth Mastholder, and had the following children in Brother's Valley Twp.: son$^{1.6.1k}$, b. about 1797; son$^{1.6.2k}$, b. about 1800; Sally$^{1.6.3k}$, b. Dec. 31, 1804, and m. Daniel Miller in Somerset Co., Berlin, Pennsylvania on April 7, 1829; Hanna$^{1.6.4k}$, b. April 6, 1806; Elizabeth$^{1.6.5k}$, b. Dec. 25, 1810.

Catherine Elisabeth Shultz

Catherine Elisabeth$^{1.7k}$ m. David Zimmerman in Somerset Co., Pennsylvania on Aug. 23, 1796, and d. in Ohio. They had the following children in Brother's Valley Twp.: Elizabeth$^{1.7.1k}$, b. April 19, 1801; Maria$^{1.7.2k}$, b. May 27, 1803.

Mary Shultz

Mary$^{1.9k}$ m. Jacob Hochstetler in Somerset Co., Pennsylvania on Oct. 16, 1798, and d. in 1855. He was b. in 1778. They had the following children in Somerset Co., Summit Twp., Myersdale, Pennsylvania: John$^{1.9.1k}$, b. in 1800; Samuel$^{1.9.2k}$, b. November 21, 1802; Adam$^{1.9.3k}$, b. Sept. 8, 1804, and m. Eve Blubaugh about 1825; Catherine$^{1.9.4k}$, b. Sept. 8, 1806; Susanna$^{1.9.5k}$, b. April 23, 1808; Elizabeth$^{1.9.6k}$, b. in April, 1812; Barbara$^{1.9.7k}$, b. in 1815; Jacob$^{1.9.8k}$, b. Feb. 28, 1817.

****

James Boyd

James^{11} and his wife d. in Bedford Co., Quemahoning Twp., Pennsylvania between 1790 and 1800 (unless he is the James Boyd listed on the 1800 census in an unidentified twp. (?Stoyestown)). He may be the James that served in Captain Paxton's Ranging Company in the Bedford Co. Militia in 1776. He was taxed in Turkeyfoot Twp. with 2 horses and 4 cattle in 1779 and 1780. In 1786, he was taxed with 150 acres in Quemahoning Twp. and 200 acres 3 horses and 3 cattle in 1788. James was believed to have had the following children, but their relationship, if any, has not been confirmed):

    Robert$^{1.11}$, b. about 1753, and d. in Turkeyfoot Twp. on Aug. 25, 1818. He was a Methodist Minister, was taxed in Turkeyfoot Twp. in 1773.

    David$^{1.21}$, b. about 1756, and served in Captain Paxton's Ranging Company in the Bedford Co. Militia in 1776.

    William$^{1.31}$, b. about 1758, and d. in Quemahoning Twp. after 1810. He received at land warrant in Quemahoning Twp. in 1786. He had 287 acres, 3 horse and 3 cattle in 1790, and had 287.5 acres 3 horses and 4 cattle in 1791. He may be the William Boyd that served in Captain Paxton's Ranging Company of the Bedford Co., Militia in 1776. In 1790, William had four females residing with him, and served in the militia on Feb. 6, 1789.

James$^{1.41}$, b. about 1760.

James Boyd

James$^{1.41}$ was b. in Scotland. He m. Anna Maria, dau. of Isaac and Anna Eva Jauler, in Bedford Co., Pennsylvania on Aug. 3, 1790 and Catherine Baer about 1815. According to family tradition, James and two brothers ran away from Scotland via Ireland to America. He may be the James that served in Captain Paxton's Ranging Company in the Bedford Co. Militia in 1776, and resided in Milford Twp. in 1783 and 1784. James was in Elk Lick Twp. in 1785. He moved to Greenville Twp. between 1810 and 1813. He had 50 acres in Elk Lick Twp. in 1798. Anna Maria d. in Somerset Co., Greenville Twp., Pennsylvania in 1814, and James d. there intestate in May, 1828. On May 24, 1828, Catherine renounced administration in favor of John Engle. James had the following children:

    Adam$^{1.4.11}$, b. in Bedford Co., Elk Lick Twp. on May 13, 1791, bapt. at Sailsbury (St. John's) Reformed Church on July 16, 1791.

    John$^{1.4.21}$, b. in Elk Lick Twp. on Aug. 10, 1794, and bapt. at Sailsbury on Oct. 18, 1794.

    Isaac$^{1.4.31}$, b. in 1795.

    Hannah$^{1.4.41}$, b. in Somerset Co., Elk Lick Twp. on April 19, 1799, and bapt. at Sailsbury on July 13, 1799.

    James$^{1.4.51}$, b. in Elk Lick Twp. on May 17, 1801.

    Douglas B.$^{1.4.61}$, b. in Elk Lick Twp. on Oct. 6, 1803, and bapt. at Sailsbury on Sept. 2, 1804.

Elizabeth[1.4.7¹], b. in Elk Lick Twp. in 1806, and m. George Shultz.
Mary Ann[1.4.8¹], b. in Elk Lick Twp. on Dec. 22, 1810, and m. Peter Shock.
Salome[1.4.9¹], b. in Somerset Co., Greenville Twp. about 1815, and m. John C. Beal.
Christina[1.4.10¹], b. in Greenville Twp. on March 28, 1816.
Edward[1.4.11¹], b. in Greenville Twp. about 1818.
Josiah W. H.[1.4.12¹], b. in Greenville Twp. in Aug., 1820.
Delila[1.4.13¹], b. in Greenville Twp. about 1822.
Franklin[1.4.14¹], b. in Greenville Twp. about 1824, and m. Sally.
Chauncey Forward[1.4.15¹], b. in Greenville Twp. on July 4, 1828.

Adam Boyd

Adam[1.4.1¹] m. Eve Catherine, dau. of Clement and Margaretta (Weimer) Engle, in Somerset Co., Pennsylvania on May 18, 1818, and d. in Clay Co., Missouri about 1839. She was b. in Somerset Co., Pennsylvania on Sept. 22, 1800, and resided in Bates Co., Missouri in 1850. They had the following children in Somerset Co., Greenville Twp.:

Eliza Sarah[1.4.1.1¹], b. in 1820, m. John Martin Lindeman in Somerset Co., Pennsylvania on Feb. 19, 1838, and d. on Oct. 6, 1895.
Michael[1.4.1.2¹], b. Dec. 9, 1822, m. Nancy Ann Gibson on Oct. 11, 1846, and d. in Oregon on Nov. 3, 1907.
Catherine[1.4.1.3¹], b. in 1826, and m. John Barns.
Adam[1.4.1.4¹], b. May 15, 1830, and m. Mary Crowthers.
Reuben[1.4.1.5¹], b. Feb. 26, 1832.
Levi[1.4.1.6¹], b. Feb. 17, 1834.
Solomon[1.4.1.7¹], b. Aug. 21, 1836, m. Nanie, and d. on May 8, 1908.
Sarah[1.4.1.8¹], b. in 1837.
Henry[1.4.1.9¹], b. Sept. 15, 1838.

Isaac Boyd

Isaac[1.4.3¹] m. Magdalena (b. 1792). They resided in Greenville Twp. in 1830, and Addison Twp. in 1850. They had the following children:
Mary[1.4.3.1¹], b. in 1827; Solomon[1.4.3.2¹], b. in 1829; Adam[1.4.3.3¹], b. in 1834.

Hannah Boyd

Hannah[1.4.4¹] m. Solomon Hutzell, and d. in Somerset Co., Greenville Twp., Pennsylvania on April 15, 1886. He was b. in Frederick Co., Maryland on April 10, 1800, and d. in Greenville Twp. on July 10, 1863. They had the following children in Greenville Twp.:

Margaret[1.4.4.1¹], b. in 1827, m. Daniel Garletz (1820-1858), and d. in July, 1888.

LaFayette[1.4.4.21], b. in 1829, and d. on May 2, 1887.
Susannah[1.4.4.31], b. in 1831, m. Daniel Swarner/Suarner, and resided in Elmhurst, Illinois.
Mary[1.4.4.41], b. in 1834, and m. Solomon Weimer on June 4, 1854.
Matilda[1.4.4.51], b. in 1837, m. Adam Caton and William Patton, and resided in Illinois in 1876.
Catherine[1.4.4.61], b. in 1840, m. Christian Steinley, and d. in La Grange Co., Indiana.
Dinah[1.4.4.71], b. in 1843, and d. in Greenville Twp. in 1864.
Harriet[1.4.4.81], b. about 1845, and m. George Weaver.

James Boyd

James[1.4.51] m. Catherine, dau. of Peter and Barbara (Garletts) Engle, in Somerset Co., Pennsylvania on March 20, 1831, and d. in Noble Co., Cosperville, Indiana on Sept. 1, 1889. She was b. in Somerset Co. on Feb. 22, 1815, and d. in LaGrange Co., Clay Twp., Indiana on Feb. 6, 1881. They had the following children:

Delilah[1.4.5.11], b. in Somerset Co., Greenville Twp. on Dec. 2, 1831, m. John Frick in 1852, and d. on March 18, 1913. He was b. in 1819, and d. on Feb. 21, 1872.

Eston[1.4.5.21], b. in Greenville Twp. on Dec. 9, 1832, m. Sarah E. Frisbey on Feb. 10, 1855, Ann Guann Gindlesparger on Aug. 19, 1866, and Magdalene Gindlesparger on Sept. 25, 1879. Eston d. in LaGrange Co., Indiana on Nov. 2, 1899. Sarah was b. March 2, 1837, and d. in LaGrange Co., Clay Twp., Indiana on Dec. 30, 1865.

Arion[1.4.5.31], b. in Greenville Twp. on Feb. 7, 1834, m. Nancy Carnaham in 1855, and d. on March 26, 1873. She was b. June 8, 1836, and d. on March 11, 1897.

Harrison H.[1.4.5.41], b. in Greenville Twp. on Aug. 14, 1835, m. Emily Landis, and d. in Noble Co., Elkhart/Albion Twp., Indiana on March 8, 1914. She was b. in July, 1838, and d. on June 24, 1907.

Edward[1.4.5.51], b. in Tuscarwas Co., Ohio on Dec. 23, 1836, and m. Lucinda A. Sayler in 1858, Eva Baumgarten on July 27, 1865, Mary Jane McBeth on Nov. 1, 1874, and Ellen Schoyer after 1891. Lucinda was b. Jan. 18, 1840, and d. on June 19, 1863. Eva was b. Aug. 20, 1846, and d. on April 9, 1872. Mary was b. in 1842, and d. on Nov. 27, 1891. Ellen was b. Nov. 18, 1854, and d. on Aug. 16, 1918.

John[1.4.5.61], b. in Tuscarwas Co. on June 24, 1838, m. Amanda Landis in Noble Co., Albion, Indiana on March 2, 1865, and d. in LaGrange Co., Indiana in 1909. She was b. in Noble Co., Eden Twp., Indiana on Sept. 15, 1846, and d. in LaGrange Co. on Dec. 20, 1931.

Charles[1.4.5.71], b. in Tuscarwas Co. in 1840, and d. in Noble Co., Indiana in 1851.

Elizabeth[1.4.5.81], b. in Noble Co., Indiana on Nov. 21, 1841, m. Cory Roger Frisbey on Oct. 27, 1867, and d. on Aug. 9, 1933. He was b. Feb. 21, 1836, and d. on May 13, 1925.

James V.[1.4.5.91], b. in Noble Co. in 1843, m. Sarah Cherry and Ruth, and d. on March 21, 1891.

Mary[1.4.5.101], b. in Noble Co. on Sept. 5, 1845, m. Andrew McBeth on April 7, 1868, and d. on Oct. 3, 1926. He was b. Dec. 10, 1845, and d. on Sept. 10, 1924.

Peter[1.4.5.111], b. in Noble Co. on June 14, 1848, m. Adelaide Fish in Tama Co., Iowa on Dec. 5, 1871, and d. in Clay Co., Clay Center, Nebraska on Dec. 28, 1928. She was b. Jan. 26, 1854, and d. on May 11, 1924.

Jacob[1.4.5.121], b. in Noble Co. on June 22, 1850, m. Julia Bell Saum, and d. on Oct. 9, 1926. She was b. April 4, 1865, and d. on May 6, 1923.

Douglas[1.4.5.131], b. in Noble Co. on April 11, 1852, and m. Susan Ann Korn in June, 1873 and Molly Moose. Susan was b. June 7, 1852, and d. on March 14, 1876.

Urias[1.4.5.141], b. in LaGrange Co., Indiana on Aug. 5, 1853, m. Ida May Clark on Oct. 30, 1880, and d. on April 18, 1941. She was b. Aug. 22, 1862, and d. on Oct. 8, 1951.

Phillip[1.4.5.161], b. in LaGrange Co. on July 14, 1856, and m. Henrietta Fleck on June 11, 1878, Elizabeth Malone on July 28, 1886, and Christine Sodquest in April, 1925. Phillip d. on March 6, 1932. Henrietta was b. April 5, 1858, and d. on March 18, 1880. Elizabeth was b. in 1860, and d. on October 29, 1922. Christine d. in 1931.

Samuel[1.4.5.171], b. in LaGrange Co. in Jan., 1860, and d. in June, 1860.

Daniel[1.4.5.181], b. in Jan., 1860, and d. in November, 1860.

Corinda[1.4.5.191], b. in LaGrange Co. on March 10, 1862, m. George Albert Coger on Aug. 14, 1879, and d. on May 7, 1950. He was b. November 11, 1856, and d. on June 27, 1938.

Douglas B. Boyd

Douglas B.[1.4.61] m. Susanna, dau. of John and Elizabeth (Miller) Lichty, in Somerset Co., Pennsylvania in Sept., 1830, and d. in Marshall Co., Iowa on July 26, 1878. She was b. in Somerset Co., Pennsylvania on May 26, 1813, and d. in Marshall Co., Iowa on Sept. 3, 1896. They had the following children in Somerset Co., Greenville Twp., Pennsylvania:

Samuel Douglas[1.4.6.11], b. Sept. 11, 1832, m. Catherine Bueghley, and d. in Glaen Rock, Nebraska in 1917. She was b. in

Somerset Co., Summit Mills, Pennsylvania on June 26, 1835, and d. in Rock Co., Nebraska on April 19, 1892.

Manasses[1.4.6.21], b. April 13, 1834, and d. in 1840.

John D.[1.4.6.31], b. May 7, 1836, m. Sarah Jane Wright on Dec. 1, 1861, and d. in Liscomb, Iowa on Feb. 17, 1918. She was b. in Pennsylvania on May 20, 1838, and d. in Liscomb on Feb. 25, 1913.

William Douglas[1.4.6.41], b. May 23, 1839, m. Barbara, dau. of Solomon and Christina (Keim) Engle, in Somerset Co., Elk Lick Twp. on Dec. 25, 1860, and d. in Liscomb, Iowa on Dec. 2, 1922. She was b. in Somerset Co. on Oct. 26, 1840 (?differs from other sources), and d. in Liscomb on May 28, 1926.

Matilda[1.4.6.51], b. Oct. 3, 1841, m. Jacob R. Johnson in Marshalltown, Iowa on Feb. 20, 1869, and d. in Liscomb, Iowa on Dec. 20, 1928. He was b. in Berks Co., Reading, Pennsylvania, and d. in Liscomb, Iowa on Dec. 22, 1924.

Francis[1.4.6.61], b. Jan. 8, 1844, and d. on Nov. 28, 1851.

James D.[1.4.6.71], b. Feb. 20, 1847, m. Elizabeth Bueghley in Liscomb, Iowa on March 10, 1870, and d. in Liscomb on July 26, 1938. She was b. in Somerset Co., Pennsylvania on May 10, 1841, and d. on July 23, 1916.

Christina Boyd

Christina[1.4.101] m. Jeremiah, son of Martin and Lovis Engle, in Somerset Co., Pennsylvania in 1838, and d. in 1893. He was b. June 26, 1816, and d. on December 9, 1871. They had the following children:

John Boyd[1.4.10.11], b. April 16, 1839, and m. Elizabeth Tressler on Oct. 27, 1860, and d. in 1912.

Josiah J.[1.4.10.21], b. May 1, 1841, m. Barbara Sarah Loury on Oct. 3, 1865, and Malinda Folk on May 14, 1871. He d. in 1906.

Catherine[1.4.10.31], b. August 23, 1843, bapt. on Oct. 22, 1843, and m. Levi Caton.

Douglas J.[1.4.10.41], b. Aug. 31, 1846, m. Sarah Anna Folk on Oct. 30, 1870, and d. on Sept. 4, 1917. She was b. in 1846.

Theodore[1.4.10.51], b. in 1850, m. Dianna Keefer, and d. in 1920.

Nancy[1.4.10.61], b. Oct. 17, 1852, and m. Washington Warner.

Jonas[1.4.10.71], b. about 1854.

Chauncey J.[1.4.10.81], b. Feb. 4, 1857, m. Julia Nedrow on Sept. 28, 1879, and d. in 1915.

Harvey[1.4.10.91], b. November 30, 1860.

Ellen[1.4.10.101], b. in 1866.

Mary J.[1.4.10.111], b. in 1867.

Josiah W. H. Boyd

Josiah W. H.[1.4.121] m. Sarah (b. 1821) about 1841, Mary Elizabeth (b.

1839) in 1859, and Catherine Bitner (b. 1842) on June 14, 1890. He d. in Somerset Co., Ursina, Pennsylvania on Jan. 18, 1901. They had the following children in Somerset Co., Southampton Twp. (unless otherwise noted): Benjamin Franklin$^{1.4.12.11}$, b. in 1842, m. Marion, Sarah, and Minerva, and d. on Dec. 22, 1894; Louisa$^{1.4.12.21}$, b. in 1844; James$^{1.4.12.31}$, b. in 1846; Lydia$^{1.4.12.41}$, b. in 1849; Jonas$^{1.4.12.51}$, b. in Somerset Co., Milford Towship in 1862, and m. Eliza Jane Holliday on Dec. 25, 1889; Franklin$^{1.4.12.61}$, b. in Milford Twp. in 1865.

Delila Boyd

Delila$^{1.4.131}$ m. Josiah Joseph Smith, and had the following children: Susanna$^{1.4.13.11}$; Sabina$^{1.4.13.21}$; Mary Elizabeth$^{1.4.13.31}$, b. in Centerville on Feb. 27, 1853.

Chauncey Forward Boyd

Chauncey Forward$^{1.4.151}$ m. Sarah "Sally" Fike in Somerset Co., Summit Twp., Pennsylvania on Nov. 6, 1853, and d. in Somerset Co. on Sept. 19, 1906. She was b. in Somerset Co., Myersdale on March 13, 1837, and d. in Somerset Co. on May 23, 1919. They had the following children in Somerset Co., Lavansville (unless otherwise noted):

John$^{1.4.15.11}$, b. Jan. 27, 1856, and d. on Feb. 23, 1871.

Savilla$^{1.4.15.21}$, b. Nov. 18, 1857, m. W. N. Barnett (b. 1855) on Sept. 11, 1881, and d. on Oct. 20, 1907.

Catherine$^{1.4.15.31}$, b. Sept. 23, 1859, m. H. A. Stahl (1859-1914) in New Centerville on Oct. 16, 1881, and d. on Sept. 8, 1933.

Mary F.$^{1.4.15.41}$, b. July 27, 1861, and m. W. W. Brown (b. 1858) in Carroll Co., Milledgeville, Illinois on July 26, 1891.

Anna G.$^{1.4.15.51}$, b. Sept. 24, 1863, and d. in Somerset Co. on Aug. 13, 1910.

Samuel H.$^{1.4.15.61}$, b. in Glade (Stoney Creek Twp.)on Jan. 9, 1866, and m. Edith Dull on May 26, 1889.

Amanda$^{1.4.15.71}$, b. Feb. 16, 1868, and d. on May 20, 1868.

Franklin William$^{1.4.15.81}$, b. in Ursina on April 5, 1870, and m. Zura E. Fike (b. 1871) on July 19, 1891.

Elmer J.$^{1.4.15.91}$, b. in Ursina on Aug. 11, 1872, and m. Ida Gnagey on Dec. 18, 1894.

Charles B.$^{1.4.15.101}$, b. in Ursina on March 16, 1875, m. Emma Groton (b. 1876) on June 17, 1903.

Emma S.$^{1.4.15.111}$, b. in Rockwood on Dec. 2, 1878, and m. Bruce B. Dickey on March 3, 1901. He was b. March 21, 1878.

****

Jacob Jauler

Jacob^{1m} m. Maria C., and had the following children: Jacob$^{1.1m}$, b.

about 1740; Isaac$^{1.2m}$, b. about 1743; Anna Dorothea$^{1.3m}$, bapt. by Reverend Jacob Lischy in York Co., West Manchester/Dover Twp., Pennsylvania on May 16, 1756, and sponsored by Adam and Anna Dorothea Bartmesser.

Jacob Jauler

Jacob$^{1.1m}$ m. Barbara, and had the following children (all bapt. at Frederick Co., Middletown Lutheran Church except the first):

    Anna Maria$^{1.1.1m}$, bapt. by Reverend Jacob Lischy in York Co., Pennsylvania on Aug. 28, 1765, and sponsored by Jacob Bohrech and Appolonica Pfeifferin. She m. Nicholas Schaeffer in Frederick Co., Maryland on May 9, 1786.

    Catharina$^{1.1.2m}$, b. in Frederick Co., Middletown, Maryland on Oct. 29, 1771.

    Eve$^{1.1.3m}$, b. in Middletown about 1772, and m. Nicholas Neihoff in Frederick Co., Maryland on Jan. 8, 1793.

    Jacob$^{1.1.4m}$, b. in Middletown on Feb. 27, 1774, and sponsored by Conrad and Margaret Gedultig.

    Magdalena$^{1.1.5m}$, b. in Middletown on Sept. 29, 1776, and sponsored by Johannes and Magdalena Link.

    Elisabetha Margaretha$^{1.1.6m}$, b. in Middletown in March, 1779, bapt. on April 11, 1779, and sponsored by Frederick and Margaret Schonholtz.

    Eleonora$^{1.1.7m}$, b. in Middletown on April 20, 1780, bapt. on July 11, 1780, sponsored by Leonora Bucher, and m. Daniel Staufer in Frederick Co., Maryland on April 11, 1803.

    Michael$^{1.1.8m}$, b. in Middletown on Oct. 9, 1781, and sponsored by Michael and Magdalena Storm.

    Johan Georg$^{1.1.9m}$, b. in Middletown on July 14, 1785, and sponsored by Nicholas Shafer.

Michael Jauler

Michael$^{1.1.8m}$ m. Catharine Shafer in Frederick Co., Maryland on Sept. 17, 1809, and had the following son in Middletown: Johannes$^{1.1.8.1m}$, b. in 1809, and bapt. at Middletown on March 6, 1810.

Johan Georg Jauler

Johan Georg$^{1.1.9m}$ m. Maria Lambrecht in Frederick Co., Maryland on Aug. 30, 1809, and had the following children in Middletown: Elenora$^{1.1.9.1m}$, bapt. on Oct. 1, 1809; Marianne$^{1.1.9.2m}$, bapt. on Jan. 12, 1812.

Isaac Jauler

Isaac$^{1.2m}$ m. Anna Eva. They moved from York Co. West Manchester Twp., Pennsylvania to Frederick Co., Middletown, Maryland between

1767 and 1771, and from Maryland to Bedford (now Somerset) Co., Elk
Lick Twp., Pennsylvania between 1775 and 1778. The name Jauler
evolved to Youler and finally Yowler. In 1787, Isaac was taxed with 100
acres, 2 horses and 3 cattle in Elk Lick Twp., and served in the Twp.
Militia on Feb. 7, 1789. He d. in Aug., 1798, and his wife survived him.
Isaac and Anna Eva had the following children:
- Anna Maria$^{1.2.1m}$, bapt. in York Co., West Manchester Twp., Wolf's (St. Paul's) Reformed Church on July 26, 1767, and sponsored by Michael and Anna Eva Lau.
- Maria Eve$^{1.2.2m}$, b. about 1770.
- Adam$^{1.2.3m}$, b. in Middletown, Maryland on April 20, 1772, and bapt. at Middletown Lutheran Church.
- Peter$^{1.2.4m}$, b. April 20, 1772, and bapt. at Middletown Lutheran Church.
- Johan Jacob$^{1.2.5m}$, b. March 10, 1775, and bapt. at Middletown Lutheran Church on March 28, 1775.
- Isaac$^{1.2.6m}$, b. in Bedford Co., Elk Lick Twp., Pennsylvania on March 1, 1778, bapt. in Berlin Lutheran Church in Brother's Valley Twp. in 1779, and sponsored by Clement Engle.
- Margaretha$^{1.2.7m}$, b. May 5, 1781, and bapt. at Berlin Lutheran Church, and m. George Newman.
- Elisabetha$^{1.2.8m}$, b. March 3, 1785, bapt. at Berlin Lutheran Church, and d. before 1798.

Maria Eve Jauler

Maria Eve$^{1.2.2m}$ m. Johan Adam Fadley in Bedford Co., Elk Lick Twp. in 1787, and d. in Somerset Co., Elk Lick Twp., Salisbury, Pennsylvania about 1792. Johan Adam was b. in Montgomery Co., New Hanover Twp., Pennsylvania on June 15, 1765. After Maria Eve's death, he m. Anna Maria$^{1.4n}$, dau. of Solomon and Maria Eva (Frensch) Glatfelter. Adam and Maria Eve had the following children:
- John William$^{1.2.2.1m}$, b. December 20, 1788, and bapt. on May 13, 1789.
- Susanna$^{1.2.2.2m}$, b. in 1790.

Johan Adam and Anna Maria had the following children:
- Adam$^{1.4.1n}$, b. in 1794; Jacob$^{1.4.2n}$, b. in 1796; Eve$^{1.4.3n}$, b. in 1798; Polly$^{1.4.4n}$, b. in 1800; Peter$^{1.4.5n}$, b. in 1802; Sally/Sarah$^{1.4.6n}$, b. in 1804/1808, and m. Samuel George Washington Shock; Adeline$^{1.4.7n}$, b. July 19, 1811.

John William Fadley

John William$^{1.2.2.1m}$ m. Barbara Krieder in 1811, and had the following children in Somerset Co.: Peter$^{1.2.2.1.1m}$, b. Jan. 2, 1812; Mary$^{1.2.2.1.2m}$, b. April 14, 1813; Elizabeth$^{1.2.2.1.3m}$, b. Nov. 17, 1814; Sara$^{1.2.2.1.4m}$, b. Sept. 28, 1816; Elijah$^{1.2.2.1.5m}$, b. April 14, 1818; Daniel$^{1.2.2.1.6m}$, b. Nov. 6, 1820; Margaret$^{1.2.2.1.7m}$, b. Oct. 13, 1822;

Alexander$^{1.2.2.1.8m}$, b. Nov. 29, 1825. Susanna$^{1.2.2.1.9m}$, b. Nov. 26, 1827; Delilah$^{1.2.2.1.10m}$, b. April 5, 1829; John$^{1.2.2.1.11m}$, b. March 3, 1832.

Peter Fadley

Peter$^{1.2.2.1.1m}$ m. Elizabeth Meyers on April 26, 1831, and had the following children: Catherine$^{1.2.2.1.1.1m}$, b. Sept. 5, 1833; Barbara$^{1.2.2.1.1.2m}$, b. Feb. 6, 1837; Henry$^{1.2.2.1.1.3m}$, b. Nov. 20, 1838; Elijah Penelton$^{1.2.2.1.1.4m}$, b. Aug. 1, 1841; Elizabeth$^{1.2.2.1.1.5m}$, b. Oct. 21, 1842; Magdalena$^{1.2.2.1.1.6m}$, b. Oct. 21 (25), 1842; Peter W.$^{1.2.2.1.1.7m}$, b. Aug. 26, 1844.

Adam Jauler

Adam$^{1.2.3m}$ had 137 acres in Elk Lick Twp. in 1798, and was on the 1830 census on Somerset Co., Milford Twp., Pennsylvania. In 1850, he resided in Somerset Co., Henry Twp. He m. Salla, and had the following children: Israel$^{1.2.3.1m}$, b. in 1813; Hannah$^{1.2.3.2m}$, b. April 20, 1817, and bapt. at Berlin Lutheran Church on May 9, 1819; Josiah$^{1.2.3.3m}$, b. in 1822.

Israel Jauler

Israel$^{1.2.3.1m}$ m. Margaret (b. 1816), resided in Milford Twp. in 1860, and had the following children: John$^{1.2.3.1.1m}$, b. in 1838; Cyrus$^{1.2.3.1.2m}$, b. in 1839; Sarah$^{1.2.3.1.3m}$, b. in 1841; Lucinda$^{1.2.3.1.4m}$, b. in 1843; Adam$^{1.2.3.1.5m}$, b. in 1845, and m. Anna Catharina Denney; Peter$^{1.2.3.1.6m}$, b. in 1847; Lydia$^{1.2.3.1.7m}$, b. in 1849; Phebe$^{1.2.3.1.8m}$, b. in 1850, and m. William Mickley; Henry$^{1.2.3.1.9m}$, b. in 1852; William$^{1.2.3.1.10m}$, b. in 1852; Elizabeth$^{1.2.3.1.11m}$, b. in 1855; Susanna$^{1.2.3.1.12m}$, b. in 1857; Margaret$^{1.2.3.1.13m}$, b. in 1857.

Josiah Jauler

Josiah$^{1.2.3.3m}$ m. Elizabeth Nedrow (b. 1826) in Somerset Co. on Nov. 16, 1845, resided in Milford Twp. in 1860, and had the following children: Christina$^{1.2.3.3.1m}$, b. in 1846; Jonathan$^{1.2.3.3.2m}$, b. in 1847; Sullena$^{1.2.3.3.3m}$, b. in 1851; Susanna$^{1.2.3.3.4m}$, b. in 1854; Louisa$^{1.2.3.3.5m}$, b. in 1856.

****

Solomon Glatfelter

Solomon^{1n}, son of Casper Glatfelter, was b. in Glattfelden, Switzerland on Feb. 1, 1738, and bapt. on Feb. 23, 1738. He and his parents came to America in 1743, and settled in York Co., Pennsylvania. He was a blacksmith, and m. Maria Eva, presumed dau. of Phillip Frensch of Codorus Twp. She was b. in York Co., Shrewsbury/Codorus Towsnhip,

Pennsylvania. They moved to Frederick Co., Maryland about 1770, and Somerset Co., Pennsylvania in 1776. Solomon d. in 1818. They had the following children:

Maria Magdalena$^{1.1n}$, bapt. at Wolf's Lutheran Church in York Co., West Manchester Twp., Pennsylvania on July 26, 1767, and sponsored by Maria Magdalena Frentsch.

Eva Margaretha$^{1.2n}$, b. April 12, 1769.

Johan Adam$^{1.3n}$, b. Dec. 15, 1770, and bapt. at Middletown Lutheran Church.

Anna Maria$^{1.4n}$, b. May 16, 1773, and bapt. at Frederick Co., Middletown Evangelical Lutheran Courch on May 16, 1773. She m. Johan Adam Fadley.

Elisabeth$^{1.5n}$, b. April 16, 1775, and bapt. at Middletown.

Casper$^{1.6n}$, b. Aug. 24, 1777.

Johan Henrich$^{1.7n}$, b. Nov. 14, 1779.

Jacob$^{1.8n}$, b. in Elk Lick Twp. on Jan. 17, 1784, and bapt. at Berlin Lutheran Church on June 2, 1784.

Catharina$^{1.9n}$, b. in Bedford Co., Elk Lick Twp., Pennsylvania on Oct. 15, 1789, and m. Frederick Diehl about 1805.

Eva Margareth Glatfelter

Eva Margaretha$^{1.2n}$ m. Lightfoot John, son of Casper and Anna Elizabeth (Lightfoot) Durst, on Sept. 26, 1790. He was b. in Berks Co., Lower Heidelberg Twp., Pennsylvania on Feb. 6, 1767, and bapt. at St. John's on March 1, 1767. They had the following sons in Somerset Co.: Solomon$^{1.2.1n}$, b. April 15, 1797; Jacob Lewis$^{1.2.2n}$, b. Feb. 7, 1806.

Johan Adam Glatfelter

Johan Adam$^{1.3n}$ m. Elizabeth Newman and Maria Diel on Feb. 9, 1797, and had the following children: Mary Ann$^{1.3.1n}$; John$^{1.3.2n}$; Elizabeth$^{1.3.3n}$; Anna$^{1.3.4n}$; Solomon$^{1.3.5n}$; Susannah$^{1.3.6n}$; George$^{1.3.7n}$; Benjamin$^{1.3.8n}$.

Casper Glatfelter

Casper$^{1.6n}$ m. Julia A. Easter, and had the following children: Jacob$^{1.6.1n}$, m. Eliza Green; Eva$^{1.6.2n}$; Henry$^{1.6.3n}$; Samuel$^{1.6.4n}$; John$^{1.6.5n}$; Catherine$^{1.6.6n}$; Jonas$^{1.6.7n}$.

Johan Henrich Glatfelter

Johan Henrich$^{1.7n}$ m. Anna Maria Heer on March 4, 1798, and had the following children: Joseph$^{1.7.1n}$, m. Barbara Magdalena$^{1.12o}$, dau. of Clement and Margaretta (Weimer) Engle; Phillip$^{1.7.2n}$; William$^{1.7.3n}$, may have m. Esther Livengood in 1832; Henry$^{1.7.4n}$; Peter$^{1.7.5n}$, may have m. Julian Peck in 1842; Daniel$^{1.7.6n}$, and m. Catherine Shirer in 1836; Elijah$^{1.7.7n}$; Eva$^{1.7.8n}$; Sally$^{1.7.9n}$;

Rebecca[1.7.10n].

Jacob Glatfelter

Jacob[1.8n] m. Mary Shawman/Showman, and had the following children: Samuel D.[1.8.1n], b. May 14, 1808. He may be the Samuel that m. Charlotte Wagner on March 7, 1830; Harriet[1.8.2n], b. June 18, 1809; Adaline[1.8.3n], b. June 7, 1811; Jeremiah[1.8.4n], b. July 2, 1812, and m. Catherine Welfley; David[1.8.5n], b. Feb. 22, 1814, and m. Harriet Schrock; Michael[1.8.6n], b. April 20, 1816, and m. Anna Maust; Elizabeth[1.8.7n], b. Jan. 1, 1818; John C.[1.8.8n], b. Sept. 4, 1819, and m. Anna Dively.

****

Clement Engle

Clement[1o] was b. in Germania, Prussia in 1747, and m. Anna Elizabeth, dau. of Peter and Anna Maria (Yost) Graeff, in 1778, and Margaretta, dau. of Martin and Catharina Barbara (Troutman) Weimer, in 1790. He d. in Somerset Co., Elk Lick Township, Salisbury, Pennsylvania on May 28, 1812. Elizabeth was b. in Germany on Jan. 21, 1757, and d. in Salisbury in 1789. Margaretta was b. in 1770, and d. in 1848. Clement came to America about 1752, and served in the Revolutionary War. He had the following children in Somerset Co.:

Anna Maria[1.1o], b. Feb. 8, 1779, bapt. at Berlin Lutheran Church, and sponsored by Gertrude (Graeff) Hay.

Peter[1.2o], b. Oct. 17, 1780, bapt. at Berlin on November 17, 1780, and sponsored by Peter Graeff.

Johan Jacob[1.3o], b. Feb. 28, 1782, bapt. at Berlin on Sept. 22, 1782.

Anna Barbara[1.4o], b. November 20, 1783, bapt. at Berlin on June 2, 1784, and sponsored by Anna Barbara Graeff.

Michael[1.5o], b. July 21, 1785, bapt. at Berlin on Sept. 7, 1785, and sponsored by Michael Engle.

John[1.6o], b. Oct. 1, 1787, bapt. at Berlin on may 18, 1788, and sponsored by Solomon and Maria Eva Gladfelter.

Adam[1.7o], b. November 18, 1791, m. Elizabeth Mellinger, and d. in 1830.

Martin[1.8o], b. Jan. 21, 1792.

Susanna[1.9o], b. Aug. 18, 1794 (93), m. Jacob Deal on April 17, 1813, and d. on April 30, 1860.

Clement[1.10o], b. Feb. 22, 1796, and d. young.

Michael[1.11o], b. Feb. 5, 1797, and d. young.

Barbara Magdalena[1.12o], b. April 6, 1798, bapt. on May 27, 1798, and m. Joseph Glatfelter[1.7.1n].

Elizabeth[1.13o], b. November 11, 1799, bapt. on November 15, 1799, and m. John Robinson.

Eve Catherine[1.14o], b. Sept. 27, 1800, bapt. at Salisbury Lutheran on Feb. 8, 1801, and m. Adam Boyd.

Frederick[1.15o], b. Feb. 28, 1802, and d. in 1848.
Margaret[1.16o], b. May 6, 1804, m. John Fuller, and d. in 1848.
Clement[1.17o], b. Nov. 13, 1807.
Samuel[1.18o], b. Aug. 26, 1809, m. Elizabeth Shirer, Rebecca Broadwater, Catherine Ridgley, and d. on July 28, 1888.
Jacob[1.19o], b. June 6, 1812, m. Susan Sides, Louisa Maria Probst in Berlin on Dec. 3, 1836, and d. in Benton Ridge, Ohio on July 16, 1859.

Peter Engle

Peter[1.2o] m. Barbara Garletts, and d. in Somerset Co., Pennsylvania on April 18, 1854. They had the following children:

John[1.2.1o], b. Nov. 20, 1807, and d. in Somerset Co. on Aug. 15, 1850. He m. Diane.
Elizabeth[1.2.2o], b. in 1809, m. Daniel (Logan), and d. in Somerset Co. on Jan. 1, 1898.
Adam[1.2.3o], b. in Greenville Twp. on March 12, 1811.
Rachel[1.2.4o], b. Sept. 12, 1812, and m. Christian Fair.
Catherine[1.2.5o], b. Feb. 28, 1815, and m. James Boyd.
Christian[1.2.6o], bapt. in 1817.
Barbara[1.2.7o], b. April 13, 1818, m. John McKenzie, and d. on March 24, 1905.
Susanna[1.2.8o], b. Feb. 11, 1821, and m. John Shock.
Sarah[1.2.9o], b. May 14, 1823, and m. John Harden.
Magdalena[1.2.10o], b. Oct. 10, 1826, m. Jonas Hutzell, and d. on May 30, 1897.
Peter[1.2.11o], b. Aug. 27, 1829, and m. Elizabeth Long.

Adam Engle

Adam[1.2.3o] m. Barbara Ann (1812-1883), dau. of Jacob Maust, and resided in Uniontown, Pennsylvania in 1881. They had the following children:

daughter[1.2.3.1o], d. young.
Hannah[1.2.3.2o], b. Sept. 1, 1837, and m. John Sickles.
Samuel[1.2.3.3o], b. Sept. 21, 1839, and m. Mary Balsinger.
Peter[1.2.3.4o], b. July 20, 1841, m. Margaret Reese, and d. on April 17, 1884.
Benjamin[1.2.3.5o], b. May 8, 1843, and m. Katherine Smith.
Katherine[1.2.3.5o], b. April 7, 1845, and m. William Burton.
James K.[1.2.3.6o], b. June 24, 1847, and m. Nancy Umbel.
Noble[1.2.3.7o], b. March 15, 1849.
William[1.2.3.8o], b. April 12, 1850.
Sarah[1.2.3.9o], b. Sept. 24, 1852, and d. in 1883.

John Engle

John[1.6o] m. Salome Sterner (1791-1847) and Catherine Lichty (1808-1895). He d. on March 1, 1863. He had the following children:

Catherine[1.6.1o], b. in 1812, m. Jacob Brenneman, and resided in McHenry, Maryland.

Solomon[1.6.2o], b. Sept. 15, 1816.

Elizabeth[1.6.3o], b. in 1822, and m. Benjamin Lowery (1816-1878).

Lydia[1.6.4o], b. Oct. 14, 1824, m. George Lowery, and d. on March 29, 1853.

Sarah[1.6.5o], b. Feb. 24, 1827, m. Daniel G. Meese (b. 1835), and d. on May 15, 1853.

Susan[1.6.6o], b. in 1835, and m. Daniel Meese.

John J.[1.6.7o], b. Dec. 15, 1839, m. Sarah E. Wagner on July 7, 1871, and d. in 1915.

Solomon Engle

Solomon[1.6.2o] m. Christina Keim on Nov. 21, 1837, and d. on Jan. 15, 1902. They had the following children:

Sally[1.6.2.1o], b. Jan. 14, 1839.

Barbara[1.6.2.2o], b. Oct. 10, 1841, and m. William D. Boyd.

Lucinda[1.6.2.3o], b. Aug. 3, 1842.

Catherine[1.6.2.4o], b. July 24, 1844.

John[1.6.2.5o], b. Jan. 13, 1846.

Christian[1.6.2.6o], b. April 17, 1849.

Nancy[1.6.2.7o], b. Oct. 5, 1851.

Lydia[1.6.2.8o], b. Jan. 15, 1857.

William H.[1.6.2.9o], b. Oct. 3, 1862.

Martin Engle

Martin[1.8o] m. Lovis, and d. in 1840. They had the following son:

Jeremiah[1.8.1o], b. June 26, 1816, and m. Christina Boyd.

Sarah[1.8.2o], b. in 1819.

Samuel[1.8.3o], b. May 16, 1822.

Clement Engle

Clement[1.17o] m. Judith before 1830, Margaret Atchison before 1849, Sarah Atchison after 1853, and d. on May 7, 1887. He had the following children: Catherine[1.17.1o], b. Aug. 1, 1830; Henry[1.17.2o], b. June 25, 1833; Margaret Ann[1.17.3o], bapt. on March 2, 1839; John[1.17.4o], bapt. on Aug. 5, 1849; William[1.17.5o], b. December 24, 1850; Samuel[1.17.6o], bapt. on July 4, 1853.

Michael Engle

Michael[2o] m. Catharina, and had the following children: Jacob[2.1o], b. Jan. 21, 1789, and bapt. in Berlin Lutheran Church on April 28, 1789;

Abraham²·²ᵒ, bapt. in Elk Lick Twp. on June 17, 1794; Adam²·³ᵒ, bapt. on March 20, 1796.

****

John Weimer

John¹ᵖ had the following children: Johann Martin¹·¹ᵖ, b. in 1738; John¹·²ᵖ, b. in 1740; Frederick¹·³ᵖ, b. in 1742.

Johann Martin Weimer

Martin¹·¹ᵖ was b. in 1738. He m. Catharina Barbara Troutman (1748-1824) in 1769, d. in Sailsbury, Pennsylvania in 1815, and had the following children:
  Margaretta¹·¹·¹ᵖ, b. in 1770, and m. Clement Engle.
  Adam¹·¹·²ᵖ, b. about 1773.
  Martin¹·¹·³ᵖ, b. in Cecil Co., Maryland in 1777.
  Godfrey¹·¹·⁴ᵖ, b. in Cecil Co., Maryland on Nov. 24, 1780.
  Frederick¹·¹·⁵ᵖ, b. in 1783.
  Elizabeth¹·¹·⁶ᵖ, b. March 1, 1785, and bapt. at Pinehill Lutheran Church in Somerset Co. on Sept. 7, 1785.
  Elizabeth Barbara¹·¹·⁷ᵖ, b. in Brother's Valley Twp. on Aug. 26, 1787.
  Eve¹·¹·⁸ᵖ, b. Dec. 11, 1790.

Godfrey Weimer

Godfrey¹·¹·⁴ᵖ m. Elizabeth Sterner, and had the following sons in Somerset Co.: John¹·¹·⁴·¹ᵖ, b. in 1806; Levi¹·¹·⁴·²ᵖ, b. in 1807.

Eve Weimer

Eve¹·¹·⁸ᵖ m. Peter Welfley in 1810, and d. in 1870. They had the following children: Israel¹·¹·⁸·¹ᵖ; Catherine¹·¹·⁸·²ᵖ; Jacob¹·¹·⁸·³ᵖ; Henry¹·¹·⁸·⁴ᵖ; Martin¹·¹·⁸·⁵ᵖ; John¹·¹·⁸·⁶ᵖ; Balthasar¹·¹·⁸·⁷ᵖ; Margaret¹·¹·⁸·⁸ᵖ; David¹·¹·⁸·⁹ᵖ.

John Weimer

John²ᵖ was b. in 1740. He m. Susanna Ackerman. She was b. May 7, 1741, and d. on Jan. 27, 1813. He d. on Jan. 24, 1831. They had the following children:
  George¹·²·¹ᵖ, b. April 1, 1762.
  John¹·²·²ᵖ, b. May 11, 1764.
  David¹·²·³ᵖ, b. April 27, 1766.
  Henry¹·²·⁴ᵖ, b. May 6, 1769, m. Barbara, and d. in Melcroft, Pennsylvania in 1833. She was b. April 1, 1776, and d. on April 17, 1835. They had no children.
  Jacob¹·²·⁵ᵖ, b. Sept. 28, 1772.
  Susanna¹·²·⁶ᵖ, b. Oct. 4, 1774.

Rosina$^{1.2.7p}$, b. March 21, 1776, and bapt. on Oct. 9, 1777. She m. John Harbaugh about 1792, and d. in Ohio in 1843.

Samuel$^{1.2.8p}$, b. Jan. 25, 1779.

Frederick$^{1.2.9p}$, b. Nov. 2, 1783, and bapt. in Westmoreland Co. on June 1, 1784.

Anna$^{1.2.10p}$, bapt. in Westmoreland Co. on Nov. 17, 1784 (mother is Margaretta?).

Catharina$^{1.2.11p}$, bapt. in Somerset Co., Somerset Twp. on April 19, 1786.

Peter$^{1.2.12p}$, b. Aug. 26, 1787.

George Weimer

George$^{1.2.1p}$ m. Catherine. She was b. Aug. 18, 1763, and d. on March 19, 1841. George d. in Montgomery Co., Ohio. They had the following children:

Susanna$^{1.2.1.1p}$, bapt. in Westmoreland Co., Greensburg on June 1, 1784, m. John Green, and d. on May 20, 1873.

Catharina$^{1.2.1.2p}$, bapt. on Aug. 30, 1785, and presumed to have m. Johannes Robinson$^{1.3c}$.

Sara$^{1.2.1.3p}$, b. in Somerset Co., Somerset Twp. on Sept. 22, 1787, bapt. on Nov. 5, 1787, and m. Daniel Wertz. She d. on March 10, 1857. Elizabeth$^{1.2.1.2p}$, b. in 1789.

John Weimer

John$^{1.2.2p}$ m. Susanna$^{1.3.3.5f}$, dau. of Johan Georg and Anna Catharina Lenhart. He was b. in Somerset Co., Milford Twp., Pennsylvania on May 11, 1764, and d. in Westmoreland Co., Ligonier Twp., Pennsylvania in 1812. Susanna d. in Stark Co., Sugar Creek Twp., Ohio on Oct. 1, 1829. She is buried in Weimer cemetery. They had the following children in Milford Twp.:

John Henry$^{1.2.2.1p}$, b. July 11, 1789, bapt. on Sept. 20, 1789.

John$^{1.2.2.2p}$, bapt. at Sanner Lutheran Church on Feb. 15, 1793.

Elizabeth$^{1.2.2.3p}$, b. about 1794, and d. before 1813.

Anna Catherine$^{1.2.2.4p}$, b. July 17, 1796, and m. David Weimer$^{1.2.3.1p}$ in Westmoreland Co., Donegal Twp., Pennsylvania on Jan. 18, 1814.

Peter$^{1.2.2.5p}$, b. in 1797.

Mary$^{1.2.2.6p}$, b. in 1799, and m. Elias Wade.

Gabriel$^{1.2.2.7p}$, b. May 13, 1801.

John Henry Weimer

John Henry$^{1.2.2.1p}$ m. Margaret Arenal Potts, and had the following dau. in Milford Twp.: Mary$^{1.2.2.1.1p}$, bapt. on April 19, 1807.

John Weimer

John[1.2.2.2p] m. Margaret Arnel, d. in 1861, and had the following children:

    Ann[1.2.2.2.1p], b. Nov. 5, 1813, and m. Peter Connelly on March 29, 1836.

    Eliza[1.2.2.2.2p], b. May 27, 1815, and d. on May 28, 1815.

    Barbara[1.2.2.2.3p], b. in 1816, m. Peter Grim on Jan. 26, 1843, and d. in Huntington Co., Roanoke, Indiana in 1888.

    Leah[1.2.2.2.4p], b. in 1818, and m. Jacob Reed Crepliver on Dec. 25, 1838.

    Christina[1.2.2.2.5p], b. in 1820, and m. Samuel Dinius on Feb. 13, 1840, and resided in Allen Co., Delphos, Ohio.

    Susanna[1.2.2.2.6p], b. in 1822, and drowned in 1823.

    Mary[1.2.2.2.7p], b. in 1824, and m. Robert Crawford Bashford on Sept. 18, 1845.

    Lydia[1.2.2.2.8p], b. in 1826, and d. age 1 day.

    Margaret[1.2.2.2.9p], b. in 1827, and m. Robert Arford on June 16, 1850.

    Elizabeth[1.2.2.2.10p], b. in 1829, and m. Josiah S. Grim on Dec. 29, 1850.

    Harriet[1.2.2.2.11p], b. in 1831, and m. O. Abraham Forney on Dec. 29, 1850.

    Solomon Arnel[1.2.2.2.12p], b. in 1832.

    Lucy Ellen[1.2.2.2.13p], b. in 1840.

Gabriel Weimer

Gabriel[1.2.2.7p] m. Anna Overholser on Dec. 22, 1821, and Elizabeth, dau. of Philip and Susanna (Weimer) Dumbauld, in Stark Co., Ohio on March 28, 1840. Anna was b. in Somerset Co., Pennsylvania on April 8, 1802, and d. in Stark Co., Sugar Creek Twp., Ohio on Jan. 15, 1839. Elizabeth was b. March 29, 1811. Gabriel had the following children in Stark Co., Ohio:

    Elias W.[1.2.2.7.1p], b. Sept. 15, 1824, m. Margaret (b.1829), and d. in Stark Co. on Sept. 6, 1898.

    Sarah A.[1.2.2.7.2p], b. about 1826.

    Susan[1.2.2.7.3p], b. about 1828.

    Louisa[1.2.2.7.4p], b. about 1830.

    Josiah[1.2.2.7.5p], b. Feb. 26, 1831, and d. on April 7, 1842.

    Orlando B.[1.2.2.7.6p], b. Jan. 22, 1835, m. Amarda Ward in Millersburg, Ohio in 1863, and d. in Stark Co. on Jan. 22, 1901.

    Franklin[1.2.2.7.7p], b. Feb. 12, 1841, and m. Catherine Crise on Oct. 14, 1873. She was b. in Somerset Co., Pennsylvania in 1851.

    Oliver[1.2.2.7.8p], b. Feb. 12, 1843.

    Rose A.[1.2.2.7.9p], b. March 24, 1845, and m. W. M. Stanford.

    Uriah[1.2.2.7.10p], b. May 26, 1847, m. Magdalena Elizabeth Burris

on Aug. 18, 1867, and d. on April 8, 1889. She was b. in Ohio in 1850.
Mary C.$^{1.2.2.7.11p}$, b. Jan. 30, 1850.
Solomon$^{1.2.2.7.12p}$, b. June 26, 1852, and m. Katherine Diedler.

David Weimer

David$^{1.2.3p}$ m. Christina Frey in Berlin on Dec. 2, 1788, and d. on July 2, 1842. David had the following children: Michael$^{1.2.3.1p}$, bapt. in Somerset Co. on May 3, 1789; David$^{1.2.3.1p}$, b. Oct. 20, 1791; Peter$^{1.2.3.2p}$, b. July 30, 1794, Susanna$^{1.2.3.3p}$, b. Jan. 5, 1797; John$^{1.2.3.4p}$, b. Nov. 10, 1799, and m. Rebecca Porch; Henry$^{1.2.3.5p}$, b. Nov. 1, 1801; Solomon$^{1.2.3.6p}$, b. Nov. 29, 1805.

Michael Weimer

Michael$^{1.2.3.1p}$ had the following children: Michael$^{1.2.3.1.1p}$; Johanna$^{1.2.3.1.2p}$; Aaron$^{1.2.3.1.3p}$; Adeline$^{1.2.3.1.4p}$.

David Weimer

David$^{1.2.3.1p}$ m. Anna Catharina$^{1.2.2.4p}$, dau. of John and Susanna (Lenhart) Weimer, in Westmoreland Co. Donegal on Jan. 18, 1814, and had the following son in Donegal:
Daniel$^{1.2.3.1.1p}$, b. Nov. 1, 1814.
John$^{1.2.3.1.2p}$, b. Nov. 1, 1814.
Juliana$^{1.2.3.1.3p}$, b. Oct. 22, 1816, and m. John Overholt.
Gabriel$^{1.2.3.1.4p}$, b. April 17, 1818, and m. Lydia Gnaga.
Joseph David$^{1.2.3.1.5p}$, b. June 2, 1820, and m. Hannah Hurraw.
Sarah$^{1.2.3.1.6p}$, b. Aug. 23, 1822., and m. David Brenninger.
Susanna$^{1.2.3.1.7p}$, b. Nov. 1, 1824.
David$^{1.2.3.1.8p}$, b. June 7, 1827, and m. Ann Blough.
Lydia$^{1.2.3.1.9p}$, b. March 25, 1829, and m. Joseph Gilmore.
Catherine$^{1.2.3.1.10p}$, b. March 30, 1831, and m. John P. Reed.
Mary$^{1.2.3.1.11p}$, b. march 30, 1831, and m. ____ Bell.
Henry C.$^{1.2.3.1.12p}$, b. Jan. 8, 1835, and m. Frances Overholtz.
Rebecca$^{1.2.3.1.13p}$, b. Nov. 11, 1836, and m. Elias B. Slexer.

Peter Weimer

Peter$^{1.2.3.2p}$ m. Catherine Berkey, and had the following dau.: Susanna$^{1.2.3.2.1p}$.

Solomon Weimer

Solomon$^{1.2.3.6p}$ m. Rebecca, d. before 1842, and had the following children in Somerset Co., Allegheny Twp., Pennsylvania:
Elizabeth$^{1.2.3.6.1p}$, bapt. on July 6, 1842; John$^{1.2.3.6.2p}$, bapt. in Allegheny Twp. on July 6, 1842.

Jacob Weimer

Jacob[1.2.5p] m. Anna Maria[1.3h], dau. of George Shock, about 1797. They had the following children in Milford Twp.:

David[1.2.5.1p], b. Dec. 30, 1797.
George[1.2.5.2p], b. Sept. 30, 1798, bapt. at Sanner Church, and sponsored by Abraham Kopp and Elizabeth Schuck.
Jonathan[1.2.5.3p], b. Nov. 4, 1800, and m. Susan Burger (b. 1804).
Jacob[1.2.5.4p], b. Jan. 20, 1801.
Elizabeth[1.2.5.5p], b. Dec. 21, 1802.
Catherine[1.2.5.6p], bapt. on Dec. 3, 1809, and m. George Pfeifer in Westmoreland Co., Pennsylvania on Nov. 8, 1827.
Margaret[1.2.5.7p], b. in 1811.

David Weimer

David[1.2.5.1p] m. Catherine Hartman in Berlin on June 4, 1837, and had the following children in Milford Twp.:

Daniel Franklin[1.2.5.1.1p], bapt. on June 9, 1838.
Susanna[1.2.5.1.2p], bapt. on July 25, 1841, and m. Frank Walter.
Lydia[1.2.5.1.3p], bapt. on June 29, 1844, and m. George Beck.
Samuel Austin[1.2.5.1.4p], b. July 5, 1846.
Eliza[1.2.5.1.5p], b. about 1848, and m. Wade H. Kinsey.
Lovina C.[1.2.5.1.6p], b. about 1850, and m. John T. Bean.

George Weimer

George[1.2.5.2p] m. Barbara Klingaman, and d. in Somerset Co., Greenville Twp., Pennsylvania on March 11, 1879. She was b. in Pocahontas, Pennsylvania on Nov. 23, 1805, and d. in Greenville on March 10, 1888. They had the following children in Greenville Twp.:

Samuel K.[1.2.5.2.1p], b. Sept. 6, 1824, and m. Drusilla Anne McKenzie. She was b. April 9, 1825.
Jacob[1.2.5.2.2p], b. Nov. 3, 1825, and d. on June 19, 1905.
Eliza[1.2.5.2.3p], b. Jan. 14, 1828, and d. in Shanesville, Ohio on May 1, 1909.
Sarah[1.2.5.2.4p], b. July 14, 1830, m. Elijah Patton in Somerset Co., Elk Lick Twp., Pennsylvania on Jan. 22, 1854, and d. in Mountain Lake, Maryland.
John[1.2.5.2.5p], b. Nov. 22, 1832.
Levi[1.2.5.2.6p], b. Feb. 6, 1835, and d. on March 16, 1835.
Cornelius[1.2.5.2.7p], b. Feb. 28, 1836, and d. in Horseshoe Run, West Virginia on April 28, 1861.
Mary[1.2.5.2.8p], b. Aug. 4, 1838, and d. on Oct. 28, 1838.
Jesse[1.2.5.2.9p], b. Jan. 18, 1841, and d. in Oakland, Maryland.
Joseph[1.2.5.2.10p], b. March 19, 1843, and d. in McHenry, Maryland on Aug. 25, 1884.
Benjamin[1.2.5.2.11p], b. Sept. 18, 1845, and d. in Deer Park,

Maryland on Oct. 16, 1869.

Silas[1.2.5.2.12p], b. Dec. 1, 1848, and d. in McHenry, Maryland.

Samuel Weimer

Samuel[1.2.8p] m. Catherine Wisebaugh, and d. in 1828. They had the following children: Joseph[1.2.8.1p], b. about 1806. Christian[1.2.8.2p], b. July 2, 1808, and bapt. on Jan. 1, 1809; David Palmer[1.2.8.3p], b. about 1810; Susanna[1.2.8.4p], b. Feb. 3, 1812, bapt. on April 26, 1812, and m. ____ Shrock; Margaret[1.2.8.5p], b. about 1814, bapt. on Oct. 24, 1819, and m. ____ Snyder; Catherine[1.2.8.6p], b. in 1817, bapt. on Aug. 5, 1817, and m. George Sutter in Somerset Co. on Jan. 2, 1842; Daniel[1.2.8.7p], b. June 27, 1819; Henry S.[1.2.8.8p], b. June 27, 1819, and bapt. on Oct. 24, 1819; Ora[1.2.8.9p], b. about 1821.

Joseph Weimer

Joseph[1.2.8.1p] m. Elizabeth, and had the following child in Milford Twp.: Delila[1.2.8.1.1p], bapt. on December 27, 1829.

Frederick Weimer

Frederick[1.2.9p] m. Sarah[1.1.6e], dau. of John and Elizabeth Lohr, and had the following children in Milford Twp.: John[1.2.9.1p], bapt. on June 7, 1807; Sarah[1.2.9.2p], bapt. on May 22, 1809; Frederick[1.2.9.3p], bapt. on Oct. 10, 1824; Emmaliah[1.2.9.4p], bapt. on May 6, 1827; George[1.2.9.5p], bapt. on March 30, 1828.

Peter Weimer

Peter[1.2.12p] m. Christina Arnel, and had the following children: Lydia[1.2.12.1p], b. Aug. 28, 1809. Margaret[1.2.12.2p], b. Aug. 15, 1811, and m. Peter Bowman; Susanna[1.2.12.3p], b. in Stark Co., Sugar Creek Twp., Ohio on Dec. 16, 1816, and m. Henry J. Sholty; Joseph A.[1.2.12.4p], b. Aug. 2, 1819, and m. Mary Forney; Mary[1.2.12.5p], b. Oct. 23, 1822; infant[1.2.12.6p], b. and d. in 1826.

Frederick Weimer

Frederick[1.3p] m. Elizabeth Ferral, d. in 1808, and had the following children: Jacob[1.3.1p], b. about 1763; Frederick[1.3.2p], b. in 1765; Margaretha[1.3.3p], b. about 1770, and m. Peter Bradford in Somerset Co., Berlin on July 13, 1790. She has not been confirmed as a dau.; John[1.3.4p], b. in Somerset Co., Milford Twp., Pennsylvania in 1775; Elizabeth[1.3.5p], b. about 1781, and m. Adam Schneider[1.1.6.3a]. She has not been confirmed as a dau.; Maria[1.3.6p], bapt. at Berlin Lutheran on Aug. 17, 1788.

Jacob Weimer

Jacob$^{1.3.1p}$ m. Catharina, and had the following children:
Susanna$^{1.3.1.1p}$, bapt. at Pinehill Lutheran Church in Berlin on Aug. 25, 1784, and m. Philip Dumbauld$^{1.1.1.3.3d}$ and Frederick Dumbauld$^{1.1.1.3.1d}$; Catharina$^{1.3.1.2p}$, bapt. in Somerset Twp. on June 13, 1786; Maria$^{1.3.1.3p}$, b. in Somerset Co. on Aug. 17, 1788.

Frederick Weimer

Frederick$^{1.3.2p}$ m. Barbara (1768-1838), dau. of Casper Harbaugh, before 1787, d. in Somerset Co. in 1814, and had the following children:
Jacob$^{1.3.2.1p}$, b. in Milford Twp. on Aug. 8, 1787 (86), and bapt. on Sept. 25, 1787.
Sarah$^{1.3.2.2p}$, b. Nov. 23, 1787, and m. Jacob Younkin.
John$^{1.3.2.3p}$, b. June 12, 1789, and bapt. in Somerset Twp. on Aug. 16, 1789.
Mary$^{1.3.2.4p}$, b. May 19, 1792, m. Henry Drushal in 1810, and d. on Nov. 21, 1852.
Elizabeth$^{1.3.2.5p}$, b. Aug. 10, 1794.
Salome$^{1.3.2.6p}$, b. in Milford Twp. on May 13, 1796.
Catherine$^{1.3.2.7p}$, b. about 1798, and m. ___ Wiltrout in 1818, and Henry Drushal in 1855.
Barbara$^{1.3.2.8p}$, b. March 29, 1800.
Margaret C.$^{1.3.2.9p}$, bapt. at Sanner Lutheran Church on May 30, 1803.
Frederick$^{1.3.2.10p}$, b. Feb. 14, 1805, and bapt. at Sanner Lutheran Church on May 26, 1805.
Henry$^{1.3.2.11p}$, b. Dec. 29, 1809, and bapt. at Sanner Lutheran.

Jacob Weimer

Jacob$^{1.3.2.1p}$ m. Susanna Shower, and had the following children in Milford Twp.: David$^{1.3.2.1.1p}$, b. Nov. 20, 1811.

John Weimer

John$^{1.3.2.3p}$ m. Margaret, and had the following children:
James$^{1.3.2.3.1p}$; Charles$^{1.3.2.3.2p}$.

Frederick Weimer

Frederick$^{1.3.2.10p}$ d. 1880. He m. Elizabeth Spiker in 1826, Mary Barron about 1838 and Margaret Buchanon on Dec. 31, 1846. Mary d. on March 28, 1846. Frederick had the following children:
Frederick$^{1.3.2.10.1p}$, b. in 1828, and m. Catherine Houston; Francis Elias$^{1.3.2.10.2p}$, b. Aug. 24, 1832, d. March 6, 1898, m. Maria Stahl on March 8, 1854; Rose$^{1.3.2.10.3p}$, b. in 1834; Elizabeth$^{1.3.2.10.4p}$, b. in 1836; John$^{1.3.2.10.5p}$, b. in 1837, and d. in 1896; Emma$^{1.3.2.10.6p}$, b. about 1847; Amanda$^{1.3.2.10.7p}$, b. about 1849.

John Weimer

John$^{1.3.4p}$ m. Maria Margaretha Schneider in Milford Twp. about 1796, and had the following children there: John$^{1.3.3.1p}$, b. March 24, 1797, and bapt. on July 9, 1797; Susanna$^{1.3.3.2p}$, b. Dec. 27, 1803, bapt. on April 15, 1804, and may be the Susanna that m. Peter Snyder on April 22, 1823; Sally$^{1.3.4.3p}$, b. Jan. 8, 1806; Isaac$^{1.3.4.4p}$, b. June 14, 1808, and bapt. on July 31, 1808; David$^{1.3.4.5p}$, b. Dec. 11, 1810, and bapt. on March 28, 1811; John$^{1.3.4.6p}$, b. June 23, 1812; Peter$^{1.3.4.7p}$, b. Jan. 11, 1816.

INDEX

-A-
ACKERMAN, 103
ADAMS, 35
AGLER, 11, 28, 32, 35
ALBERT, 19, 75, 85
ALBRIGHT, 37
ALLEN, 75
ALLMAN, 33
AMBROSHER, 78
ANDERSON, 9
ANGST, 77
ANKENY, 21, 22, 23, 48
ANSCHUETZ, 79, 81
ARENFERT, 47
ARENFRET, 46
ARFORD, 41, 105
ARNEL, 105, 108
ARNER, 18
ASH, 34
ASHBROOK, 51, 52
ATCHISON, 102
AULT, 9, 31

-B-
BAER, 90
BAILEY, 15
BAKER, 25, 29, 31, 51, 57, 89
BALEY, 17
BALL, 28
BALSINGER, 101
BALTZELL, 7, 8
BALYEAT, 39
BANSE, 37
BARGMAN, 56
BARKLAY, 16
BARKLEY, 3, 74
BARKMAN, 12
BARNES, 25
BARNETT, 95
BARNHART, 60
BARNS, 91
BARR, 45
BARRICK, 13
BARRON, 15, 24, 34, 109
BARTHOLEMI, 18
BARTHOLOMEW, 79
BARTMESSER, 96
BARTRUFF, 33
BASHFORD, 105
BASHORE, 87
BATES, 23
BATTENBURG, 66
BAXTER, 37, 75, 76
BAY, 11
BAYLEY, 71
BEAL, 91
BEAN, 107
BEARL, 13
BEATTY, 38
BECK, 107
BEIDER, 13
BEIDLER, 33
BEITZELIN, 69
BELDEN, 12
BELKNAP, 52
BELL, 106
BERGER, 77
BERKEY, 44, 64, 106
BETTY, 3
BICKEL, 43
BIER, 19
BINFERT, 26, 31
BINKLEY, 76
BITNER, 25, 95
BITTNER, 22
BLEYMEHL, 81
BLISH, 11
BLOUGH, 106
BODFIELD, 55
BOHRECH, 96
BONESY, 45
BONSEY, 37
BOSSERT, 47, 72
BOTZIN, 72
BOUCHER, 15
BOUDEMONT, 5, 20, 35, 63
BOURGEY, 5, 20
BOVEY, 29
BOWMAN, 26, 60, 108
BOWSER, 70
BOYD, 74, 88, 89, 90, 91, 92, 93, 94, 95, 100, 101, 102
BOYER, 45, 48, 55, 56
BRADFORD, 108
BRADLEY, 67
BRAHAM, 18
BRANT, 14
BREIMER, 87
BREINER, 50
BRENNEMAN, 102
BRENNINGER, 106
BREWER, 32, 35
BROADWATER, 101
BROOKS, 8, 14, 15, 38
BROUGHER, 17
BROWN, 53, 66, 95
BRUBAKER, 12, 27, 28, 60
BRUNER, 25, 26, 31
BUCHANON, 109
BUCHER, 96
BUEGHLEY, 93, 94
BUMGARDINER, 25
BUNSEY, 45
BURFORD, 52

BURGER, 107
BURRELL, 66
BURRIS, 105
BURTON, 101
BUTCHER, 50
BUTTMAN, 21, 63
BUTTMANN, 23, 25, 27, 30, 31

-C-
CABLE, 13, 54
CANFIELD, 55
CARL, 33
CARNAHAM, 92
CARR, 75
CARTER, 42
CARVER, 49
CASEBEER, 31
CATON, 92, 94
CHAMBERLAIN, 21
CHAPLINE, 20
CHERRY, 93
CHERRYHOLMES, 77
CHRONISTER, 66
CLAPPER, 56
CLARK, 93
CLOSE, 68
COCHRAN, 58
COGER, 93
COLBERN, 15
COLEMAN, 22, 24, 64, 88
CONN, 17, 40
CONNELLY, 105
COOPER, 55
COOPERIDER, 49
COPELAND, 3
COSMER, 2
COST, 29
COVER, 35
CRAWFORD, 47
CREPLIVER, 105
CRIMES, 26

CRISE, 105
CRIST, 56
CRISWELL, 4
CRITCHETT, 52
CRITCHFIELD, 17, 18, 34
CRITES, 75
CROSSON, 17, 56
CROTINGER, 13, 50
CROWTHERS, 91
CUMMINGS, 83
CUMMINS, 52
CUNNINGHAM, 22
CURTIS, 33
CUSHMAN, 10
CUSHWA, 10

-D-
DAGUE, 42, 43
DAILY, 53
DAVIS, 15
DEAL, 100
DEANER, 29
DEHAAS, 86
DELABAR, 36
DELABARRAS, 36
DENNEY, 98
DICK, 33
DICKEY, 22, 34, 95
DIEDLER, 106
DIEHL, 64, 99
DIEL, 99
DILBONE, 8
DILVONE, 7
DINIUS, 105
DIXON, 36, 51
DOBSON, 7
DOLL, 1, 2, 4, 19
DOTTERER, 2
DOTY, 37
DREINER, 87
DROMM, 2
DRUM, 19
DRUSHAL, 109

DUFFIELD, 52
DULL, 3, 4, 5, 6, 8, 9, 10, 11, 12, 14, 15, 16, 17, 18, 20, 22, 28, 32, 34, 39, 40, 41, 42, 49, 54, 63, 95
DUMBALL, 40
DUMBALT, 46
DUMBAULD, 8, 13, 16, 37, 40, 44, 45, 46, 48, 49, 51, 52, 53, 54, 55, 56, 57, 105
DUNCAN, 36
DURST, 99
DYSINGER, 23

-E-
EAKLE, 29
EARL, 23
EASTER, 99
ECKER, 29
EDELMAN, 19
EDSON, 40
EISAMAN, 54
EISHELMAN, 44
ELLIOT, 39
EMREY, 65
ENCILL, 40
ENGLE, 74, 90, 91, 92, 94, 99, 100, 101, 102, 103
ESCH, 18
ESTELL, 10
EUNTZ, 71
EVERETT, 7
EWERS, 58
EXLINE, 10

-F-
FABRA, 66
FADLEY, 17, 76, 97, 98
FAIDLEY, 54

FAIR, 101
FAUVER, 29
FEDEROLFF, 5
FEG, 82, 84
FEINACAER, 54
FERMAN, 18
FERRAL, 108
FIKE, 70, 95
FINLEY, 36
FISH, 93
FISTER, 62
FITZGERALD, 84
FLECK, 93
FLICH, 15
FLICK, 17, 18
FLICKINGER, 22
FLUKE, 65
FLYNN, 29
FOLK, 94
FORNEY, 105, 108
FORRY, 51
FORTNEY, 35, 40, 42
FOUS, 60
FOUST, 60, 64
FOX, 25
FRANK, 79
FRAZIER, 8
FRENSCH, 97, 98
FRENTSCH, 99
FREY, 79, 106
FRIBLEY, 28
FRICK, 92
FRIEDLINE, 16, 47, 64
FRIEND, 86
FRIM, 62
FRISBEY, 92, 93
FROCK, 77
FRY, 59
FRYSINGER, 7, 8
FULLER, 101
FULTON, 48, 53

-G-
GABRIEL, 33
GAFF, 53
GAIER, 35
GARDNER, 13, 33, 60
GARLETTS, 74, 92, 101
GARLETZ, 91
GAY, 47
GEDUTIG, 96
GEETING, 29
GENTZEL, 87
GENTZLER, 87
GERHARD, 55
GIBSON, 91
GIFT, 87
GILBERT, 18
GILMORE, 106
GINDLESPARGER, 92
GITTINGER, 86
GLADFELTER, 100
GLATFELTER, 76, 97, 98, 99, 100
GLATTFELDEN, 98
GNAGA, 106
GNAGEY, 95
GOHN, 60
GOOLY, 46
GORDON, 55
GRADY, 64
GRAEFF, 100
GREBAUER, 20
GREEN, 104
GRESSINGER, 88, 89
GRIFFITH, 33, 65
GRIM, 105
GRIMES, 27, 49
GROSS, 23, 63
GROTON, 95
GRUWELL, 39
GUISE, 34
GUNSETT, 28

-H-
HAAS, 81, 87
HAGER, 45
HAHL, 62
HALL, 31, 50
HAMEN, 62
HAMMERLY, 62
HANCOCK, 52
HANEY, 40
HARBAUGH, 9, 49, 104, 109
HARDEN, 101
HARDSTOCK, 43
HARGAUGH, 71
HARMON, 45
HARNETT, 17
HARP, 7
HARRAH, 63
HARTMAN, 107
HARTZELL, 14
HASSELTON, 36
HASSINGER, 87
HAUSER, 5
HAWK, 68
HAWKINS, 49
HAY, 18, 22, 46, 47, 48, 100
HEER, 99
HEIL, 5, 19
HEILMAN, 79
HEINLY, 62
HEITZ, 80
HELL, 80
HENRICI, 81
HENRY, 48
HERGAT, 20
HERRING, 70, 75
HESSER, 5
HEYLMANN, 79
HILEMAN, 11
HINES, 46
HIS, 78
HITE, 34
HOBBS, 34
HOCHSTETLER,

89
HOETH, 4
HOFFMAN, 33
HOLLIDAY, 95
HOLTZ, 5
HOLTZINGER, 71
HOMBERGER, 62
HOOKS, 6, 7, 8
HOOVER, 18, 51, 52
HORNER, 60
HORNING, 4
HOUSEHOLDER, 83
HOUSTON, 109
HOWENSTEIN, 17
HOY, 60, 81
HUMBERT, 22, 23
HURD, 13
HURRAW, 106
HURROW, 28
HUSTON, 22
HUTZELL, 75, 91, 101
HYATT, 70

-I-
ICKES, 35
ILES, 50
INMAN, 23

-J-
JAULER, 74, 90, 95, 96, 97, 98
JENNINGS, 4, 46
JOHN, 99
JOHNSON, 94
JUNKER, 77
JUNKIN, 3

-K-
KALB, 57
KALP, 57
KAPPEL, 1
KAUFFMAN, 69

KAYLOR, 34
KEEFER, 94
KEEL, 61
KEIM, 24, 94, 102
KEPLINGER, 30
KERSHNER, 85
KESLER, 38, 40
KESSLER, 43, 60, 71
KIEM, 64
KIMMEL, 14, 15
KINDAR, 87
KINDLE, 85
KING, 13, 14, 31, 35, 42, 66
KINSEY, 107
KIRACOFF, 76
KISSINGER, 86, 88
KLEIN, 19
KLINGAMAN, 107
KLINGENSMITH, 69
KLINN, 48
KNABLE, 12, 14, 70
KNEPPER, 17, 18
KNIESZ, 80
KNIGHT, 11
KNOGEY, 15
KNUPP, 22
KOCHER, 60
KONIG, 80
KOOSER, 13, 15, 24, 25
KOPCHA, 21
KOPP, 107
KOPPENHEFER, 86
KORN, 93
KRAMER, 61, 63
KRAUGH, 11
KREAGER, 15
KREGER, 52, 54, 55
KREILING, 25
KRICK, 9, 32
KRIEDER, 97

KRING, 22
KRUMBOLTZ, 10
KUHBORTS, 78
KUHL, 61
KULHMAN, 15
KUNTZ, 48

-L-
LAIRD, 3
LAMBRECHT, 96
LANDIS, 24, 92
LAU, 97
LAUB, 22
LAVENGEYER, 68
LEIB, 80
LEIBY, 62, 63
LEICHTEN-
BERGER, 30
LEMMING, 50
LENHART, 6, 13, 25, 26, 28, 31, 34, 39, 41, 53, 61, 62, 63, 64, 65, 66, 67, 68, 69, 70, 71, 104, 106
LEONHARD, 45, 60, 71
LEONHARDT, 61
LEWELLEN, 11
LICHTY, 93, 102
LIGHTFOOT, 99
LINDEMAN, 91
LINHARD, 66
LINK, 96
LINT, 47, 74
LINTERMOOT, 10, 12
LINXWEILER, 81
LIPPIN, 81
LISCHY, 96
LIVENGOOD, 99
LOBE, 18
LOGAN, 29, 34, 101
LOHR, 23, 44, 48, 56, 57, 59, 60, 108

LONG, 23, 51, 101
LOSHER, 62
LOURY, 94
LOWERY, 102
LOWRY, 13
LOZIER, 37
LUTGE, 44
LYON, 51
LYTLE, 49

-M-
MCBETH, 92, 93
MCBRIDE, 76
MCCLINTOCK, 32
MCCLURE, 35
MCCORMICK, 14
MCCOY, 33
MCCRACKIN, 52
MCGOUGH, 40
MCINTURF, 46
MACKENDORFER, 46
MCKENZIE, 101, 107
MCKILLIP, 10
MACKLIN, 4
MCKLVEENE, 23
MCMEAL, 4
MCMILLAN, 69
MCMULLIN, 37, 38
MCNEIL, 54
MCPHEARSON, 71
MAGILLAND, 58
MALONE, 93
MARTIN, 10, 46, 103
MASON, 15
MASTHOLDER, 89
MATHEWS, 47
MATHIEU, 2
MAURER, 30, 60, 72, 78, 79, 80, 82
MAUST, 100, 101
MAYER, 68
MECHLING, 49

MECKENDORF, 38
MECKLING, 51
MEDAUGH, 11, 41
MEESE, 21, 102
MELLINGER, 100
MEUER, 85
MEYER, 81
MEYERS, 98
MICKLEY, 98
MIHM, 12, 35
MILLER, 7, 8, 10, 29, 55, 57, 59, 62, 63, 69, 74, 76, 88, 89, 93
MILLIGAN, 50
MITCHEL, 37
MITCHELL, 25
MONG, 30
MONTGOMERY, 51
MOORE, 13, 43
MOOSE, 93
MORGAN, 68
MORRISON, 25, 39
MOWRY, 30
MOYER, 61
MUELLER, 30, 81, 82, 83, 85
MUHLENBERG, 2, 4
MUMBAUER, 1
MUNCH, 68
MURRAY, 58
MYERS, 46, 50, 51

-N-
NAGLE, 59
NEDROW, 94, 98
NEEL, 37
NEFF, 30
NEIFERD, 32, 35
NEIHOFF, 96
NELCHER, 21
NELSON, 50
NEUNKIRCHEN, 80

NEWMAN, 97, 99
NIKOLAS, 88
NITTS, 72
NORTH, 28
NOWMAN, 25

-O-
OATLEY, 65
OGG, 69
OLDAKER, 51
O'LEARY, 7
OLMSTEAD, 25
OLVERHOLTZ, 106
OTTERBEIN, 20
OVERHOLSER, 105
OVERHOLT, 106

-P-
PACKER, 51
PAINTER, 53
PALMER, 46, 48, 58, 108
PARKER, 30
PARR, 46
PATTERSON, 39, 57, 58
PATTON, 16, 50, 74, 92, 107
PAXTON, 90
PECK, 99
PEITZEL, 68
PERKEY, 43
PETERMAN, 72
PETERS, 60, 71
PETERSON, 60, 67
PFEIFER, 107
PFEIFFERIN, 96
PHILLIPPI, 48
PHILLIPS, 83
PICKERING, 10
PILE, 12, 13, 31
PISELL, 48
PORCH, 38, 106
POSTLEWAIT, 4
POTTS, 104

POUNDSTONE, 52
PRATT, 52
PRICE, 3
PRITZ, 56
PROBST, 101
PUSSET, 20
PUTMAN, 7, 12, 13,
  15, 21, 23, 24, 25,
  26, 29, 30, 31, 32,
  33, 34, 35, 41, 42,
  56
PYLE, 54

-R-
RALSTON, 55
RAMBO, 65
RAMER, 65
RAMLER, 78, 86
RAMSEY, 9, 53
REAM, 9, 10, 11, 17
REBER, 62
REED, 28, 52, 106
REESE, 15, 101
REICH, 72
REICHELEDER-
  FER, 62
REIDT, 84, 85, 86
RESSLER, 14
REUTER, 79
RHODES, 54
RICE, 50
RICHSICKER, 25
RICHTER, 25, 64
RIDGLEY, 101
RIEK, 1
RINER, 87
RIPPETT, 9
ROBERTS, 65
ROBESON, 44
ROBINSON, 6, 10,
  32, 37, 38, 40, 44,
  45, 48, 57, 100, 104
ROBISON, 40
ROEBUCK, 8
ROEMER, 85

ROHRER, 27, 29
ROMESBERG, 55
ROSE, 39
ROSS, 18
ROW, 50
ROWLAND, 26
RUMPLE, 76
RUNDIO, 5
RUNNELS, 14, 50
RUPERT, 23
RUSH, 17, 68
RUTH, 2
RUTLEDGE, 65

-S-
SAFERCER, 26
SAGER, 28
SAIN, 37
SALZGEBER, 87
SAMILDA, 32
SANBOUR, 17
SAUM, 93
SAVAGE, 83
SAYLER, 92
SAYLOR, 17
SCHAEFFER, 96,
  84
SCHALTER, 37
SCHIFFLER, 80
SCHLAG, 34, 35
SCHLATER, 6, 11,
  32, 36, 37, 38, 39,
  40, 42, 43, 44, 45
SCHLEY, 20
SCHMIDT, 71
SCHNEIDER, 21,
  23, 27, 30, 31, 108,
  110
SCHOCK, 72, 79
SCHONHOLTZ, 96
SCHOYER, 92
SCHRIBNER, 52
SCHROCK, 18, 54,
  100
SCHUCH, 1

SCHUCK, 107
SCHULTZ, 70
SCHUTZ, 86
SCHWENGEL, 85
SCHWINGEL, 72,
  79, 80, 81, 82, 84,
  86, 87
SCHWINGELL, 80
SCRITCHFIELD, 22
SEARLE, 53
SECHLER, 15
SEIBERT, 21
SEISSTER, 85
SEYMOUR, 51
SHACKLEY, 67
SHAFER, 96
SHAFFER, 7, 11,
  31, 33, 35, 41, 53,
  59
SHAKE, 72
SHANKS, 27, 65
SHAW, 33
SHAWMAN, 100
SHEA, 49
SHECK, 72
SHEEK, 72
SHENK, 34
SHICK, 72
SHINDELDECKER,
  8
SHIRER, 99, 101
SHOCK, 72, 73, 74,
  76, 77, 78, 87, 89,
  91, 97, 101, 107
SHOEMAKER, 52
SHOLTY, 108
SHOLTZ, 19
SHOOK, 72
SHOOKE, 72
SHOPE, 75, 76
SHORT, 60
SHOUP, 51, 56, 67
SHOW, 37
SHOWER, 109
SHOWMAN, 100

SHRADER, 52
SHROCK, 108
SHUCK, 72
SHUE, 23
SHUK, 72
SHULTZ, 16, 73, 87, 88, 89, 91
SHUMAKER, 64
SHUNCK, 24
SHUNK, 24, 34
SHURTLEFF, 49
SICKLES, 101
SIDES, 101
SIEBERT, 15
SIMPSON, 73
SINDER, 32
SIPE, 15, 16
SKINNER, 36
SLEXER, 106
SLIFE, 51
SMITH, 9, 12, 33, 40, 41, 42, 43, 72, 77, 78, 85, 95, 101
SNAVELY, 29
SNOW, 38
SNYDER, 29, 108, 110
SODQUEST, 93
SPANGLER, 18
SPARKS, 30
SPEECE, 3
SPEER, 47
SPEICHER, 16
SPIDEL, 43
SPIDELL, 28
SPIDLE, 32, 33
SPIEKER, 80
SPIKER, 109
SPOTZ, 86
SPYKER, 85
STAHL, 95, 109
STAIRS, 47
STAMBAUGH, 34
STANBACH, 9
STANBAUGH, 9

STANFORD, 105
STANLEY, 2
STAUBS, 29
STAUCH, 64, 68
STAUDT, 19
STAUFER, 96
STEEN, 42
STEINLEY, 92
STEPHENS, 8
STERNER, 102, 103
STEWART, 10, 33
STOCK, 87
STOCKBERGER, 51, 55, 56
STOLTZ, 5
STONE, 67
STONEBREAKER, 82, 83
STOPHLET, 8
STORM, 96
STOUGH, 13
STOVER, 72, 77, 79
STOYESTOWN, 60
STRASSER, 20
STROEHER, 77
SUARNER, 92
SULLIVAN, 55
SUTTER, 108
SWARNER, 92
SWEITZER, 17
SWINGLE, 82, 84
SWITZER, 47
SYLVANIA, 11
SYLVESTER, 65

-T-
TAYLOR, 55
TEMPLE, 7, 35
THAMBALD, 49
THEIL, 59
THEISS, 83, 85
THOMA, 82
THOMAS, 29, 66
THOMPSON, 38
THORP, 53

TICE, 84
TREESCH, 65
TRENTOR, 26
TRESSLER, 94
TROUTMAN, 30, 100, 103
TUMBALD, 40
TURNEY, 70

-U-
ULLOM, 29
ULREY, 37
UMBEL, 101
UNDERWOOD, 47

-V-
VAN HORN, 77
VAN ZANDT, 3
VANDERSALE, 23
VICKERS, 65
VOLTER, 56
VOUGHT, 53

-W-
WADE, 104
WAGERS, 11, 41
WAGNER, 43, 55, 100, 102
WAGONER, 76
WALKER, 18, 26, 35, 52, 75
WALLACE, 34
WALLRICK, 77
WALTER, 14, 24, 30, 64, 107
WALTERS, 2, 9, 11, 42, 49
WARD, 105
WARNER, 27, 28, 33, 66, 94
WAYNE, 36
WEAVER, 56, 58, 92
WEBER, 44
WECHTEN-

HEISER, 22
WEIGLEY, 60
WEIMER, 24, 30, 34, 44, 48, 53, 56, 63, 73, 91, 92, 99, 100, 103, 104, 105, 106, 107, 108, 109, 110
WEIR, 85
WEISER, 85
WEITMANN, 85
WELFLEY, 100, 103
WELLER, 15
WELLS, 72
WERNER, 81
WERTZ, 104
WETZEL, 5
WEUTLER, 71
WHIPKEY, 58, 63, 64
WHITE, 34
WHITMORE, 32
WHITNEY, 55
WILHELM, 28, 70
WILKIE, 23
WILLIAMS, 45, 53
WILLS, 70
WILSON, 29
WILTROUT, 109
WINNETT, 58
WISE, 52
WISEBAUGH, 108
WITZSTEIN, 73
WOLFE, 8, 48
WOY, 59
WRIGHT, 9, 30, 43, 94
WYANDT, 27, 28, 29, 30, 34

-Y-
YARD, 57
YARGER, 21
YETTER, 38
YORTY, 63

YOST, 100
YOULER, 97
YOUNG, 46, 47, 49
YOUNKIN, 3, 16, 33, 54, 109
YOWLER, 97

-Z-
ZELLER, 86
ZIMMERMAN, 29, 64, 89

www.ingramcontent.com/pod-product-compliance
Lightning Source LLC
Chambersburg PA
CBHW070505100426
42743CB00010B/1767